QAWWALI

THE CALL OF HEARTS IN LOVE

CONCEPTUALISED, CURATED AND EDITED

By

MANJARI CHATURVEDI

First published in 2025 by

Om Books International

Corporate & Editorial Office
A-12, Sector 64, Noida 201 301
Uttar Pradesh, India
Phone: +91 120 477 4100
Email: editorial@ombooks.com
Website: www.ombooksinternational.com

Sales Office
107, Ansari Road, Darya Ganj,
New Delhi 110 002, India
Phone: +91 11 4000 9000
Email: sales@ombooks.com
Website: www.ombooks.com

Book designed by
I ME AM DESIGN

Cover calligraphy by
Khursheed Ahmad, Tonk, Rajasthan

ISBN: 978-93-6395-486-1

Printed in India

10 9 8 7 6 5 4 3 2 1

QAWWALI

THE CALL OF HEARTS IN LOVE

Om Books International

Advance Praise for The Book

Qawwali, an apparently humble folk tradition is not taken seriously by scholars and practitioners of Indian music. As a popular, little culture of music, it is now identified with Sufism, Muslims, and older Bombay films. Though a few of the performers in recent years did become well-known public figures.

In this world has entered Manjari Chaturvedi, the distinguished Kathak dancer and choreographer, and found that the so-called little culture was not so little, but a vast world waiting to be explored and preserved for the music lovers of India.

This half-forgotten world of qawwali crosses borders of religions, cultures, politics and nations with ease. Manjari has found qawwalis on not only Ganesh, Ram and Krishna, but even on Kashi Viswanath, Hanuman-ji and Ganga-ji. Manjari has also found a large number of Muslim women who took to qawwali, too, and I was pleasantly surprised to find in the book a few Bengali Hindu women who sang qawwalis that were recorded.

Manjari's majestic effort has made her a pioneer and trendsetter, and coming generations will be grateful to her for widening the range and the scope of Indian music.

Ashis Nandy

Manjari Chaturvedi's book is a masterpiece that offers a unique and comprehensive exploration of this soulful Indian art form. Being the first academic and visual record of qawwali in India, it skilfully and sensitively connects oral traditions, historical development, and modern practice.

This book traces the origins of qawwali from the courts of Sufi saints to contemporary manifestations throughout India, beautifully capturing its spiritual, cultural, and musical aspects. The rich photographs, scholarly essays, and personal narratives create a multidimensional portrayal that educates, while also deeply moving the reader.

In a time when it's essential to remember our roots and celebrate India's rich history, I recommend this book to anyone seeking a deeper connection with our traditions and, through the lens of qawwali, a deeper connection with themselves.

Amitabh Kant

The culture of India is very rich. It is the land of gurus, pirs, qalandars, spiritual guides, saints, sages, and ascetics. Punjab is a state where many great Sufi mystics have emerged, including Baba Bulleh Shah, Shah Hussain, Sultan Bahu, Waris Shah, Baba Ghulam Farid, Baba Shaikh Farid.

Qawwali was started by Amir Khusrau sahab, who was the most beloved disciple of Nizamuddin Auliya. He established the tradition of qawwali, but it truly flourished, matured, and reached its peak when it came to Punjab, where many great qawwals and Sufi saints were born. The poetry of Sufis has been echoing for centuries. But preserving such a valuable work needed an effort of equal calibre in the shape of a book or document.

We have such a luminary in Manjari Chaturvedi. She has done such credible work in the form of a book, with excellence and research, about India's history before partition, even earlier than that—centuries-old history, regarding Sufi poetry, especially qawwali. She deserves all praise and congratulations. Because qawwals themselves cannot document their own work, this work becomes necessary for coming generations and for history.

Whoever the Lord grants ability to, whoever He bestows His grace upon, such enormous and great work comes to their share. So, it is not surprising that this beautiful work of preserving their work (the work of Sufis) came to Manjari-ji's share. I take pride in the fact that whatever she did, whenever she did it, she did creative work while maintaining a completely non-commercial mindset. This book, too, which is for everyone to see, will be preserved for centuries in the form of a document. May Allah grant, may the Lord grant, may God grant Manjari-ji a long life.

This work will be useful for us, and also for new generations who are not familiar with Sufism. Because Sufism is above any kind of religion. Neither can any border stop it, nor is it for any particular class or caste. When they pray, Sufis pray for the entire humanity, for all creation, for the entire universe.

While I express gratitude, I also give my good wishes to her. May God grant her the ability to do more such work, may God bestow upon her legendary talents, may God give her the strength and power to continue to distribute legendary knowledge and art.

Hans Raj Hans

Manjari Chaturvedi's labour of love, this book on Qawwali, is a remarkable document like none other! Manjari has put together an inspired piece of work tracing the history of the music form and the practitioners involved in shaping its form and style and also about the lost qawwali ustads including women, who were never acknowledged or recognised for their brilliance!

Manjari has dug into musty archives, libraries, and personal collections like a badger on steroids! Her single-minded pursuit of the real history of the art form is as spellbinding as a mystery thriller.

The work is not only academic, but takes you on a fantastic journey in history and is beautifully, immersive. A collector's piece, for lovers of poetry, art, music, and the amazing artists involved! Congratulations!

Prahlad Kakar

For

my pir

Hazrat Nizamuddin Auliya (RA)

and

Hazrat Amir Khusrau (RA)
inseparable from the Pir

and for

Hazrat Maula Salim Chisti (RA)
Khwaja Bakhtiyar Kaki (RA)
Baba Bulleh Shah (RA)
Shamz-e-Tabriz (RA)

and

a fakir

of those who have sung the songs of love

A journey traversing the many stages of love,
finding refuge in the poetic path of qawwali

dilkashi - attraction
uns - attachment
mohabbat - love
aqidat - trust
ibadat - worship
junoon - madness
maut - death

and for
Naazo
A blessing from the Pir

Manjari Chaturvedi

Contents

Foreword

Qawwali: A World of Surrender

Muzaffar Ali

◆

Poet: Hazrat Shah Niyaz

◆

Aql ke madarse se utth
ishq ke maikade mein aa
Jaam e fana o bekhudi
ab to piya jo ho so ho

(Leave the school of knowledge, enter the tavern of love,
Drink the wine of annihilation and surrender,
let whatever happens, happen...)

Qawwali is the essence of the soul connecting with the divine in a state of sama. All senses surrender with a feeling of deep peace as the ascent begins with the sound of the voice and the rhythm of clapping hands. You enter into the realm of a sacred art perfected by masters in spirituality, music and poetry. It is born in a dargah or a khanqah before a realised pir. You embark on a mystical journey with the qaul of the Prophet (PBUH).

◆

Mann kun to Maula fa haza Ali yun Maula

◆

(Of whom I am the Master,
Ali is the Master)

With Ali at the helm, the ascension begins with a composition of Hazrat Amir Khusrau that blends Bhupali with Yaman Kalyan to explore stages of union, surrender and separation.

Laali morey laal ki jit dekhuñ tit laal,
Laali dekhan mai gayi mai bhi ho gayi laal

(Becoming one with the Beloved)

◆

Poet: Amir Khusrau

◆

Chhap tilak sab chheeni re mosey naina milayeke

(Total surrender to the Beloved,
casting off the differences man has made between men)

Gori soye sej par mukh par daale kes,
Khusrau chal ghar aapne rayen bhayi chahudes

(Complete annihilation with the Beloved)

◆

Poet: Ghalib

◆

Ishrat e qatra hai darya mein fana ho jaana...

(The pleasure of the droplet is to become as
nought with the ocean...)

This is the state of sama and the trajectory of the qawwali. The metaphors are deeply rooted in the Indian ethos with Krishna both divine lover and the Beloved, touching the emotional sensibility of the people, striking a chord of harmony, and building bridges across the diverse cultural landscapes of the Indian subcontinent.

A realised master believes that all performing art forms, thought, calligraphy, sound are connected deep within. Spiritual art is the art of divine ecstasy, not just holy, but soulful and beautiful. This passion is beyond the realm of worldly passion known to us, not just as a day-to-day experience. In the eyes of the saint, it is a passion that joins souls and buries manmade differences. The essence of Sufi music is the liberation of art from the structure of knowledge, ushering it into the realm of surrender. Human beings are blessed with voices that take you through the path of the unseen and this invariably finds its way to the heart and soul.

Qawwali is this gift and the path of the gift is both sacred and blessed. How it came to be thus is a miracle of the age and has been passed down through those who possess human qualities that are beyond description and definition. They materialise from inclusivity of all human beings. Thus, all music emerges from the same source, opening us all to influences of divine origin.

It is for this reason that the qawwali has been a binding factor in India's cultural fabric from the time of Hazrat Khwaja Moinuddin

Photo: Mustafa Quraishi

Chishti before evolving to great artistic heights with Hazrat Amir Khusrau, the disciple of Hazrat Nizamuddin Auliya, the third saint of the Chishti order.

It saw the human race as one. It embraced the Bhakti metaphor as embodied in the ancient dhrupad. Poets like Amir Khusrau and many other Sufi poet saints that followed him positioned it in its rightful and organically natural place. The sitar, the sarod, the sarangi and the tabla emerged as accompaniments to this spiritual art form.

The Sufis found in Radha the epitome of devotion. Krishna became a cultural bridge. Krishna was the muse of the Sufis and he traversed freely in their realm of imagination with a sense of belonging to all. The Sufi's Krishna did not become a visual image but found attributes in mystic metaphors and music. He began to coexist with Ali and the Khwaja freely as the masters celebrated the oneness of the human race through the beauty of the arts, the voice, the music and the sacred dance.

The thumri entered shyly in a Sufi's khanqah and ruled the hearts of all without any division of the high and the low. Classical music entered the soul of the meekest, elevating them to the highest possible station a human being can attain. The poet in the Sufi created miracle after miracle with words that stirred the soul. The vocabulary of the ghazal crossed the boundaries of the ego and entered the realm of love and total surrender. Thus, poetry became the everlasting miracle of a fakir's darbar. Khusrau ascended dizzying heights with his ghazals like:

⬩ ◆ ⬩

Nami daanam che manzil bood
shab jæy kay man boodam
Ba har su raqs-e-bismil bood
shab jæy kay man boodam

⬩ ◆ ⬩

(I know not where I was,
where I spent the night gone by
All around, the wounded danced
where I spent the night gone by)

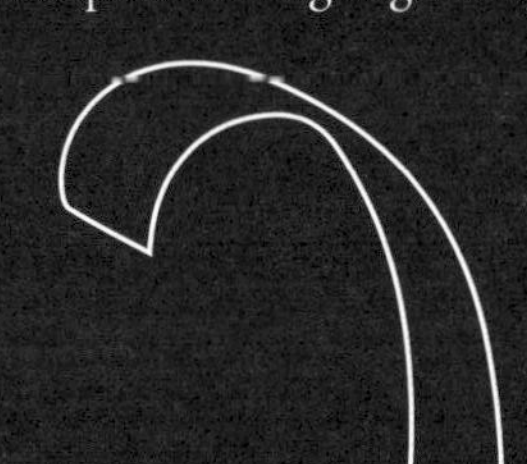

◆

Pari paikar nigaray
sarv o qadday lala rukhsaray
Saraapa aafat-e-dil bood
shab jæy kay man boodam

◆

(The fairy-formed beloved, like a stately cypress appeared,
face aglow like tulips in bloom
From head to toe a sight that became an aguish for the heart
where I spent the night gone by)

◆

Raqeebañ gosh bar awaaz ou,
der naaz-o-man tarsaan
Sukhan guftan chay mushkil bood
shab jæy kay man boodam

◆

(I trembled at the apparition of the Beloved,
which left my rivals aghast, overpowered by this stance and pride,
In silence I stood in awe, I spent the night gone by)

Thus, the qawwali through Khusrau's ghazal takes you on a mesmerising journey through time and space, (the) soul whirling in the body becoming an overwhelming experience. The master knows the secret of the words and how each word can have the deepest effect. He measures it through his own journey of ecstasy.

These melodies have journeyed through time. The qawwal at a dargah knows the order in which the kalaam is to unfold to the audience. They are a part of the divine journey.

◆ ◆ ◆

Khuda khud Mir-e-majlis bood
andar laa makaan Khusrau
Muhammad shamm-e-mehfil bood
shab jæy kay man boodam

◆ ◆ ◆

(Over the congregation, God presided,
and Khusrau was nowhere found
Where Muhammad became the candle's flame,
I spent the night gone by)

Manjari (Chaturvedi) has over the years internalised the essence of the qawwali and the kalaam, and has added her own sense of surrender to its beauty.

Muzaffar Ali
February 2025
New Delhi

Photo: DINESH KHANNA

Introduction

Qawwali Unveiled: A Realm of Love

Manjari Chaturvedi

Qaul is an utterance.
Qawwal is the one who sings a qaul.
Qawwali is the music form that a qawwal sings.
Qawwali is the performance art and qawwal is the practitioner.
The central themes of qawwali are love, devotion and longing of man for the Divine.
The ritual of qawwali is deeply rooted in the Sufi tradition.
Qawwali is experiential.

Qawwali, is a means of spiritual elevation, a music form associated with the Sufi traditions of the Indian subcontinent. It is a religious ritual that has been shaped over the years by many cultural influences and when performed in the setting and premises of Sufi shrines it is clearly a form of worship and devotion.

Sufism is a profound journey, mystical and spiritual, that desires an intimate connection with the divine and a personal enlightenment, within a religious practice. At the core of the practice is a mystical state known as wajd (ecstasy), which signifies an experience with the unknown divine. It inculcates an overwhelming sense of momentary transcendence from the material world. Sufi saints have been of the opinion that music, in its varied forms, can function as a bridge between the personal and the divine, a medium that facilitates spiritual elevation and healing. Sufi music is an integral aspect of mystical traditions and a potent force in traditional, cultural, and religious contexts.

Qawwali is a musical genre of Sufi music, a devotional music form, which within the Indian subcontinent exhibits common features with the light classical music found in north India. Shaped by centuries of historical and cultural confluences, it possesses a distinct attribute linked to its spiritual purpose. Through it, Sufis aspire to attain an ecstatic state that brings them closer to the divine. With a musical heritage spanning hundreds of years, qawwali is associated with performances at Sufi shrines or dargahs across the Indian subcontinent. However, over time, it has transcended its spiritual roots to also achieve mainstream recognition, popularity, and appeal.

Qawwali incorporates mystical poetry and is integral to the Sufi tradition of sama (assembly of listeners), a practice involving spiritual listening at a gathering with vocal renditions and poetic recitations with specified instrumental accompaniment and at times dance with rhythmic body movements. Sama is clearly an act of devotion, meticulously curated over centuries to bring the desired state of wajd. In qawwali, the repetitive rhythms and emotional poetry are essential musical features that can take the listener to this state of spiritual ecstasy.

Characterised by emotionally charged lyrics imbued with symbolism conveying the soul's insatiable longing for union with the divine, a qawwali evokes extreme emotions in listeners. People are found swaying to music, clapping in rhythm with the qawwals, crying. The qawwals become the voice for prayers of the hundreds of people at the shrine, each seeking grace in their own way. Qawwali's significance however lies in the broader cultural and religious meanings attached to the performance with the shrine as a symbolic sacred space. Here, qawwali transcends mere entertainment, and becomes a sacred ritual that helps the people connect with the saint as a shared spiritual and emotional experience.

Prof. Tanvir Anjum looks at the origin of qawwali and the musical tradition known as sama and the contribution of Amir Khusrau, a Sufi belonging to the Chishti order, who is credited with merging the musical traditions of Persia and India to form qawwali as we recognize it today. Amir Khusrau established the Qawwal Bachche Gharana, a lineage of twelve disciples who were personally trained by him. These disciples laid the foundation and Khusrau started the formalization of qawwali as a distinct musical genre, remarkably different from the existing musical gharanas. These twelve disciples also ensured the transmission of qawwali through successive generations following the guru-shishya parampara (master-disciple tradition). Khusrau collaborated and interacted with intellectuals and musical artists of his time and developed a musical style that blended relevant elements from different cultures and traditions, Persian, Arabic, and Indian, fundamentally establishing the unique musical and literary qualities that define contemporary 'Indian qawwali' as we see today.

In the Indian subcontinent, a qawwali session is formally referred to as Mehfil-e-Sama. A traditional mehfil encompasses various types of poetry and hymns, each serving a distinct purpose. These include compositions in praise of God (hamd), in praise of the Prophet (PBUH) (naat), in praise of Hazrat Ali (RA) (qaul), honouring Sufi saints (manqabat), and for Nizamuddin Auliya (rang). A qawwali performance invokes the memory of the entire lineage of spiritual masters and at the same time traces the history and spiritual journey, back to the founder of Islam. Syed Zia Alvi discusses the Islamic roots of qawwali in his essay.

Initially, it was Arabic and Persian, with their rich literary tradition of mysticism, that became closely associated with Sufism in the subcontinent. However, Amir Khusrau, freely incorporated other dialects, such as Purbi, Awadhi and Braj Bhasha, into his compositions. Further north, in undivided Punjab, Baba Farid and Baba Bulleh Shah introduced Punjabi into traditional qawwali music. 'Damadam Mast Qalandar' became a cult song for generations. Prof. Kumkum Srivastava unravels the meaning of the song in her essay.
Today, while compositions in Arabic, Persian, or Urdu may be included in the opening of a traditional qawwali performance, subsequently, the qawwal uses a varied language and cultural milieu for his musical expression and for nisbat (connection) with the listeners. This use of different vernacular languages serves to build bridges between diverse linguistic and cultural regions. In regions like the Deccan, Urdu is employed, and in Punjab, Punjabi is used, replacing the use of Braj or Purbi in those specific contexts. This book covers the spread of qawwali in regions such as Punjab and Sindh, as well as Hyderabad, Delhi, Ajmer, Lucknow and various other parts of India. Dinesh Khanna traces the traditional qawwali in Delhi, Punjab, Ajmer and Deccan through photo essays. Mustafa Quraishi travels to the interior of the Awadh region to visually document qawwals. This linguistic diversity reflects the adaptability of qawwali as it resonates with audiences across a broad cultural and linguistic spectrum. Prof. Salil Misra, Yousuf Saeed and Suman Mishra discuss the poetic traditions and the languages used in qawwali.

A qawwali ensemble, referred to as a 'qawwali party', typically comprises eight or nine musicians, seated cross legged on the ground. Traditionally, the group consists only of men, as qawwali is largely an androcentric, familial tradition. They are dressed in kurta-pyjama or for more formal occasions in a sherwani with a topi (cap) that covers their head, especially in the shrine setting. This group includes a lead singer, the primary qawwal, lead vocalist, who sets the tempo and rhythm for the performance. There are also one or two side singers, and/or harmonium players, and a very prominent percussion section. The group is well versed in raag and taal and provide cues about the specific raag and taal that will be used in the musical composition. The percussionist may play the tabla and dholak simultaneously, cradling both between his legs. In instances where there are two percussionists, one may handle the tabla, while the other manages the dholak. Additionally, there is a chorus consisting of four or five men responsible for repeating key verses and contributing to the percussion through hand-clapping. Improvisation is a crucial aspect of qawwali presentations in melodies and in the skilful amalgamation of shers extracted from pertinent poems.

The opening section of the qawwali composition is an aalap, a form of melodic improvisation where the performer explores and develops the raag. This is followed by the naghma, which is the melody or the tune, played with the percussions, focussing on the rhythmic structure of the composition, though not necessarily the same rhythm which would be played in the composition. The aagaaz, commencement of the poetry, is with a couplet, typically a four- or eight-line poetic form known as rubai, which is sung in a free style without adhering to a strict rhythm. This particular couplet encapsulates the central theme or thought of the qawwali. It marks the initiation of the qawwali composition, setting the tone for the rest of the performance. This dynamic creative process showcases the expertise and artistry of the qawwal. The qawwal often delves into a particular phrase or sentence, bringing attention to both its apparent and concealed meanings. This is achieved through the emphasis on and repetition of various words and syllables. Following the conclusion of the rubai, the actual qawwali commences.

Typically centred around a primary poetic composition, the lead qawwal sings this main poetry in a specific raag and taal. After delivering the main poetry, the lead qawwal incorporates additional verses from other poems into the qawwali, a practice known as girah lagana. These verses often carry similar meanings to the main poetry. During *girah lagana*, the lead qawwal introduces new elements seamlessly into the ongoing performance, maintaining the same raag pattern. Multiple girahs can be incorporated, and they may be in different languages, and originate from diverse regions, and may possess varied textual qualities. This process resembles the creation of a quilt, where different pieces are stitched together, forming a cohesive and rich tapestry of musical expression in the qawwali tradition. This is discussed in detail in an essay with Late Ustad Meraj Nizami of Qawwal Bachche Gharana and Late Ustad Iqbal Ahmad Khan of the Dilli Gharana.

A significant aspect of the performance is the use of a refrain. The lead qawwal selects a particular line, the refrain, which he sings first. It is then repeated by the chorus. This repetition of the refrain by the chorus contributes to the creation of a trance-like mood for the listeners. In the midst of the refrain, the lead qawwal has the freedom to introduce a different couplet, using vocal expression and creativity to lead the poetry in a new direction. This spontaneous shift in the lyrical content and musical expression adds to the overall improvisational nature of qawwali.

A question arises about whether there exists a standardised structure for qawwali or what factors actually influence a qawwal in structuring a performance. While there are no strict written rules, the oral training of the tradition plays a significant role in passing down the conventions and guidelines for structuring a qawwali performance. Qawwals learn the sequencing of rhythm, girah, and refrain as part of their training. However, unlike the standardised structure found in classical music, the overall structure of a qawwali is more fluid and allows for improvisation. The lead qawwal's intuition, creativity, and the collective mood of the performance can influence the direction the qawwali takes. This fluidity allows qawwals to adapt their performances based on the audience's response, the atmosphere, and their own artistic impulses.

An intriguing aspect of qawwali lies in its ability to use music to establish a meditative environment. The combination of powerful and emotive words, along with the distinctive manner in which they are sung, creates a pattern that resonates with the listeners at a deep emotional level. This aims to evoke a profound emotional response, often touching the hearts of the audience and creating a heightened state of meditation or contemplation. Qawwal Dhruv Sangari traverses this aspect of qawwali in detail in his essay.

A pivotal moment in the history of qawwali occurred during the doctrinal and political disputes between Hazrat Nizamuddin Auliya and the conservative religious authorities of his era. These conflicts intensified as the saint's spiritual teachings and his advocacy for sama drew charges of religious deviation. The controversy culminated when he was summoned before the royal court to justify his position, where he defended the legitimacy of sama before Sultan Ghiyasuddin Tughlaq which is discussed in the essay by Prof. Raziuddin Aqil.

Sufism underwent significant development, transforming into a sophisticated movement with the establishment of Sufi silsilas, or spiritual orders, around the twelfth century. While most qawwals largely belong to the Chishti Sufi order, even here they distinguish their connect with a shrine or the pir, the saint. Qawwals associated with the Nizamuddin shrine add 'Nizami' to their names, those associated with Waris Pak at Dewa Sharif call themselves 'Warsi', those owing allegiance to Hazrat Shah Niyaz at Bareilly add 'Niyazi' to their names, thus showing their own sense of belonging to the shrine or the pir. Sufi scholar Affan Yesvi discusses Sufism and the Sufi orders of the subcontinent in his essay.

The historical interaction between Hinduism and Islam is complex and cannot be easily chronicled. However, certain similarities can be identified between the Bhakti movement in Hinduism and the Sufi movement in Islam. Though the Bhakti movement emerged a few centuries earlier than the Sufi movement, the two share some common characteristics. One notable similarity is the support they received from the lower rungs of society. People traditionally neglected and considered outcaste by the upper castes, thronged Sufi shrines, establishing their own soul connections and a feeling of belonging to the pir, a belonging, which was denied to them in a society ridden with caste and regional distinctions. Both these movements appealed to people across social classes, providing a more accessible and direct approach to spirituality. The anthropology of qawwali by Prof. Vinay Kumar Srivastava and Scholar Rachna Atri Saxena discusses this in detail.

A spirit of mutual understanding and tolerance developed as a result of the Bhakti and Sufi movements. Followers of both traditions often emphasised the universal nature of divine love and sought to transcend religious and social boundaries. This spirit of inclusivity and acceptance influenced literature, music, arts, and spiritual rituals. In literature, the poetry of Bhakti saints like Kabir and

Mirabai, as well as the works of Sufi poets such as Rumi and Khusrau, often expressed similar themes of divine love, unity, and transcendence. The concept of bhakti in qawwali and how it evolved with Khwaja Muinuddin Chishti is discussed in the essay by Reema Abbasi.

One significant example of the influence of bhakti on Sufism can be seen in the story of the revered Sufi saint Amir Khusrau. The Basant festival at the shrine of Hazrat Nizamuddin Auliya in New Delhi, going back 700 years, is a vibrant and deeply symbolic annual celebration. Attended by thousands, the festival is a unique confluence of devotion, culture, and music, reflecting a centuries-old tradition rooted in a beautiful historical narrative. The Bhakti and Sufi movements, while rooted in different religious traditions, shared common themes, using music as a means to connect with the divine, and contributed to a cultural and spiritual exchange that fostered mutual understanding and tolerance. A detailed photo essay by Dinesh Khanna showcases the resplendent Basant celebration at Nizamuddin Dargah.

This interaction played a role in shaping the diverse cultural landscape of the Indian subcontinent. This aspect of syncreticism was not limited to Delhi, it flourished further in Awadh, at the Kakori shrine, where Sufi saint Shah Turab Ali Qalandar wrote on Lord Krishna in documented volumes of diwan (a collection of poetry) which is sung till date by qawwals all over the subcontinent. A popular qawwali written by Azeemullah Shah Safipuri, '*Jhoomat aave nand ke lala, galin mein najariya lag jayein*', dedicated to Lord Krishna, is ecstatically sung by qawwals in Awadh. The Warsis of Dewa, followers of Sufi Saint Haji Waris Pak, play with resplendent colours on Holi, while qawwals sing on Holi and rang, a tradition that is alive even today. In this book several collective and individual issues are examined through academic studies on qawwali by scholars. Especially the unifying and syncretic nature of qawwali, which reflects the rich, diverse cultures of India. Photo essays by Mustafa Quraishi on Dewa and Safipur document these Awadh traditions of qawwali.

The composite nature of Indo-Islamic society of the subcontinent, the shared culture and the obvious similarity between the qawwali and the Indian ritualistic temple singing known as bhajan-kirtan are all embedded in this music tradition. This book discusses this in multiple essays and especially through the archival document 'Kauwali Bahar' and the essay on the Sanatani qawwali

Qawwali, a deeply kinship-oriented art form, is undergoing significant transformation as it moves beyond the confines of religious institutions and khanqahs (Sufi shrines) into broader cultural and global contexts. This book studies the impact of modernity on the performance of qawwali, a critical endeavour since oral traditions are often the first casualties in times of technological advancement. Qawwali in the twentieth century has moved from its original place of the khanqahs to a more secular space which has been extensively promoted by theatre, films, and even social media. It is no longer limited to specially trained singers from definite musical lineage. Today anyone can sing a qawwali. Once devoid of the role and the spiritual purpose it was created for, a qawwali is a song that any singer can sing. The 'sacred' vs 'secular' is a debate between tradition and modernity. For the sake of modernity is it essential that the essence of the form should be compromised?

It's a question that needs to be addressed. It is a journey from ishq-e-haqiqi, denoting the love of the Divine, the pursuit of ultimate truth, and ishq-e-majazi, traversing the realm of love of human affection underlined with sensual desire, and becoming a performative art, rather than an act of devotion. Sufi doctrines lay emphasis on the mystical and divine love but contemporary reinterpretations of qawwali have largely moved into the domain of sensualisation of human love that was not in the ambit of the qawwali form when it was created hundreds of years back.

Personally for me it is an unfortunate development, but academics are of the opinion that this change would help qawwali live and survive in a more secular format. This adaptability is also a reason for qawwali's global appeal, whether in traditional Sufi shrines or modern settings. A qawwal's flexibility in transforming the context from spiritual love to worldly love ensures that the music will remain relevant. It can now be moulded and performed in any setting, as we discuss in the essays here, at shrines, at religious mehfils, in cinema, in unconventional contexts like Hindu festivals or secular gatherings, and even in the growing pub culture, with or without losing its spiritual connect. Pragya Tiwari discusses the modern space of qawwali performances and her own personal experience.

While some like me, may lament this commercialization of qawwali, that it takes away from the spiritual essence of the form, it is undeniable that these changes have allowed the qawwals to sustain themselves with more economically viable performances, enabled this music to thrive in new spaces, reaching newer secular audiences that might otherwise have remained outside its influence. I grudgingly see the global spread of qawwali as a form of entertainment, instead of the spiritual purpose it was created for many centuries back, but at the same time it works for cultural preservation, allowing the traditional qawwals to survive in a changing world.

Notably, a unique manifestation known as 'filmi qawwali' has surfaced in Hindi films, sharing thematic elements with its traditional counterpart but distinguishing itself in presentation and contextual integration within the cinematic sphere. While the musical framework remained intact, changes have been made to suit the cultural context with an eye on popular audience reception. This commercial expansion brought out an array of compositions that deviated from the spiritual orientation completely. The popular qawwali '*Jhoom barabar jhoom sharabi*', clearly alluding to the drunkenness not of the divine love but of the material world, can be seen as an example of compositions designed for mass consumption. The commodification of qawwali is complete when we see it in the context of entertainment in Hindi cinema. The poetry used in cinema is often not associated with spiritual content and can exhibit a wide variety of poetic content completely unrelated to Sufism. The poetry, formerly a refined interplay of metaphysical themes and philosophical concepts, is now simplified to appeal to mass audiences and blasé popular tastes. This book explores the malleable nature of qawwali and its cultural elasticity, which allows it to incorporate diverse traditions and concepts, and its highly adaptive character which led to its easy integration into Hindi cinema, unlike the more strictly structured classical music traditions.

In Hindi cinema, qawwalis have been strategically incorporated into movie narratives to captivate audiences, add cultural richness, and infuse emotional depth into scenes. These qawwalis became memorable moments in films, contributing significantly to their overall appeal and success. The famous qawwali '*Na toh karwan ki talaash hai*' (Barsaat ki Raat, 1960) took qawwali to unbelievable heights of popularity. Filmi qawwalis represent a fascinating musical category, not only adapting the centuries-old Sufi tradition to the cinematic realm but also reinterpreting and portraying it in a distinctly modern, popular, and more secular context. In early Hindi cinema, qawwali emerged as a prominent form of entertainment in the format of the *sawaal-jawaab* qawwali, featuring two teams engaging in poetic exchanges. These teams, comprising either both male groups or one male and one female group, would select a qawwali and respond to each other through couplets or poetry. This format gained immense popularity and became a defining feature of the music of Hindi cinema. This improvisation within the sawaal-jawaab format was a departure from traditional qawwali performances, highlighting its adaptation for cinematic entertainment. A term 'secular qawwali' was used for film music where music contributed to and established a unique multicultural context, avoiding the depiction of a single culture or religion in isolation. Yousuf Saeed discusses this aspect of qawwali in detail in his essay.

Qawwali in cinema has also been used to foster stereotypes of a Muslim ethos or narrative. In earlier times it was used to establish a Muslim family wedding or celebration, with a distinctly Muslim attire and visual themes. Even in such instances, the qawwalis remained intensely popular with many legendary music directors creating unforgettable melodies. In more recent times songs such as like 'Kun Faya Kun' (Rockstar, 2011), 'Bhar Do Jholi Meri' (Bajrangi Bhaijaan, 2015), and 'Khwaja Mere Khwaja' (Jodhaa Akbar, 2008) bring the association of qawwali back to the shrine and to its spiritual foundations.

In many instances, traditional qawwali has been adapted in cinema, often with changes to the lyrics to suit the context of the movie, with blatant misuse and no respect for the original copyright of any qawwal family or tradition. Interestingly, there is one notable exception that marked a departure from this norm. Kaifi Azmi wrote original poetry for a qawwali, '*Maula Salim Chisti*' (*Garam Hawa*, 1974). This song became a part of the traditional qawwali repertoire and is now sung as a prayer by qawwals at the shrine of Hazrat Salim Chishti at Fatehpur Sikri. This is a rare instance where poetry written for entertainment purpose for Hindi cinema became integrated into the qawwali tradition itself, showcasing the enduring influence of cinema on cultural practices. This book looks at the qawwals of Hazrat Salim Chishti, Fatehpur Sikri, in the photo essay by Mustafa Quraishi.

An intriguing aspect of qawwali in Hindi cinema is the inclusion of women qawwals, because traditionally qawwali has been largely androcentric, with male performers dominating the tradition. Even historical figures like Amir Khusrau, who trained qawwals, focused primarily on male disciples. and the Qawwal Bachche Gharana started by him consisted of only male students. Prof. Danish Iqbal discusses the aspect of the feminine in the qawwali tradition. The inclusion of women qawwals in Hindi cinema challenged this norm, highlighting a departure from traditional gender roles and making a significant social statement. A notable example of this is a classic qawwali from *Mughal-e-Azam*. This qawwali, '*Teri mehfil mein kismet aazma ke hum bhi dekhengey*', pioneered the introduction of women into qawwali and a poetry that centred on love, and subsequently became immensely popular. In traditional qawwali, women performers have been few in number. In recent times figures like Shakila Bano Bhopali and Chanchal Bharati gained popularity in the traditional qawwali scene, but often did not receive the same recognition as their male counterparts who performed in Sufi shrines or dargahs. However, through cinema, this gender distinction became blurred, highlighting the significance of women's inclusion in the qawwali tradition.

In this volume, archivist and collector Amarnath Sharma shares from his private collection records from the gramophone era to establish the presence of women singers who were actively performing and recording qawwali from 1905 onwards as gramophone artists. This serves as a revelation of the popularity of women singing qawwali as sacred religious compositions, as well as songs for entertainment on themes of love and romance. Qawwali as we know today academically is understood as an androcentric form whereas the sound recording history proves it otherwise, where a large number of tawaifs and baijis were actively singing qawwali as part of their concerts and recordings. Ironically, in present times women performers have been denied being a part of qawwali, citing history and tradition.

Qawwals are not merely performers but also custodians of a rich heritage passed down through generation. Qawwali being an oral tradition works on a lineage system of passing the skill within the familial structure and hence brings the focus on the qawwal as the sole preserver of the from. The role of the qawwal has not received the recognition it deserves. Qawwals remain the 'unseen faces' at the shrine, singing their hearts out, as people stop by and handout some money as nazrana. The role of the qawwal is central to understanding the tradition of qawwali. Ironically, qawwals are not academic and their study is limited to the form of music and hence documentations like this gain significance. Qawwals are highly skilled musicians often with a deep knowledge of both music and Sufi traditions. The qawwal's relationship with the audience is dynamic and carries a mutual exchange of emotions. In the shrine setting, the qawwal is not merely a performer but a medium who facilitates the spiritual experience of the many listeners present.

In the modern context, however, the role of the qawwal has been compromised with the rise of qawwali as a commercialized genre in popular media. Increasingly, singers who are not qawwals and do not belong to the tradition are singing commercial qawwali. The pressure is on the traditional qawwal – he must perform for both sacred and commercial audiences. Anyone can sing a qawwali, but anyone cannot be a qawwal. Therein lies the difference. While commercialization has expanded the reach of qawwali, it has also altered the authenticity of the tradition and the spiritual purpose of qawwali. There is a clear distinction between shrine-based and non-shrine performances with the altering of its inherent spiritual essence. This book addresses the longstanding neglect of qawwals in the broader narrative of Indian performance traditions. By bringing academic aspects of tradition and photographs to light, this endeavour seeks to ensure that the brilliance and stewardship of a centuries-old art form is recognised, celebrated, and preserved in the digital age.

In an era marked by growing animosity between communities, the significance of the qawwali cannot be overemphasised. Qawwali goes beyond being a mere musical expression. It serves as a poignant reminder of our shared cultural heritage, diversity, and collective potential for harmonious coexistence. The inclusive and multicultural contexts created by qawwalis showcase that, despite differences, there exists a common thread that binds communities. Qawwali offers a positive narrative that emphasises the potential for peaceful and harmonious coexistence, promoting a shared cultural ethos that transcends religious and ethnic boundaries. Qawwali persists as a dynamic tradition, continually negotiating its place between spiritual authenticity and popular culture. This musical tradition has played a vital role in encapsulating and conveying the essence of emotions, cultural belonging and shared narratives across the Indian subcontinent. And it still does.

Sufism and Sufi Orders in the Indian Subcontinent

Affan Yesvi

oday, Sufism is a name without a reality; formerly it was a reality without a name.' Nearly a thousand years ago, the great Sufi saint Hazrat Ali al-Hujwiri (1009–77), known reverentially as Data Sahib in South Asia, wrote this in his *Kashf-al-Mahjub*, one of the most definitive of the classic manuals of early Sufism.

The essence of Sufism is the transformative experience of divine love and truth through direct personal experience with God. The trappings of the material world have always troubled seekers who yearn to break free and search for the Almighty. Over centuries, through its myriad interpretations and explanations, Sufism continues to be regarded as one of the highest spiritual pursuits of man to find God.

Persian Sufi saint Hazrat Abu Hamid al-Ghazali (1058–1111), a prominent and influential jurisconsult, philosopher and mystic in Islamic history, said this of Sufis: 'I learnt with certainty that it is above all the mystics [Sufis] who walk on the road of God; their life is the best life, their method the soundest method, their character the purest character. It became clear to me, however, that what is most distinctive of mysticism is something which cannot be apprehended by study, but only by immediate experience (*dhawq*, literally "tasting"), by ecstasy and by a moral change.'

Etymologically, the origin of the word Sufi has been linked to '*Suf*', meaning wool. This refers to the coarse woolen garments which were worn by the early ascetics and mystics in the Middle East. Wearing wool was a sign of poverty, simplicity, and detachment from worldly comforts—values that have always been embraced by the Sufis. The association of this path with purity and good actions continues to resonate with its core principles.

The Sufi path takes an individual on the journey of liberation. It provides man the roadmap for his personal bond with the Almighty. Adherence to the Sufi philosophy enables man to break free from the limitations of a life bound by material desires and worldly concerns, and to turn towards a profound connection with God in the landscape of his heart and soul.

Purity of heart, purity of mind and purity of action have always defined the Sufi way of life. In the late tenth century, Persian Sufi saint Abu Bakr al-Kalabadhi, the author of *Kitab at-Ta'arruf*, one of the most important works of Sufism composed during the first three hundred years of Islam, wrote: 'The Sufis were only named Sufis because of the purity *(safā)* of their hearts and the cleanliness of their acts *(athār)*.' Connecting the seeker to 'athār' (good actions, traces) aligns with Sufi thought, as Sufis strive to live ethically and leave a positive impact.

Sufi mysticism has always encouraged its practitioners and followers to focus on divine love and self-purification. The endeavour of the Sufis was always to live in accordance with the teachings of Prophet Muhammad (PBUH), emphasising upon spiritual growth and closeness to God. Through the centuries, Sufis have sought to emulate the virtues of the Prophet (PBUH), renouncing worldly desires to attain spiritual purity and unity with the Almighty. This path includes practices like dhikr (remembrance of God) and tazkiya (self-purification). Sufis take the long, arduous journey of self-purification, aiming to return to one's original state of purity (fitra).

Sufism is deeply rooted in Islamic values. Sufi masters encourage their followers to forge a personal connection with God and strive to embody the Prophet's (PBUH) character in daily life. Their emphasis is on the concept of sunnah as a way of life, devoutly incorporating the traditions, practices, sayings, silent approvals and the character of Prophet Muhammad (PBUH) as the faithful model for Muslims to follow.

Significantly, the emphasis of Sufi saints is not only on the outward facets of sunnah but also the inner transformation that it can bring about, achieving khuluqin azim (exalted character). Sufis view the inner qualities of the Prophet (PBUH), such as his piousness, humility, altruism and humanitarianism as fundamental to understanding and integrating the sunnah. They regard following the example of the Prophet (PBUH) as the path to cleanse the heart of impurities and ego (tazkiya), seeking and aspiring for inner perfection (ihsan).

While the Indian subcontinent shaped its own Islamic vocabulary, many Arabic words continued to be used. Among them is ihsan, meaning 'to do beautiful things'.

Ihsan is one of the three dimensions of the Islamic religion. Islam shows man the path—what one should do. Iman shines light on the reason—why one should do. Ihsan is primarily associated with intention. It encompasses excellence in every aspect. Like many other Arabic words, ihsan too is a word with many layers. As one Sufi writer notes, 'Ihsan is excellence. It is perfection. It is beauty. It is balance, harmony, discipline, good character, softness, gentleness, improvement, drive, willpower. Ihsan is a human reflection, a human attempt to achieve a high level in the areas covered by the revealed 99 beautiful names of Allah (SWT). It emphasises upon the pursuit of moral and spiritual perfection.'

Hazrat Ibn Hajar Al-Haythami (1503–66) wrote: 'Worship Allah (SWT) as if you see Him; if you do not see Him, He sees you.' Herein, one is instructed regarding the dual levels of ihsan: the direct perception of Allah (SWT) and the awareness of His omnipresence. Striving for ihsan elevates the pursuit of excellence into a habit, urging all seekers to cultivate a deep awareness of God's presence and strive for moral and spiritual excellence in every aspect of life.

Sufi meditative practices such as dhikr (remembrance of God) and embodying outward goodness in all ways are anchored in Quranic injunctions and the sunnah. Cultivating these practices guide the Sufis towards the path of spiritual elevation and achieving divine closeness while following the example of Prophet Muhammad (PBUH).

The Journey Within

◆

Thou sheddest light for me to travel by.
How many of earth's forms Thou makest Thine...

◆

The journey to God realisation is internal and profoundly personal. On the Sufi path to the Almighty, Sufi saints have described three essential dimensions. The first, and most familiar to many, is the 'journey towards God'. This marks the soul's ascent from the world of people to the presence of the Almighty.

The second is 'journeying in God', in which the seeker experiences the presence of God the Almighty. For one who has embarked on this journey, the divine experience of 'journeying in God' continually deepens without interruption.

The third dimension is 'journeying from God', in which the Master returns to the world to guide ordinary seekers on their path to God, to show them the way to finding the Almighty. This transformative mystical experience has been captured thus:

◆ ◆ ◆

Mosaafer-am be-shahr-e-man
Shaayad ke baaz na-gardam

◆ ◆ ◆

(I am a traveller to my place of origin
Perhaps I shall not return)

Each Individual Finds His Own Way towards God

Since ancient times, religious mystics have sought a connection with the divine. Those who are truly mystical often find that their experiences are beyond words and cannot be adequately described. For centuries, Sufis have related a parable to illustrate how an individual can only develop a limited and skewed understanding of God. It is derived from the *Hadiqat-ul-Haqiqah* (The Walled Garden of Truth) by Hazrat Hakim Abu'l-Majd Majdud Sana'i Ghaznavi (1080–1141), who hailed from Ghazna, a city in south-eastern Afghanistan.

The parable also illustrates how different individuals perceive Sufism differently, and that their understanding is based on their personal experiences and perspectives. Verily, Sufism is a diverse and multifaceted spiritual journey that can be traversed in different ways, depending on one's focus. The whirling dervishes of Mevlevi saw Sufism through the lens of devotional music and dance, to connect with the Almighty and express spiritual ecstasy. Sufi masters like Hazrat Rumi and Hazrat Bulleh Shah expressed their spiritual longing and love for God through their profound articulation of spiritual yearning.

For Sufi saints like Hazrat Nizamuddin Auliya, Sufism was the path of introspection and meditation. They devoutly practised dhikr (remembrance of God) in order to find inner peace and spiritual awareness. Other seekers focused on the philosophical and theological experiences of Sufism. They contemplated on wahdat al-wujud (unity of existence) and the nature of God and humanity.
The parable is as follows:

Not far from Ghur once stood a city tall
Whose denizens were sightless one and all
A certain sultan once, when passing nigh
Had pitched his camp upon the plain hard by
Wherein, to prove his splendour, rank and state
Was kept an elephant most huge and great
Then in the townsmen's minds arose desire
To know the nature of this creature dire
Blind delegates by blind electorate
Were therefore chosen to investigate
The beast, and each, by feeling trunk or limb
Strove to acquire an image clear of him
Thus each conceived a visionary whole
And to the phantom clung, with heart and soul.

When to the city they were come again
The eager townsmen flocked to them amain
Each one of them—wrong and misguided all—
Was eager his impressions to recall
Asked to describe the creature's size and shape
They spoke, while round about them, all agape
Stamping impatiently, their comrades swarm
To hear about the monster's shape and form.
Now, for his knowledge, each enquiring wight
Must trust to touch, being devoid of sight
So he who'd only felt the creature's ear
On being asked, 'How doth its heart appear?'

'Mighty and terrible,' at once replied.
'Like a carpet, hard and flat and wide.'

Then he, who on his trunk had laid his hand
Broke in, 'Nay, nay! I better understand
'Tis like a water-pipe, I tell you true
Hollow, yet deadly, and destructive too.'
While he, who'd had but leisure to explore
The sturdy limbs which the great beast upbore
Exclaimed, 'No, no, to all men be it known
'Tis like a column tapered to a throne.'

Each had but known a part, and no man all
Hence into deadly error each did fall
No way to know all man's heart can find
Can knowledge ever accompany the blind?
Fancies and phantoms vain as these, alack!
What else you can expect from fool in sack
Naught of God Almighty can creatures learn
Nor e'en the wise such mysteries discern!

Sufism in the Indian Subcontinent

In *The Clear Fountain on the Forty Paths*, a compilation by Muḥammad al-Sanūsī al-Idrīsī (1787–1859), an Algerian Muslim theologian and leader who founded the Senussi mystical order in 1837, wrote, 'The ways to God most High are many—the Shadhiliyya, the Suhrawardiyya, the Qadiriyya, and so forth—so that some say that they are as numerous as the souls of human beings. Nevertheless, although they have many branches, they are in reality one, since the goal of all is one.'

Islam arrived in India in the early eighth century and the mystical traditions of Sufism gained prominence in the Indian subcontinent during the eighth and ninth centuries. Sufism significantly gained in strength during the Delhi Sultanate in the tenth and eleventh centuries and subsequently spread across the rest of India.

Altaf Hussain Hali (1837–1914), the famous poet, writer and critic wrote a couplet that well illustrates the spread of Sufism in the Indian subcontinent.

'Jab Islam Hindustan mein aaya, uska rang badal gaya. Logon ne usay apne rang mein rang liya.' (When Islam came to India, its colour changed; people coloured it with their own hues.)

For over a millennium, Sufism has steadily evolved within India and has played a significant role in expanding the reach of Islam throughout South Asia. The widespread appeal of Sufism began in the twelfth century with the rise of established Sufi orders (silsilas). The migration of Sufis to the subcontinent increased in the thirteenth century, spurred by scholars and teachers fleeing Mongol invasions in Iran and Central Asia.

This influx led to the Indian subcontinent, especially Delhi, becoming a vital centre for the Sufi movement. Sufi Shaikhs integrated into Indian society through their open beliefs, respect for local customs, and incorporation of various belief systems. At Sufi khanqahs in medieval India, people professing different religions and enjoying different social status met and rubbed shoulders. Distribution of food (langars) was free for all.

The spread of Sufism in south India can be traced back to Arab traders and Sufi saints who arrived along the coastal areas, particularly during the tenth and eleventh centuries, coinciding with the rise of the Delhi Sultanate. Sufi orders such as the Qadiriyya and Chishtiyya established numerous dargahs across south India, which became centres for spiritual gatherings and community activities.

Around 1430, Sultan Ahmed Shah Al Wali Bahamani of Bidar Sultanate in the Deccan invited Hazrat Shah Nimatullah Wali, the famous spiritual leader or Qutb of the Nimatullah Order in Iran. Shah Nimatullah was more than a hundred years old by then, so he sent his son Hazrat Shah Khalilullah to India. Hazrat Shah Nimatullah Wali had opened the door of his tavern to seekers of all hues. He used to say: 'We are like the sea, people our waves; necessarily we are associated with everyone.' This philosophy aligned with the prevailing spiritual beliefs and played a key role in the spread of Sufism here.

In the extreme north, Sufism deeply influenced Kashmir and merged with the local traditions and culture to create a distinctive and flourishing spiritual heritage. A curious fact about Kashmir and the thriving tradition of Sufism there finds echoes in a book written in the twelfth century by Kalhana, a chronicler of

Kashmir. Kalhana wrote the following about Kashmir in his book *Rajatarangini* (Sanskrit, The River of Kings), a legendary and historical chronicle of Kashmir: 'The country which may be conquered by spiritual merit, not armed force.' And so it was that Islam spread in Kashmir.

Introduced by revered Sufi saints like Hazrat Bulbul Shah of the Suhrawardi order in the thirteenth century, Sufism gained ground by promoting love, compassion, and humanity, resonating with Kashmiris. Islam spread further in the region with the arrival of Mir Syed Ali Shah Hamdani, a Sufi saint from Central Asia and Persia. Saints, called rishi in the local language, were revered people in Kashmir. Sufi saints were also referred to as rishis. They advocated communal harmony and even mediated disputes. Sufism's impact led to a syncretic culture known as Kashmiriyat, where Hindu and Muslim communities coexisted harmoniously. This unique form of Sufism incorporated elements of Kashmiri Buddhism and Shaivism, merging with local traditions and flowing as shared spiritual heritage.

Sufi Orders in the Indian Subcontinent

Rooted in a network of spiritual lineages or silsilas, the Sufi tradition in the Indian subcontinent blossomed into diverse orders, each known as a tariqa. Over the centuries, various Sufi orders, or silsilas, emerged. Each of them contributed to the rich tapestry of Sufi thought and practice in India.

Sufi orders in India historically branched into two main categories. A large number of them emerged as the Ba-shara orders, with strict adherence to Islamic law. The second kind were the Be-shara orders, who chose not to be constrained by Islamic law. Both kinds of order held sway and influence across the Indian subcontinent.

Sufi silsilas are spiritual lineages and many of them have traversed several centuries, connecting the disciples and followers to their revered masters. All Sufi silsilas ultimately trace their roots to Prophet Muhammad (PBUH).

The Sufi orders evolved as structured groups with their dedicated following, distinct spiritual practices and meditational traditions. To join a silsila and to convey their lifelong allegiance (bay'ah) and surrender, it was a usual practice for the disciples to place their hands on the master's hand. This simple and profound gesture conveyed the disciple's readiness to draw wisdom and clarity from the master through submission and spiritual connection.

Simplicity of the Heart, Natural Flow of the Soul

Sufism is a deeply personal connection with the divine. The mysticism of the Sufis cannot be discerned by a worldly eye. These connections are forged with emotions that lie deep in our subconscious, and which rise to be part of our energy circle, our vibe—making the whole mystical and miraculous for the Sufi. Poetry and mysticism intertwine in Sufism. Hazrat Bu Ali Shah Qalandar, Hazrat Rumi, Hazrat Amir Khusrau gave expression to their deeply mystical experiences in verses that have guided seekers for centuries.

Can one know the divine without the simplicity of the heart and natural flow of the soul? What the Sufi masters called veils are the layers of the world that settle upon our heart. These layers cloud our vision, and we cannot witness the Divine shining forth around us in all His glory. Those who have known the Almighty have first unlearned all the learning that they carry. This may be achieved by highly committed spiritual practice, or this experience may descend upon an individual as a grace of God the Almighty.

There is a beautiful story relating to the time when Hazrat Nizamuddin Auliya, master of Hazrat Amir Khusrau, directed Khusrau to keep visiting the gatherings of another famous Sufi saint Hazrat Bu Ali Shah Qalandar.

One fine day, Hazrat Qalandar jokingly teased Khusrau: How is it that I have never seen your master Hazrat Nizamuddin at the heavenly gathering conducted by Prophet Muhammad (PBUH) in heaven? Hazrat Khusrau was crestfallen and dejected, but he had no reason to doubt this assertion. When Hazrat Nizamuddin Auliya met his favourite disciple, he perceived something amiss. Upon questioning, he got to know what had happened. He laughed and said, 'When the Qalandar asks you this very question again, tell him that he should take you to the gathering in heaven and that you will yourself seek out your Master (me) there.'

When Hazrat Bu Ali Shah Qalandar asked the same question next time, Hazrat Khusrau asked to be taken to the heavenly gathering where he would himself seek his master Hazrat Nizamuddin. Hazrat Bu Ali Shah Qalandar agreed and put his hand on Hazrat Khusrau's heart. Instantaneously, Hazrat Khusrau found himself in an unimaginable place where shining figures were in attendance. But he was disappointed to find that Hazrat Nizamuddin Auliya was not there Sad and despondent, Hazrat Khusrau asked the Master of Ceremonies, the Holy Prophet Muhammad (PBUH) if his master was present there. The Prophet (PBUH) pointed upwards and said, 'You won't find him here, try searching higher.'

Hazrat Khusrau progressed to the second stage and saw a similar gathering. Again, the Prophet (PBUH) was conducting the holy gathering. The kamaal (calibre) of these saints was higher than those who were present at the first gathering. Again Hazrat Khusrau couldn't find Hazrat Nizamuddin there. He continued to ask for him till they went up all the seven levels. At the seventh level he still was unable to see his master. At this gathering, which was the highest of all, he saw beneath the feet of the Holy Prophet Muhammad (PBUH) two mysterious personalities. Upon approaching them, Hazrat Khusrau saw his master as one among them. The two were the masters of the masters he had encountered during his journey. Hazrat Khusrau tried to fall at the feet of his master with a cry of delight. As he fell, the Qalandar withdrew his hand from Khusrau's heart, the brilliant lights vanished, and they were back where they had been sitting.

When Hazrat Khusrau next visited Hazrat Nizamuddin Auliya, he took along his musical instruments and presented his poem:

◆

Nami danam chi manzil bood shab jaay ki man boodam;
Baharsu raqs-e-bismil bood shab jaay ki man boodam.
Pari paikar nigaar-e-sarw qadde laala rukhsare;
Sarapa aafat-e-dil bood shab jaay ki man boodam.
Khuda khud meer-e-majlis bood andar laamakan Khusrau;
Muhammad shamm-e-mehfil bood shab jaay ki man boodam.

◆

(I wonder what was the place where I was last night.
All around me were half-slaughtered victims of love,

> tossing about in agony. There was a nymph-like beloved with cypress-like form and tulip-like face, ruthlessly playing havoc with the hearts of the lovers. God himself was the master of ceremonies in that heavenly court, Oh Khusrau, where [the face of] the Prophet (pbuh) too was shedding light like a candle).

The poem is lush with metaphors, imagery and symbolism, in which the heavenly court and the divine presence symbolise the spiritual and sublime love that encompassed the palace. Through these striking, inspired verses, Hazrat Khusrau gave the timeless message that all talk of divine experiences or the other realm are meaningless unless one experiences them oneself. But these divine experiences are real and one can seek and find them only if one starts from the premise that 'I know nothing'.

Notably, Hazrat Nizamuddin Auliya, known for his pious insistence on love and service to humanity for attaining closeness to the Almighty, was revered by his followers as 'Mehboob-e-Ilahi' (Beloved of God). The title spoke of his illustrious and noble spiritual status, his closeness to the Almighty and his stature as a guiding light of faith and devotion.

Sheikh Abd al-Qadir al-Jilani, a renowned Sufi saint of the Qadiriyya, one of the oldest Sufi orders, was revered as Mehboob-e-Subhani to highlight his lofty position among Sufis and his role as a spiritual leader and guide. Sheikh Abd al-Qadir al-Jilani was lovingly called Ghawth al-A'zam (the greatest helper) by his disciples and followers. Both titles reflect the profound spiritual reverence and regard for these great saints.

The limits of human understanding veil the Almighty from man's reach. When one does not know, one knows all that is to be known. The Sufi heart surrenders to the mystery of the divine, because true knowledge lies not in books but in realms beyond human comprehension. As Hazrat Bulleh Shah sang:

◆

Parh parh ilm te faazil hoya
Te kaday apnay aap nu parhya naai

◆

(You have studied tomes and tomes of books and have become a learned man. But have you ever studied yourself? Have you ever gone into yourself?)

Spiritual truths cannot be grasped through the prism of logic or rational knowledge. Spiritual truths shine through when an individual trusts the unknown and embraces it, surrendering to the divine glory that shines in everything we perceive through our senses. The pir can guide us to those magical realms where one may experience the Almighty, and our tears of surrender and acceptance may flow.

It is believed that the pirs, who illuminate with the power of their meditative and spiritual strength, intercede for their followers in the afterlife. In this way, deep bonds of surrender and acceptance are forged between the disciples and their spiritual guides. The traditions, rituals, poetry and devotional expression of each silsila create meaningful and fulfilling legacies for their followers through centuries.

Sufi Orders in India

Several prominent Sufi orders (silsila) established their presence in India, each with unique characteristics and teachings that were intricately linked to the socio-political landscape of the region. By the twelfth century, Sufi orders had evolved into well-established religious institutions that offered spiritual guidance to communities in both urban and rural areas. Sufi khanqahs served as important hubs for social interaction and cultural exchange, fostering a sense of unity among people from different backgrounds. Inclusive Sufi teachings, which stressed upon the universal philosophy of brotherhood, fostered dialogue among various religious communities, encouraging peace and mutual understanding.

Chishti Order: Founded by Khwaja Moinuddin Chishti in Ajmer during the twelfth century, this order is renowned for its emphasis on love, tolerance, and inclusiveness. The Chishti order attracted followers from diverse backgrounds and became a significant force in spreading Sufism throughout India. Notable figures of the Chishti order include Hazrat Qutubuddin Bakhtiyar Kaki, Baba Fariduddin Ganjshakar, and Hazrat Nizamuddin Auliya who further propagated its teachings across the subcontinent.

The teachings of Hazrat Nizamuddin Auliya advocated renunciation and trust in God, promoting a vision of unity among mankind that transcended social and economic distinctions. He encouraged his followers to engage in altruism, particularly through acts of charity, such as feeding the poor and supporting the oppressed. Hazrat Nizamuddin also maintained a distance from political power, focusing instead on the spiritual upliftment of the common people. His gatherings, characterised by zikr and langar, fostered inclusivity among diverse faiths and backgrounds, making his dargah a sanctuary for all seekers of truth and solace.

Suhrawardi Order: This is a significant Sufi order founded by Hazrat Abu 'l-Nadjib Suhrawardi in the twelfth century. It gained prominence in India through the efforts of Sheikh Bahauddin Zakariya, who established major centres in regions like Delhi, Bengal and Multan, and was influential in shaping local Sufi practices. The order emphasises a balance between mystical practices and scholarly pursuits, advocating for community engagement and ethical living. The Suhrawardi order gained prominence for its rigorous adherence to Islamic law (Sharia) while also emphasising spiritual discipline.

Sheikh Bahauddin Zakariya was awarded the title of Sheikh-ul-Islam by Sultan Iltutmish. The Suhrawardis maintained a structured approach, organising khanqahs for spiritual learning. The order played a crucial role in the spread of Islam in India, influencing both rulers and common people, and remains active in various regions today.

Hazrat Sayyid Djalal Bukhari, also known as Djalal Surkh, was a notable disciple of Hazrat Bahauddin and founded the Jalali branch of the order.

The Firdausi order was also a branch of the Suhrawardi order established in the fourteenth century in Rajgir, Bihar.

Qadiri Order: This order, founded by Abdul Qadir Gilani in Baghdad in the twelfth century, is one of the most prominent Sufi orders in India. It became popular among South Asian Muslims, especially during the Mughal period. It emphasises upon piety and spiritual cleansing, adherence to Islamic fundamentals and the pursuit of spiritual enlightenment through love and devotion to God. The order gained significant traction in India, particularly through the efforts of figures like Sultan Bahu, who popularised its teachings through poetry and writings.

The Qadiri order has numerous suborders, including Qadiri Naushahi and Qadiri Sarwari, which further disseminated its principles across the Indian subcontinent. Today, it remains influential, promoting a message of peace and spiritual unity among diverse communities.

Naqshbandi Order: This was founded by Hazrat Baha al-Din Naqshband in the fourteenth century in Central Asia. The Naqshbandi order is distinguished by its practice of silent zikr and for its emphasis on adherence to Islamic law. It gained prominence during the Mughal period due to its close ties with the ruling elite, particularly under Emperor Akbar's reign.

The order gained significant influence in India during the late sixteenth century, primarily through Khwaja Baqi Billah and his disciple Hazrat Ahmad Sirhindi, who played key roles in its propagation. The Naqshbandi order has produced various suborders and remains a vital force in contemporary Sufi practices, promoting spiritual reform and unity among Muslims.

Music as a Form of Ibadat in Indian Sufi Traditions

Hazrat Abu Hamid al-Ghazali famously said, 'The study of text alone is not sufficient preparation for spiritual union with God.' Hazrat al-Ghazali, considered to be the eleventh century's Mujaddid (renewer of the faith) and so highly acclaimed by his contemporaries that he was awarded the honorific title 'Proof of Islam' (Ḥujjat al-Islam), believed that music and dance—and the rituals associated with them—are necessary tools to prepare for the mystic experience.

Many Indian Sufi saints embraced music as a vital aspect of their spiritual practice, believing it could facilitate a transformative experience that brings individuals closer to God. Hazrat Nizamuddin Auliya utilised music in his gatherings to foster a sense of closeness to God. His disciple Hazrat Amir Khusrau blended various musical elements from different cultures and developed the musical genre of qawwali for sama gatherings. He also helped in establishing a rich tradition of Sufi devotional music in India. The lyrical content of Sufi music often expresses longing for the divine, as seen in the works of poets like Hazrat Baba Bulleh Shah.

James Mayer, a strategic communications assistant at the Smithsonian Center for Folklife and Cultural Heritage and a Fulbright Fellow in Konya, Turkey, has noted that in many Sufi orders, music plays an essential role in ritual, practice, and community building. Mayer writes that while the music from the sama and zikr rituals is strikingly different, both utilise music and ritualised movement to empower participants to achieve transcendence or mystical union with God.

As Hazrat Rumi, the globally famous thirteenth-century Sufi mystic sang:

Don't worry about saving these songs!
And if one of our instruments breaks,
it doesn't matter.
We have fallen into the place
where everything is music.

When everything is music, everything is God, everything is the Divine, all that flows are his notes, his play, his rhythm and flow. What miracles shall flow in His sohbat (company)? How hardened hearts may melt and tired minds may find solace in the divine sohbat when He holds our hand and shows us the way. The deep connection to Almighty the Beloved must never be lost, and times and technology must enable us to deepen this bond. In our rushed life space, we may not be able to physically partake of the divine nectar of sohbat. And hence there are alternatives like digital sohbat, virtual gatherings, which have been chosen by seekers to engage in spiritual discourses that uplift the soul and show the way.

One may choose one's way. One may choose one's music. The way may be ibadat (worship), encompassing acts of devotion such as prayer, fasting, and dhikr. One may get lost in the magic of wajd, the state of divine ecstasy that often arises during practices like dhikr or Sufi music, reflecting an intense spiritual connection. Or one's journey to the divine may be through tariqat, the path. The structured journey within a Sufi order or the way of the wandering dervish, all may lead towards ma'rifah (knowledge of God) and ultimately fana (self-annihilation in God).

As the spirit flows through the amazing freedom found in surrender to the divine, one encounters fleeting touches of ihsan, excellence or perfection in worship. In this blessed state, the veils drop, and one may worship God as though one may see Him with eyes of love, faith and devotion. Sincerity and purity must flow through every breath in our being. Ihsan encapsulates the essence of Sufi thought. It captures the glorious space of those who have been able to experience the divine in their heart and soul. With unwavering devotion and a heart that thirsts for unity with the divine, one moves forward to seek the divine through self-purification, love and deep, abiding surrender.

Hazrat Ali (RA)

Syed Zia Alvi &
Manjari Chaturvedi

Shah-e-Mardan,
Sher-e-Yazdan,
Quwwat-e-Parwardigaar,
La Fatah ila Ali,
la Saif illa Zulfiqar

he voice of a single qawwal rises in aalap (musical notes set in raga) singing the above verses, calling out to Hazrat Ali (RA), the Lion of the God, the brave one, the one who is blessed with the strength of the God himself. Another voice from the chorus joins in and repeats the verse, the repetition is not merely a musical need but is the firm belief of the qawwal himself, this time at a higher pitch. He believes in Hazrat Ali (RA), and is calling out to him. Then a third voice brings the last line of the verse on a lower pitch, there is no one like Ali and there is no sword like Zulfiqar, and thus starts the beginning of Qaul, the composition that epitomises the musical form of qawwali and the bravery and generosity of Hazrat Ali (RA). Both intertwined and inseparable. The phrase expresses the belief that Ali is unmatched in his bravery and strength.

Ali imam-e-man-ast-o-manam ghulam-e-Ali
hazar jaan-e-giramī fida ba-nam-e-Ali

(Ali is my imam, and I am his slave,
innumerable revered souls are all devoted to Ali)

Hazrat Amir Khusrau is credited with the specific composition of the Qaul, *'Man kunto maula fa-haza Ali yun maula'*, a Hadith, a saying of Prophet Mohummad (PBUH), which also has the musical stanzas of tarana, a musical composition with rhythmic syllables set to a specific raga and rhythm, interspersed between these lines, which is popularly sung by qawwals as a tradition till date, during a performance.

man kunto maula fa-haza Ali yun maula
da-ra-dil-da-ra-dil dar-dani
ham-tum ta-na-na-na na-na-re
yala li yala li yalali-yalali ya la li

(Whoever accepts me as their Maula [Master/Lord],
Ali is also their Maula)

The above lines reverberate in the multiple voices of the qawwals, creating layers of sound, till there is nothing audible but the sound of the name of Ali. This is an often heard qawwali and a very popular composition, known as Qaul and we can frequently hear the audience request simply asking to sing 'Ali Maula' especially during the shrine performances. It is a composition that has the power of creating the spiritual ecstasy that qawwali is originally created for and is sung at all Sufi shrines and sama mehfils (assembly of listeners). The nisbat (connect) between a qawwal and Hazrat Ali (RA) is one of spiritual offerings and there are many compositions written in praise of Hazrat Ali (RA). Most poetry refers to the power, might, or the divine ability attributed to Hazrat Ali (RA), the Supreme Being. It is common in Islam to praise and glorify Hazrat Ali (RA), who is the fourth caliph in Islam but is considered the first Imam.

◆

Ana Madina-tul-ilm wa Ali-un-babuha

◆

(मैं इल्म का शहर हूँ, और अली उसका दरवाज़ा है।
I am the city of knowledge and Ali is it's gate)

The above lines by Prophet Muhammad (PBUH) for Hazrat Ali (RA) underline the status of Hazrat Ali (RA) in the hierarchy in Islam. He is also known as Ali Ibn-e-Abu Talib and was born at the sacred Kaaba in Mecca (now in Saudi Arabia) in AD 599. A revered figure for Muslims, he is respected for his bravery in many battles during the tumultuous times in Islamic history. He also played a pivotal role in reviving Muslim culture and traditions in the region and died in AD 661 in Kufa (now in Iraq).

A relative and a constant companion of Prophet Muhammad (PBUH), Ali is one of his first four successors who are called 'caliphs'. The Prophet gave his daughter, Faṭimah to Hazrat Ali (RA) in marriage. He also designated him as one of the scribes who would compile the text of the Quran, which had been revealed to Prophet Muhammad (PBUH). Hazrat Ali (RA) further worked all his life to spread the teachings of Islam. Most Sufi orders trace their lineage to Prophet Muhammad (PBUH) through Hazrat Ali (RA). Sufis believe that Ali inherited from the Prophet the spiritual power (wilayah or walayah).

Ekai suratiya ki dui hai muratiya
Ek Mohammad ek Ali
Ali Maula, Maula Ali Ali

The multiple voices of the qawwals keep repeating the above lines referring that Prophet Muhammad (PBUH) and Hazrat Ali (RA) are inseparable. The frenzy in their voices is the belief in their hearts, as the multiple chorus of the voices and the sounds rise up from their hearts to the listeners, the belief transcends to the listener with the same intensity as it is being called out by the qawwals. What is it about Hazrat Ali (RA) that makes the qawwals go into an ecstatic state of mystical frenzy while singing?

Kabhi diivaar hiltii hai, kabhii dar kaanp jaataa hai,
Ali kaa naam sun kar ab bhii khaibar kaanp jaataa hai,
Ali ji veer ho, balwan ho, dhartipita tum ho,
Kathin haarey jagat ke ishwar ke soorma tum ho,
Anokhi tumhari leela hai, koi kya jaane kya tum ho
Kahi dharmatma tum ho, kahi
parmatma tum ho,

According to a very popular legend, Ali is said to have torn off the door of the fort (khaibar) with one hand and used it as a shield during the battle. The qawwals often recite the above lines in praise of the bravery of Hazrat Ali (RA). Loosely translated it would mean that the moment you utter the name of Hazrat Ali (RA), walls tremble, the threshold shudders, the door shivers. The compassion of Ali is spoken of alongside, each time his bravery is referred, for he is the saviour for people, he is the one who will fight for their right and will solve their problems. Mushkil Kusha, he is the one who untangles life's knots, the many complexities of life, and liberates souls from the trappings of this world. He can further unfold the mysteries of the universe, for he is the one illuminated with divine grace.

In every language, long poems are written in praise of him and they tell us about his life story through incidents thereby keeping the Islamic history alive. These poems are further repeated by the qawwals through their singing, generation after generation as a living tradition. These accounts of Hazrat Ali's (RA) strength and courage in the many battles fought and also his own desire for justice, made him an epitome of humanity throughout the Islamic world. The qawwals continue to chant in multiple repetition, as if in a frenzy, expressing their complete surrender to Hazrat Ali (RA), their voices raised at a high pitch proclaiming that each pore of their body takes the name of Ali. Their voice utters the same name, even the day they die, they seek the name of Ali written on the kafan (the shroud used to wrap the dead body).

Tan mein Ali Ali, toh zabaan par Ali Ali
Mar jaaon toh likh dena kafan par, Ali Ali

Hazrat Ali (RA) is known within the Islamic tradition by a number of titles, some reflecting his personal qualities and others derived from particular episodes of his life like Murtaza, Asad Ullah, Haydar, Amir al-Muminin. Most names are derived from the word 'lion' as in Arabic there are more than a hundred names of lion based on specific situations.

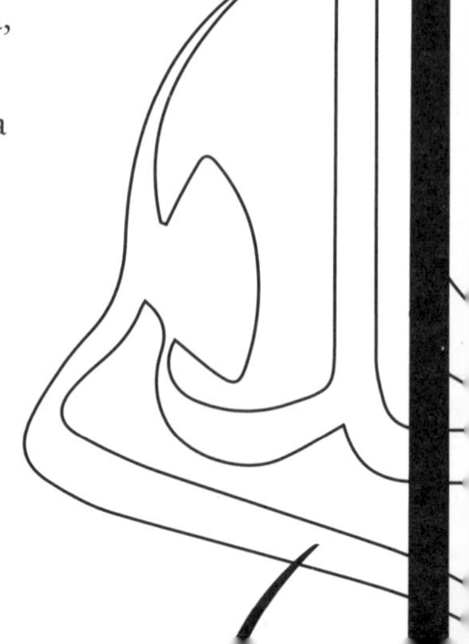

Panjtan: The Holy Five

Kismet ka Sikandar hun, muqaddar ka dhani hun
Taqdeer ka yavar hun, muqaddar ka dhani hun
Main panjtani, panjtani, panjtani hun
Ghulam e panjtani hun

The above lines are from a very famous and much sought-after qawwali sung by qawwals all over the subcontinent, one that is completely in surrender to the Panjtan. Hazrat Ali (RA) is celebrated in qawwalis in multiple ways, even the poetry sung often refers to the term Panjtan, the Holy Five persons, in Islam. The Prophet Mohammad (PBUH), his daughter Bibi Fatima, his son-in-law Hazrat Ali (RA) and their sons Hasan and Husayn.

The Battle of Karbala

There were many battles fought during that period, but the 'Battle of Karbala', fought in AD 680, at Karbala (now in Iraq) was a defining battle that has been kept alive in public memory till date. The historical stories of this battle are full of pathos and pain and the suffering that the Imam had to go through while fighting for justice. This was a fierce military battle between Yazid I and the supporters and family members of Imam Husayn Ibn Ali, son of Hazrat Ali (RA), grandson of Prophet Muhammad (PBUH). Most of the supporters and family members of Imam Husayn Ibn Ali were massacred and killed or were taken prisoners by a large army of Yazid I. Imam Husayn was tragically killed while he was in namaz (praying).

Imam Husayn Ibn Ali and his supporters were deprived of water before being murdered. The army of Yazid I was guarding the river Faraat (now called Euphrates) so that even water was not available to them and hence this extreme thirst of Imam Husayn is referred to in most elegies written for Karbala. The incidents of this battle have been kept alive through collective memory, in the literature of almost all languages and it finds prominence in the history of Islam. Imam Husayn's suffering and death during the battle became a symbol of sacrifice in the struggle for right against wrong and for seeking justice. The memory of Karbala continues to inspire resistance against tyranny and oppression.

Muharram and Marsiya

Muharram is a sacred month, the first month of the lunar calendar in Islam, and it is the beginning of the new Islamic year. It is the most revered month being associated with the martyrdom of Imam Husayn Ibn Ali, son of Hazrat Ali (RA). During the month of Muharram, the mourning includes fasting and majlis (religious gatherings) where marsiya (elegies) are recited by members of the community including the qawwals, to keep the memory of the sacrifice of Imam Husayn and battle of Karbala alive. There are processions of people carrying the miniature replicas of Imam Husayn's tomb, called tazia. These tazias are symbols of grief, mourning for the dead, which are taken out on the tenth day of Muharram, known as the Day of Ashura, a day of public mourning, memorizing the battle of Karbala, and the qawwals walk along reciting the marsiyas (elegies) without using any musical instruments.

Marsiya (elegy), is a poem which is written in lamentation of the the martyrdom of Imam Husayn, his family and supporters at the Battle of Karbala. Marsiya is a distinct style of religious poetry with a specific religious purpose, and is largely written in Urdu and Persian language. It is used by Muslims to mourn the tragedy. There are long poems that describe the battle scenes, the suffering and the martyrdom of Imam Husayn. *Waqia-e-Karbala* by Meer Anees and poems by Mirza Dabeer are very long and even extend to eight hundred lines. 'Noha' is a marsiya specifically written as lamentation and is recited in praise of Imam Husayn as part of collective mourning in gatherings. The valour of Imam Husayn and the memory of death is passionately kept alive till this day and a dramatic recitation of these elegies is meant to move the audience to tears.

In the subcontinent, during this holy month of Muharram especially till the tenth day of Ashura, the qawwals do not perform with instruments and they do not give qawwali performances. During this period every year, the qawwals only recite marsiya and sozkhwani (the tradition of narrating the story of the battle of Karbala in song) and salaam in reverence to shaheeds (martyrs) of Karbala, 'Shaudaye Karbala' to express their grief and devotion. Imam Husayn and his companions are widely regarded as martyrs by Muslims all over the world.

Woh salaam kahiye Husayn ko, ki bahisht jiska sila miley,
Ye talab to apni taraf se hai, mujhe dekhiye wahan kya miley,
Jo dar-e-Husayn ka ho gada, usey ho rasai Ali talak,
Jo Ali miley to Nabi miley, Jo Nabi miley to Khuda miley

The same voices of qawwals that ecstatically sing the praise of Hazrat Ali (RA), using various instruments and percussions and raising their sound to reach the skies, as part of qawwali, remain silent all through this period mourning the death of the sons of Hazrat Ali (RA), their allegiance to him remains paramount.

◆ ◆ ◆

Poet: Syed Zia Alvi

◆ ◆ ◆

Dekho sar-e-yazid, andheron mein gharq hai,
Dekho chamak rahey hain, mere panjtan ke paon.

In history, the head of Yazid lies in darkness, he the one, who killed the Imam, he is the one forgotten. While the panjtan, the holy five, the ones who were massacred, they are shining bright and are alive in the memory of people till today. They are eternal.

QAWWALI AT NIZAMUDDIN

Sing for My Pir, Sing for My People

Hazrat Nizamuddin Auliya is referred to as Mahboob-e-Ilahi or the Beloved of God. He is recognised as the greatest Sufi saint of his times. Born in a small town Badaun, in present-day Uttar Pradesh, he lived his life in Delhi, where his dargah is thronged by visitors of all religions, genders and social status even today. The words of Sufi Saint Baba Farid Ganjshakar were prophetic, 'You will be a tree, under whose soothing shadow, people will find rest and comfort.' As the successor of Baba Farid, Nizamuddin Auliya became that towering tree, under whom the mystical tradition, the Chishtiya silsila and the Sufi tenets flourished.

Hazrat Nizamuddin was fond of sama (mystical gatherings) and listened to qawwali daily and hence till date music is performed every day at the shrine. The daily informal music sessions are intimate gatherings in which the assembly of listeners sit on the ground right next to where the qawwals perform. There is no amplification of sound, and the voices rise from the hearts of the singers to the listeners, both moved to rapturous heights of spiritual ecstasy. The qawwals sit facing the shrine and perform for their pir (the master) and yet qawwali becomes the means of prayer for some and for others the balm that soothes their souls. The prophecy was true, hundreds of years have passed and yet people throng the shrine to seek comfort for their souls. Qawwali was designed to be an inclusive and accessible form and hence it draws people from diverse backgrounds into a shared spiritual space, especially the dargah.

The dargah compound, situated in an area that is named Hazrat Nizamuddin, after the saint himself, has the shrines of both Hazrat Nizamuddin Auliya and Hazrat Amir Khusrau. Hazrat Amir Khusrau, known as 'tuti-e-hind', the parrot of India, established the 'Qawwal Bachche Gharana', a lineage of twelve disciples who were personally trained in qawwali by him. These musicians laid the groundwork for the formalisation of qawwali as a distinct genre. Qawwali has been kept alive by them through their unbroken lineage and successive generations. Like other oral musical performance traditions, the qawwal gharanas (musical lineages of qawwal bachche) adhere to codes of conduct at the shrine and the musical principles that keep the spiritual authenticity and purpose of the form intact.

All qawwals of the subcontinent pay respect as a musical haziri to the Sufi saint whose abode is said to have been the place where the present form of qawwali originated. Poetic compositions abound in praise of Hazrat Nizamuddin Auliya sung daily at the shrine. The qawwals who owe allegiance to the saint write 'Nizami' along with their names as their identification, establishing nisbat (connection) and becoming the followers of the saint.

Photographer: Dinesh Khanna
Qawwali Practitioners: Qawwal Saqlain Nizami, Qawwal Hasnain Nizami, Ustad Ghulam Rasool Nizami, Ustad Meraj Ahmad Nizami, Qawwal Dhruv Sangari, Haider Qawwal, Ather Hayat Qawwal.
Text: Manjari Chaturvedi
Place: Dargah Hazrat Nizamuddin, New Delhi, India
Project: The Qawwali Project

qawwali at
nizamuddin

LAHORE MUSIC HOUSE

Hazrat Khwaja Nizamuddin Auliya's Defence of Sama and Qawwali at Sultan Ghiyasuddin Tughluq's Court

Raziuddin Aquil

ishq ra bu hanifa dars na-guft
shafi'i ra dar riwayat nist

(Abu Hanifa did not teach lessons of love
Shafi'i is also not reported to have done so)

Sufi music is about love for God and care for all his creations. Struggles over Sufi music and dance has a long history, with artists and connoisseurs running into difficulties with the custodians of public morality backed by political regimes. Yet for all their powers, they have not been able to suppress the artists and art forms. This chapter deals with the troubles faced by Delhi's foremost Chishti Sufi saint, Hazrat Khwaja Nizamuddin Auliya on account of his interest in qawwali. Though there might have been some other political issues behind the harassment, he was called to defend his interest in Sufi music, sama and qawwali, in the light of the shari'at, or Sunni-Hanafi interpretation of Islam presented as law, at a judicial interrogation (mahzar) at Sultan Ghiyasuddin Tughluq's court (darbar). Nizamuddin Auliya's arguments more or less settled the issue of the legitimacy of Sufi music as a popular and devotional art form, though naysayers have continued with their tirade. Some even attack Sufi practices in general.[1]

According to Amir Khwurd Kirmani, the author of the mid–fourteenth-century Sufi text, *Siyar-ul-Auliya*, Hazrat Nizamuddin identified four kinds of musical practice: halal (lawful), haram (forbidden), makruh (abominable) and mubah (permissible). If the connoisseur (sahib-i wajd o haal) is fairly attracted towards the divine, his practice of sama is mubah; if he is inclined more towards majaz (this—worldly concerns), it is makruh; if his interest is entirely for majaz, it is haram; and if he is fully devoted to God, sama is halal for him. The practitioner of music (sahib-i sama) should be capable of understanding these distinctions.[2]

Amir Khwurd further writes, quoting from Hazrat Nizamuddin's remarks (recorded in *Fawa'id-ul-Fu'ad*), that the singer (musma) should be an adult male, and not a boy or woman. The heart of the listener (mustame) should be full of love and devotion for God. The content (masmu) should not be vulgar (fahash, hazl). Musical instruments (ala-i sama) such as chang and rabab should not be used in majlis-i-sama.[3] Hazrat Nizamuddin emphasised during his conversations with disciples that whatever was being heard was for remembering God (yaad-i-haqq) and, thus, it was a valid (halal) act.[4] Hazrat Nizamuddin is also reported to have outlined the adab or norms for sama: it should be held at an appropriate time when the heart is free from any anxiety; it should be organised at a place where the environment is soul-refreshing; the participants should belong to the same group of male adults known for their addiction (zauq) for sama, which in practice was a blend of poetry, music and dance. At the time of settling down in the majlis (musical assembly), one should wear a neat and perfumed attire.[5]

The above norms are supplemented with suggestions made by Fakhruddin Zarradi, a khalifa (one of the spiritual successors) of Hazrat Nizamuddin Auliya who actively participated in the discussion on the legitimacy of Sufi music. According to Zarradi, sama should be listened to with full attention. The participants of the majlis should not look at each other or be conscious of each other's presence. Clearing one's throat and yawning should be avoided. The heads should be lowered and completely lost in contemplation. There should not be any movement of the body and one should keep one's nafs (the sensual aspect of one's being) in control so that dancing and clapping are avoided. However, if one is so lost or moved while listening to music that one suddenly starts crying, shaking or dancing, and the intention is not marred by any sense of ostentation or hypocrisy, the actions will be treated as mubah. For, crying and wailing drown one's sorrows (gham), and dancing is equivalent to surur (cheerfulness, exhilaration) which is a valid movement or activity.[6] Among the recommended norms in adab-i-sama is included the suggestion that if a fellow participant stands up in wajd, moved or transported in an ecstasy of love for God, others in the majlis should follow him in standing up to be by his side. And, while dancing in ecstasy (raqs), he should maintain a certain degree of grace so that others are not put off by his vulgar movements and intention.[7] Though it takes two to tango the dance companion's role should be to help him, as if, in reaching out for God above.

Hazrat Nizamuddin Auliya is also quoted as saying that the body movement that is generated in remembering God in ecstasy is mustahab, a recommended or allowed practice, and if the intention is for some carnal pleasure (fasad), it is haram.[8] However, if a person gets really ecstatic (raqs and harkat) in sama and even tears his clothes, he may be treated as one overpowered by ecstasy and so he may not be questioned. But those who pretend to be lost in ecstasy just to show off their spiritual bent of mind will be accused of indulging in haram.[9] Sufi circles did identify the pretenders who would be the cause of embarrassment, especially when the ulama were ready to interrogate anyone departing from norms of proper conduct. Qalandars and related groups particularly attracted attention for their behaviour, which could be identified as deviance.

Also, Hazrat Nizamuddin's followers themselves would be reported to be part of musical jamborees where not only instruments were used, but also women were present—much to the disappointment of the khwaja. However, it might appear that Nizamuddin maintained some ambiguity in the matter, or at least let the followers decide for themselves what was good for them, recalling here reports of his dearest disciple, Amir Khusrau, inventing not only ragas, khayal and tarana, but also being instrumental in creating the sitar, sarod, etc.

Amir Khwurd has noted that certain jurists and ulama who were opposed to sama would also come to observe the majlis organised by Hazrat Nizamuddin Auliya. Looking at the manner in which the shaikh would be standing at one place, crying silently and wiping his tears, even as the singers—two of whom were named Hasan Paihadi and Samat Qawwal—were reciting heartrending Persian poetry in their distinctive intonations, the ulama would fall at his feet and accept as legitimate what they would otherwise condemn as un-Islamic.[10] Despite being deeply touched by the poetry of love being recited by the singers and all but lost in the thought of the divine, Hazrat Nizamuddin would not only come out of the hall, taking a break at the time of prayers, but also keep a watch on the activities of the other participants. He once noticed Amir Khusrau raising his hands during raqs as a Sufi would do, and asked him not to do so as he was attached to this-worldly concerns. Thereafter, Khusrau would dance with his hands down and palms closed, appearing as if his hands were tied and, unlike the Sufi, unable to break free and attempt to reach out for God.[11]

Hazrat Nizamuddin's interest in music and particular verses which touched his soul and created ecstasy in him would become very popular in the large circle of his followers. Some very good singers attached themselves to the khwaja. They would spend a lot of time to train themselves, composing new ghazals, creating new ragas, and taking the art to newer heights.[12] According to reports, not only sophisticated Persian poetry of love, but also Hindi verses would create ecstasy for Hazrat Nizamuddin. On one occasion the shaikh was overwhelmed by ecstasy (haal) for a long period after listening to some Hindi poetry composed by one of his Chishti successors (khalifas), Maulana Wajihuddin Yusuf.[13]

Eventually, Amir Khwurd writes, the Naib Hakim of the Sultanate under Ghiyasuddin Tughluq, Qazi Jalaluddin Lawanji, who was opposed to the lovers of God (ahl-i-ishq), encouraged Shaikhzada Husamuddin, a disgruntled disciple of Hazrat Nizamuddin Auliya who had access to the sultan's court, to build a case against the shaikh. It was reported to the sultan that Hazrat Nizamuddin, who was a leading religious personality of the time, indulged in music that was considered haram in the mazhab of Imam Abu Hanifa, founder of the Hanafi school of jurisprudence which the Sultanate ulama followed in their practice of Islam. The sultan was told that following Hazrat Nizamuddin, thousands of others were fascinated by the unlawful practice of music. Amir Khwurd states that Sultan Ghiyasuddin had no idea of the legality of music (halal/haram) and, therefore, wondered how it was that a leading religious authority could indulge in an un-Islamic (ghayr mashru) act.[14]

In order to convince Sultan Ghiyasuddin, Hazrat Nizamuddin's opponents collected the works relating to music in the shari'at which were used to issue fatwas against Hamiduddin Nagauri and presented them to the ruler. The sultan was already uncomfortable with Hazrat Nizamuddin's attitude, especially over the dispute regarding the recovery of cash-grants doled out by the usurper Khusrau Khan, who had killed the last Khalji Sultan Mubarak Shah. He announced that if the religious scholars have issued fatwas against the legality of sama, the Sufi shaikh should be brought to his presence and the leading ulama of the city should also be summoned so that the problem could be discussed or debated in an assembly of the learned and the truth of the matter established. Hazrat Nizamuddin's followers who were employed in the sultan's court informed the shaikh, who apparently did not show any concern over the development. However, a number of other leading religious scholars of the time who had joined the discipleship of Hazrat Nizamuddin Auliya, such as Maulana Fakhruddin Zarradi and Maulana Wajihuddin Pa'ili, began to scan the relevant texts to collect arguments in favour of the validity of the practice of sama.[15]

Hazrat Nizamuddin eventually appeared in the court on the appointed date, with Maulana Fakhruddin, who was superior in reputation to the Naib Hakim Qazi Jalaluddin, and Maulana Muhiuddin Kashani, another leading scholar of the age. As the arguments began, Qazi Jalaluddin lectured the shaikh on the need to mend his ways and warned him of being punished if he continued to organise music assemblies. Amir Khwurd notes that Hazrat Nizamuddin listened silently to all the accusations levelled in a harsh language, but Jalaluddin's warning of punishment provoked the shaikh to curse the opponent, first for his removal from the position of the Naib Hakim and death soon after. Whatever may be the rational, historical account, Jalaluddin actually lost his position and died not long after the inquest.[16]

As the debate proceeded in front of the leading ulama of the city and a full house of nobles, Shaikhzada Husamuddin took over from the silenced Qazi Jalaluddin and asked the shaikh whether he would organise sama in his assemblies in which the participants danced, cried or raised slogans. Hazrat Nizamuddin advised Husamuddin to refrain from showing his overenthusiasm, and instead of making unnecessary statements, explain what he meant by sama. Hazrat Nizamuddin's question on the need to first clarify the meaning of the term sama itself would test any theoretical grounding of the opponents in the terms and categories being deployed by them. Instead of explaining his understanding of the validity or otherwise of music, Husamuddin continued in a rhetorical mode and said that he did not know the meaning of sama, but so many great ulama had said that it was haram. Hazrat Nizamuddin replied that if Husamuddin did not know the meaning of sama, he was not fit to discuss the matter. Thus, the main opponent in the case was also silenced.[17]

Amir Khwurd records that Ghiyasuddin Tughluq was all along carefully following the debate, and was asking the noisy opponents to keep quiet and listen to what the shaikh was saying. Of all the ulama present there, Maulana Hamiduddin and Maulana Shahabuddin Multani remained silent; they did not say anything scandalous from the point of view of the Sufi facing the inquest. According to Amir Khwurd, Hamiduddin in fact intervened to say that the reports of the opponents regarding the details of the activities in Hazrat Nizamuddin's majlis were not true, and that he had himself closely observed the participants, including shaikhs and dervishes. However, during the course of the discussion, another official alim, Qazi Kamaluddin, interjected to say that he had seen a report quoting Imam Abu Hanifa that sama was haram and raqs was fasq (sinful). Hazrat Nizamuddin replied that there was no prohibition in the matter.[18]

As the arguments and counterarguments continued, Maulana Ilmuddin, a grandson of Bahauddin Zakariya (the thirteenth-century Suhrawardi saint of Multan), arrived at the court. The sultan turned towards Ilmuddin and, referring to him as a scholar and traveller, inquired whether sama was halal or haram. Ilmuddin replied that he had written a tract on the issue wherein he has collected all the arguments for or against music. His conclusion was that sama was permissible for those who take it as a matter of heart, and it was unlawful for those who indulge in it to satisfy their nafs, the lower self. The sultan further asked Ilmuddin whether during his travels to Baghdad, Damascus and Rum, he had seen the Sufis of those cities listening to music, and whether anyone had stopped them from doing so. Ilmuddin said that the Sufis of those cities did listen to music, which was sometimes also accompanied by instruments like daf and shababa, but no one prevented them from following this practice which was inherited from the time of the earliest masters, Shaikh Junaid and Shibli.

The sultan was silenced on hearing this response from Ilmuddin, but the Naib Hakim spoke again, insisting that the sultan must announce a ban on music, keeping in mind Imam Abu Hanifa's opinion in the matter. However, the sultan eventually followed Shaikh Nizamuddin's request not to issue any order in this regard, and thus concluded, for Hazrat Nizamuddin on a happy note, the acrimonious debate in the darbar, which lasted for roughly the whole of the first half of the day, from chasht to zuhar prayers.[19]

Amir Khwurd's above narrative on the sultan being favourably disposed towards Hazrat Nizamuddin and his accepting the shaikh's suggestion not to issue an order is derived from a reliable report of Fakhruddin Zarradi, who was present at the inquest and recorded the details in a text of his own. Amir Khwurd notes that according to another less reliable report, the sultan had ordered that Hazrat Nizamuddin could continue with his practice of sama and no one should prevent him from doing so, but others like the Qalandars and Haidaris, who were suspected of listening to music for fun, should be prevented.[20] According to another report, unlike Imam Abu Hanifa who is believed to have disapproved of sama as a whole, Imam Shafi'i, founder of the Shafi'i school of Sunni jurisprudence, not only considered sama a legitimate devotional practice, but also approved the use of musical instruments.[21]

Referring to the report in *Hasrat-nama* of Ziyauddin Barani, another important contemporary figure who, like Amir Khusrau, doubled up as a courtier as well as disciple of Hazrat Nizamuddin Auliya, Amir Khwurd further writes that after returning from the sultan's court at the time of the afternoon (zuhar) prayers, Hazrat Nizamuddin called Maulana Muhiuddin Kashani and Amir Khusrau and told them of the disgusting behaviour of the ulama—not only of their personal opposition to him, but also of their disrespecting prophetic traditions (hadis) by privileging a report by a jurist, Imam Abu Hanifa. All the hadis referred to by Hazrat Nizamuddin justifying the validity of his interest in Sufi music were dismissed as important only for Imam Shafi'i and the Shafi'i school of jurisprudence was characterised as opposed to the Hanafi mazhab followed by the official ulama in Delhi. Expressing his concern that the ulama's approach could mislead the people into not having enough respect for the prophetic traditions, Nizamuddin prophesied that there would be a divine retribution for the wrong faith of the ulama of the city.[22]

Amir Khwurd concludes that within a period of four years, all the ulama of the opposing group were forced to migrate to Deogiri (renamed Daulatabad), most of them dying there. This is with reference to an order of the next sultan, Muhammad bin Tughluq, who had considerable respect for Hazrat Nizamuddin. The city itself was faced with famine and epidemic. The shaikh's prophecy proved true and the legitimacy of his practice was not only approved by the sultan, but also confirmed through divine intervention.[23] Indeed, Sultan Ghiyasuddin himself died under mysterious circumstances in a camp outside Delhi; this, once again, happened at a time when he was ordering the shaikh to leave the city, provoking the latter to utter that proverbial phrase, *hunuz dilli dur ast* (Delhi is far away for you)!

Irrespective of the exact historicity of the incident and whether those developments were related to Hazrat Nizamuddin's curse or political connections, what cannot be denied is that the shaikh was considerably irritated by the opposition to his mystical practices. In *Fawa'id-ul-Fu'ad* itself, which was being compiled by Amir Hasan Sijzi during the period that coincided with the debate in Ghiyasuddin's court, the shaikh is found explaining his position in self-restrained agitation (neither cursing nor abusing the antagonists, but deploying the language of the jurists). It is recorded that one of the members of the audience mentioned that the ruler had given orders to the effect that the shaikh could listen to music whenever he liked, and that it was lawful for him. Hazrat Nizamuddin replied that what was halal could not become haram and vice versa just because someone has issued orders to this effect. However, the shaikh added, in a case like the current controversy over sama and the ruler's order, since Imam Shafi'i has termed sama as permissible even when accompanied by instruments like daf and chaghana which is not in conformity with the majority Hanafi position, it was the ruler's discretion to follow whichever position he found appropriate in his opinion.[24] Sultan Ghiyasuddin clearly followed the Shafi'i position in the matter, allowing the shaikh to continue with his practice, despite the uncomfortable relation between the Sufi and the sultan.

Yet, in continuing to defend the legitimacy of music, Hazrat Nizamuddin insisted that musical instruments such as chang and rabab should be completely avoided. When it was reported that some dervishes were found dancing (raqs) in a musical programme in which instruments were used, Hazrat Nizamuddin maintained that it was not the right thing to do. He was informed that when confronted, the dervishes explained that they were so lost (in remembering God) that they had no idea musical instruments were being played there. According to Hazrat Nizamuddin, this justification was not valid and could be used for covering any gunah or sin.[25]

Further, referring to the differences of opinion within Sufi fraternities on the validity of music as a legitimate spiritual exercise, Amir Hasan has mentioned that he had participated in the ongoing discussion at Hazrat Nizamuddin's jama'at-khana. He had opined that while one could understand the ulama's opposition to sama, how should one explain the opposition of certain Sufis to the practice. He had also remarked that even if some Sufis considered sama as haram, they could avoid it and not fight with fellow Sufis, which was not the way of the dervishes. According to Amir Hasan, Hazrat Nizamuddin liked these observations and stated that there were many ulama who were not saying anything and yet an ignorant fellow (na-waqif) was fighting (the shaikh was clearly referring to the disgruntled disciple who had lost the case in the sultan's court).[26]

Amir Hasan further noted that the shaikh also liked his remark that the opponents of sama were known to him and that they would not have taken any interest in music even if there were no two opinions on its lawfulness. Hazrat Nizamuddin opined that such people actually lacked the zauq or taste for music, and had no basis or orientation for its appreciation.[27] The pleasure of music is appreciated better by someone who is filled with pain (dard) for the divine beloved and endures it gracefully. In exceptional cases, an outward expression of madness, as in Majnun's love for Layla, is also recommended.

The reports of Hazrat Nizamuddin Auliya's struggle to defend Sufi music and elimination of the key opponents in quick succession became a part of Sufi memory. While recounting the proceedings of the mahzar from the *Siyar-ul-Auliya*, Shaikh Jamali has provided the background of the conflict in his early sixteenth-century text, *Siyar-ul-Arifin*. He writes that after the brutal murder of Qutbuddin Mubarak Shah, his usurping successor Khusrau Khan had distributed large sums to the dervishes in the city. Three Sufis of note had refused to accept these offerings, but Hazrat Nizamuddin Auliya took the five lakh tankas which had been sent to him and distributed the amount amongst the poor. Others who had received the grants kept them in trust. Four months later, when Ghiyasuddin Tughluq defeated Khusrau Khan and ascended the throne, he sought to recover the funds, which had left the treasury depleted. Hazrat Nizamuddin Auliya argued that the money he had received was from the public treasury. He had, therefore, given it to the deserving, spending nothing on himself. The sultan was silenced by this reply, but his heart turned against the shaikh. The controversy over the legality of sama came in handy for the king to call a mahzar. The proceedings came to an end with the ruler expressing his regret for summoning the saint to the court. No sooner had the shaikh returned to his hospice, news arrived that the sovereign was much ashamed and had dismissed Qazi Jalaluddin from his post.[28]

In conclusion, through this inquest, Hazrat Nizamuddin was forced to break the Chishti principle of not visiting the sultan's court. He was compelled to appear at the monarch's court and submit to judgement. This had serious repercussions as the naib hakim, who was instrumental in calling the mahzar, was removed from the post. The ulama who had opposed the saint were forcibly sent off to Daulatabad. Famine and epidemic haunted the capital city, dar-ul-khilafat, for decades. The sultan himself did not last for long. His death at the outskirts of the capital shortly after the event and bestowal of kingship upon prince Juna Khan (Muhammad Tughluq) by Hazrat Nizamuddin Auliya are mentioned in the *Qiwam-ul-Aqa'id*, an early biography—anecdotal and hagiographic—but they are not linked to the above encounter.[29] However, as mentioned above, all the opponents were soon eliminated, dying unnatural deaths—believed in Sufi memory as the result of Hazrat Nizamuddin's curse. Provoking the wrath of accomplished Sufi saints could be a flawed strategy.

Love for God and service to humanity are among the main features of Sufism. In doing so, the Sufis unite the people into an emotional, devotional, or spiritual community—creating conditions for respectful coexistence of all the diversity the society is known for. Thus, uniting people and not dividing them has been the cardinal mantra. On their part, the qawwals have continued to sing the songs of love for God and devotion for the Prophet (PBUH). As a leading Sufi poet rhetorically put it: only a donkey has no sense of music; and some others counterpoised that even the donkey loved music.[30] Only some heartless men could oppose it, legally or otherwise. In either case, it was a scandal that was resolved in favour of friends and lovers of God, led by the leading Chishti saint of Delhi, Hazrat Nizamuddin Auliya. Disappointed over the unsavoury episode, Hazrat Nizamuddin could tell the opponents that if you thought that sama was haram, it may remain haram for you:[31]

• ◆ •

gufti ke beh nazad-i man haram-ast sama
gar bar tu haram-ast haramat bada

• ◆ •

Endnotes

1. For the couplet cited above, see, *Fawa'id-ul-Fu'ad*, Conversations of Hazrat Khwaja Nizamuddin Auliya, Compiled by Amir Hasan Sijzi, Persian text with Urdu translation by Khwaja Hasan Sani Nizami, New Delhi: Urdu Academy, 1990, p. 312. For a good introduction to the early phase of Sufism, see Ahmet T. Karamustafa, *Sufism: The Formative Period*, Edinburgh: Edinburgh University Press, 2007; also see, William C. Chittick, *Sufism: A Short Introduction*, Oxford: Oneworld Publications, 2007. For a general history of Chishti Sufism, see Carl W. Ernst and Bruce B. Lawrence, *Sufi Martyrs of Love: The Chishti Sufi Order in South Asia and Beyond*, New York: Palgrave Macmillan, 2002; for discussion on relevant issues, also see Raziuddin Aquil, ed., *Sufism and Society in Medieval India*, New Delhi: Oxford University Press, 2010.

2. *Siyar-ul-Auliya* of Amir Khwurd Kirmani, Islamabad: Markaz Tahqiqat-i-Farsi Iran wa Pakistan, 1978, p. 645.

3. Ibid., p. 646; *Fawa'id-ul-Fu'ad,* pp. 418-19.

4. *Fawa'id-ul-Fu'ad,* p. 419.

5. *Siyar-ul-Auliya,* p. 647.

6. Ibid., p 648.

7. Ibid., pp. 648-49.

8. Ibid., p. 658; *Fawa'id-ul-Fu'ad,* p. 419.

9. *Siyar-ul-Auliya*, p. 658.

10 Ibid., pp. 664-65.

11. Ibid., pp. 662, 665.

12. Ibid., pp. 666-67.

13. Ibid., pp. 667-68.

14. Ibid., p. 686.

15. Ibid., p. 687.

16. Ibid., p. 687.

17. Ibid., p. 688.

18. Ibid., p. 688.

19. Ibid., pp. 688-89.

20. Ibid., pp. 689-90.

21. Ibid., p. 690.

22. Ibid., pp. 690-91.

23. Ibid., p. 691.

24. *Fawa'id-ul-Fu'ad,* p. 384.

25. Ibid., pp. 384-85.

26. Ibid., pp. 385-86.

27. Ibid., p. 386.

28. *Siyar-ul-Arifin* of Shaikh Jamali, Ms., I.O. Islamic 1313, British Library, London, fols. 97b-99b. Ziyauddin Barani refers to the recovery of the amount distributed by Khusrau Khan, but makes no mention of Nizamuddin Auliya in this context, see *Tarikh-i-Firuz Shahi*, British Museum Ms. 6376, fols. 199b-200a.

29. For the bestowal of kingship upon the prince shortly before the death of the sultan, see *Qiwam-ul-Aqa'id* of Muhammad Jamal Qiwam, translated from Persian into Urdu by Nisar Ahmad Faruqui, Rampur: Idarah Nashr-o-Isha'at, 1994, p. 96; Ibn Battuta, *Aja'ib-ul-Asfar*, Urdu translation by Maulwi Muhammad Husain, Islamabad, 1983, p. 92. For Barani's account of the ruler's accidental death, see *Tarikh-i-Firuz Shahi*, fols. 209b-210a.

30. *Kashf-ul-Mahjub* of Abul Hasan Ali bin Hujwiri, ed. Mahmud Abedi, Tehran: Soroush Press, 2013.

31. *Fawa'id-ul-Fu'ad,* p. 385.

---

*Earlier versions of this ongoing work of mine have been previously published in the *Social Scientist* (Vol. 40, Nos. 3-4, 2012) and in Vijaya Ramaswamy, ed., *Devotion and Dissent in Indian History* (Chapter 12), New Delhi: Cambridge University Press, 2014.

Sacred Music and Dance, and Khusrau's Poetics of Sufi-Mystic Transcendence

Tanvir Anjum

hough the concept of sacred music is found in many great religious traditions of the world, music or mawsiqi in Islam has been theologically and juristically a controversial issue, and its legality or otherwise has been fiercely contested and debated. Eminent scholars and philosophers of Islam such as Yaqub ibn Isḥaq al-Kindi (d. 873), Ikhwan al-Ṣafa (lit. the Brethren of Purity; a group of philosophers who lived in Basra during the ninth and tenth centuries), Abu Bakr al-Razi (d. 925), Abu Naṣr al-Farabi (d. 950), Abul Farj al-Iṣfahani (d. 967), Bu Ali Sina (d. 1037), Ibn Ḥazm (d. 1064), and Ibn Rushd (d. 1198) elaborated the philosophy and science of music, hence arguing for its permissibility. Contrarily, theologians like Ibn Abi Dunya (d. 894), Ibn al-Jawzi (d. 1201) and Ibn Taymiyyah (d. 1328) asserted its non-permissibility, arguing that it might lead to sensuality instead of spirituality.[1]

In Sufism or taṣawwuff, the mystical or esoteric tradition of Islam, devotional Sufi music (referred to as sama in Arabic or sema in Turkish and Persian, literally meaning hearing or audition) has not only been practised but its doctrine has also been theorised. Sufi masters such as Zun-Nun of Egypt (d. 861), Abu Said Abul Khayr (d. 967), Imam Qushayri (d. 1072), Saiyyid Ali Hujwiri (d. 1077), Imam Abu Ḥamid al-Ghazzali (d. 1111), Ibn al-Arabi (d. 1240) and Jalal al-Din Rumi (d. 1273) asserted the legality and permissibility of music, albeit with conditions, for which rules and regulations were developed for Sufi musical assemblies.[2] The ninth-century Sufi of Egypt, Zun-Nun stated about sama that it is a divine influence which stirs the heart to seek God; those who listen to it spiritually (ba-Haqq) attain God, and those who listen to it sensually (ba-nafs) fall into heresy.[3] In a nutshell, according to the Sufis, sama was not permitted for laypersons, but allowed for the advanced Sufi seekers, who must focus on God while attending these assemblies. Summing up the Sufi position on music, Shiloah notes that music is neither monogenetic nor monovalent, and it includes both the divine and the satanic, the celestial and the terrestrial.[4]

The practice of sama originated in Persia and Turkey, where some of the Sufi groups promoted the use of music for religious purposes. The tenth-century Sufi master, Abu Said Abul Khayr is said to have permitted the use of music in his Sufi lodge in Nishapur (Khurasan). Historically, the Mevleviyya and Rifaiyya in Turkey, Shadhliyya in North Africa, as well as Khalwatiyya and Qadriyya in many parts of the world, and Chishtiyya in South Asia are particularly known for the use of music for sacred purposes. Sufi music was often accompanied with raqs[5] (sacred Sufi dance) or daur (rotatory dance), and it became an integral part of musical assemblies in some Sufi circles.[6] Whirling dervishes in Turkey,[7] haḍra in North Africa, the Middle East and beyond, and dhamal in South Asia are varied forms of raqṣ. However, this is not to deny that some Naqshbandi Sufi masters have been averse to sama.[8]

Sacred Purpose of Sama and Raqs

Being champions of the esoteric aspect of Islam, Sufis have always emphasised the inner meaning of all religious rituals, practices and observances. Highlighting the inner meaning of sama, the Sufis as well as the philosophers have stressed its divine dimension, and argued that the notes of the earthly music necessarily imitate those of the divine or heavenly melody (sawt-i Sarmadi).[9] Moreover, relating sama with Sufi cosmology, Ernst observes that according to the Sufi view, the moment of primordial covenant in pre-eternity was the first time when God's voice was heard by human souls, and the resonance of that Divine voice is faintly recalled in all beautiful voices and in song. Thus, every Sufi musical assembly is, in essence, an attempt to connect to that moment of primordial covenant with God.[10]

To the Sufis, sama serves a sacred purpose: it is a form of zikr (remembrance of God) and a method of worship and developing proximity with God. It is considered a means of activation of link with a living spiritual guide, with the departed Sufis of one's spiritual genealogy, and ultimately with God. The Sufis believe that music heightens what is in the heart and mind of a Sufi seeker, whether it is longing for the vision of or union with the Divine. Thus, sacred Sufi music becomes a vehicle for Sufi or mystic transcendence, or an instrument of revelation of higher truths, which can be understood as attaining a higher level of consciousness. So, in short, sacred Sufi music and dance are interpreted as the language of spiritual quest, at times leading to spiritual awakening and ultimately spiritual enlightenment.

The practice of raqṣ or sacred Sufi dance induces wajd (often translated as ecstasy or rapture), which is understood as a mystical experience in which an individual feels exalted in spiritual terms, and acquires direct knowledge of divine mysteries. It is considered a mystery between the seeker and the sought (God). Hujwiri argued that wajd could produce two very different responses or states: one creating agitation owing to ardent longing in the state of occultation, and the other characterised by calm contemplation in the state of revelation.[11] Defining wajd, Armstrong notes that ecstasy is the 'descent of immense spiritual energy (*barakah*) upon the slave. It overwhelms the senses, causing extreme physical reactions ... *Wajd* may manifest as intense joy, when Allah's beauty dominates, or as intense grief, when His Majesty dominates.'[12] It is during a sama gathering that a Sufi may experience ecstasy, which is a gift of Allah's grace upon a Sufi.

The spiritual state of wajd makes a seeker oblivious of himself and the surroundings. *Siyar al-Awliya*, a fourteenth-century Sufi text, informs that a Sufi-minded preacher of Badayun, when asked about sama and raqṣ, replied that all he knew was that when one falls in a state of ecstasy, one could even dance on a hot plate (tawa).[13] Wajd can also be understood as an altered state of mind or consciousness,[14] characterised by partial or total suspension of sensory perception, enabling the seeker to have a transcendental experience through expansion or dissolution of time-space boundaries. Consequently, a Sufi seeker may have a unitive experience, considering himself as part of a greater whole—an integral part of the universe—or merging and losing his individuality and ego in the Supreme Self or God.

Chishtis and the Practice of Sama and Raqṣ

A tenth-century Sufi, Khwaja Abu Isḥaq Shami or Syrian (d. 940), is regarded as the founder of the Chishti silsilah (spiritual lineage or initiatic genealogy). The name of the silsilah is derived from Chisht, a village near Herat in the province of Khurasan (eastern Persia) in present-day Afghanistan, where the Khwaja settled at the instance of his spiritual preceptor, Khwaja Alu of Dinawar (d. 941). The Sufis of this silsilah later came to be known as Chishtis. Khwaja Abu Ishaq was also the first Sufi of the Chishtiyyah tradition to acquire the epithet Chishti when he was advised by his preceptor to change his identity from Shami (Syrian) to Chishti (meaning resident of Chisht).[15] Likewise, his followers also adopted the soubriquet Chishti.

The use of music in spiritual practices of the Chishtis was their characteristic feature from the earliest days. According to one view, the wandering Chishti Sufis were known as chist or chisht. It was customary among them to enter a town and play musical instruments such as flute and drums in order to attract an audience, and then recite a tale or legend of initiatory significance. Similar practices have been traced in Europe as well, where the Spanish chistu is referred to as a kind of itinerant jester with almost similar garb and instruments.[16] Therefore, the epithet Chishti might have been derived from the title of the wandering Chishti Sufis playing musical instruments. However, the earlier view that the epithet Chishti was derived from the name of a village called Chisht seems more plausible.

Historically, the Chishtis have been known for their fondness of sama. Among the Chishtis, it is not only permissible but highly recommended for seekers of the divine truth. The Chishti masters paid more attention to Sufi music than meditation, which was preferred by their contemporary Suhrawardi Sufis of Uch and Multan. The Chishtis advocated sama as a communal ceremony and as an 'extroverted contemplative practice.'[17] The Chishti masters sought ecstatic inspiration in sama. However, it is a mistaken assumption that the Chishtis started practising music after their advent in India. In fact, sama was practised by the Chishtis long before their arrival in India.[18] In medieval north India, sama was introduced by Khwaja Muin al-Din Chishti of Ajmer (d. 1236) in the late twelfth century. He was fond of sama,[19] and used to fall in ecstasy during sama sessions. Moreover, under his influence, many ulama (theologians and jurists) in the Sultanate of Delhi had become fond of sama.[20] Among the ulama associated with the state, there were defenders of Sufism, and supporters of Sufi practices like sama. One such example is Minhaj al-Siraj Juzjani, the author of *Tabaqat-i Naṣira*, who was himself inclined towards Sufism, and had a profound interest in sama.[21] He was the head of the Sultanate's judiciary under Sulṭan Shams al-Din Iletmish (r. 1211-36). In those days, sama sessions or assemblies were held in the Chishti lodge of Khwaja Muin al-Din's successor in Delhi, Shaykh Quṭb al-Din Bakhtiyar

Kaki (d. 1235), who was very fond of sama as well as raqṣ. Raqṣ became a part and parcel of the sama sessions of the Chishtis. Later, Shaykh Burhan al-Din Gharib (d. 1340), the spiritual successor of Shaykh Niẓam al-Din Awliya (d. 1325), introduced a new style of raqṣ, known as Burhani raqṣ after his name.[22]

Soon the Chishti practice of sama and raqṣ became a bone of contention between the Sufis and the ulama in the Sultanate of Delhi, as the latter raised objections to such practices. Nonetheless, it was due to the presence of Qazi Juzjani, that despite objections, the sama assemblies of the Chishtis were permitted in Delhi. It is said that he had legalised the institution of sama in Delhi during his tenure.[23] However, later the Chishtis had to face vehement criticism, and sometimes public debates in the royal courts were held on the question of legality of sama. The ulama kept on pressuring the kings for altogether banning these practices, but remained unsuccessful.[24]

Amid these controversies surrounding the Sufi practices of sama and raqṣ, the early Chishti Sufis wrote treatises in their defense. Khwaja Muin al-Din's successor, Shaykh Ḥamid al-Din Suwali (d. 1274), composed *Risala-i Sama* in Persian.[25] It was followed by Shaykh Fakhr al-Din Zarradi's two legal treatises on the subject, one of which was titled *Uṣul al-Sama*.[26] Amir Khurd (d. 1368 or 1369), the renowned Chishti hagiographer, also authored *Risala-i Sama* to further endorse the Chishti stance.

The Chishti silsilah is considered the most Indianised of all the Sufi silsilahs of South Asia. The Chishti practice of sama and raqṣ bore resemblance with Hindu and Buddhist religio-spiritual traditions, wherein sacred music has been a persistent tradition. It was one of the reasons of the popularity of the Chishtis among the non-Muslims. Moreover, raqṣ resembled with shamanistic dance prevalent in many parts of Central Asia,[27] from where some of the early Chishti masters had come.

It is interesting to note that many renowned Sufi masters are said to have died in a state of ecstasy or rapture while attending a sama session. Zun-Nun of Egypt, Abu Bakr Shibli (d. 946), and Ruzbihan Baqli Shirazi (d. 1209) died in a sublime state of ecstasy caused by sama.[28] In addition, Quṭb al-Din Bakhtiyar Kaki of Osh in present-day Kyrgyzstan in Central Asia, where existed the tradition of shamanistic dance, also died in a state of ecstasy while performing raqṣ in a sama assembly in his Sufi lodge in Delhi in 1235.[29] In fact, for the Chishtis, Sufi music was a means of achieving spiritual enlightenment and life-transforming Sufi-mystic transcendence. It was for the same reason that Shaykh Niẓam al-Din Awliya once expressed his wish to die in a state of ecstasy caused by sama. Four centuries later, Shah Abd al-Laṭif Bhitai (d. 1752) of Sindh chose to leave for his eternal abode while the faqirs were playing music and singing around him at his behest.[30]

Amir Khusrau as the Father of Qawwali

The late thirteenth and early fourteenth century witnessed the emergence of a new tradition of sama, referred to as qawwali, derived from qawl, literally meaning an utterance. Amir Khusrau (1253-1325), the close disciple of Shaykh Niẓam al-Din, is considered the pioneer of this new genre of sacred Sufi music. The Amir was not only a skilful musician and music theorist, he was also an eloquent poet and a court historian. He composed captivating poetry in the honour of his preceptor, and sang it in his presence, improvising and appropriating classical Indian musical ragas (melodic frameworks or modes) and musical instruments.

Qawwali can be seen as a unique South Asian vernacular form of Sufi musical tradition. Sykes observes that qawwali as a genre of music 'straddles our standard genre distinctions between folk, classical, sacred and popular' genres.[31] Qawwali is performed in mehfil-i sama (assembly for listening to Sufi devotional music), which is an occasion of sharing individual spirituality. It provides an opportunity for an intense personal and subjective experience to each listener.

For the Chishtis, qawwali became one of the central rituals of Sufism, and is a living tradition which continues till date. The Ajmer shrine complex, the foremost Chishti centre in South Asia, includes a naqqar-khana having hereditary musicians, and meḥfil-khana or sama-khana.[32] Khusrau's famous composition, '*Aj rang hei ri maṇn*' (also referred to as *rang*, literally meaning colour) is often sung at Chishti shrines along with other poems.

Qawwali has a religious/spiritual function, and seen as an act of worship, in which the qawwali performers as well as the listeners participate. It arouses a profound sense of love of God among the listeners. The primary purpose of qawwali, according to Qureshi, is inducing spiritual arousal,[33] which serves as a means of spiritual advancement, and a feast for the soul. The spiritual arousal may lead to wajd or trance states and divine ecstasy,[34] and eventually, result in achieving mystical experience. To Kugle, qawwali is a way to empower the spiritual relationship between a Sufi-minded listener and the divine source of spiritual power.[35]

Magic of the Lyrics: Sufi Poetry Sung in Qawwalis

The significance of Sufi poetry along with its singing and dancing as medium of popular culture cannot be overstated. The cultural embeddedness of poetic compositions increases their receptivity, while their high degree of musicality makes it easy to remember them by heart and sing. When sung in qawwalis, the message of the Sufi poetry is enhanced, particularly when the singer knows what and where to stress on and what to repeat in order to evoke a range of meanings as well as help generate or sustain ecstasy. This is primarily done in view of the listeners' responses and states. Qureshi opines that the song text in qawwalis cannot be separated from music. That is why, she calls qawwali a 'the musical performance of texts'.[36]

Thematically, Sufi poetry is of a wide variety, covering subjects such as moral didacticism and Sufi ethics as well as Sufi cosmology and divine love. The poetry sung in Sufi assemblies is often a love poem, having love of God (ishq) as its central theme, along with notions of beauty, separation, desire/longing, vision, and union. The Persian word ishq cannot be adequately translated in English as mere love. Safi, who renders it as 'radical love', argues that the term love seems insufficient, as the 'word love, that most divine of qualities, has become flat, ubiquitous, and, ironically, cheap ... [*'ishq*] is something more fiery, fierce, and alchemical...'[37] Ishq can be understood as intensified love coupled with a passionate longing for vision of or union with God. Believing that the metaphorical (majaz) can serve as a bridge to the real (ḥaqiqah), Sufi poets have often expressed the concept of divine love in their poetry in an idiom of human love. Moreover, the articulation of transcendent experience of divine love is beyond words. Therefore, Sufi poets have resorted to the use of figurative language to convey the subtleties of divine love in their highly symbolic verses.

In their poetic verses replete with Sufi symbolism, the Sufis have often employed gendered imagery and feminine voice. Acquiring female persona, the Sufi poets, often males, identified themselves with ardent female lovers (often depicted as a lover, bride, or a wife waiting for her husband), while God has been imagined in masculine terms (as groom, lover/beloved or husband). In addition, the human soul has also been depicted in feminine terms. The idea of depicting the human soul as God's bride, or the bridal metaphor for human-God love relationship in early Sufism, has parallels in many religio-spiritual traditions of the world.[38] The Persian Sufi Bayazid of Bistam (d. 874) was the first Sufi who self-identified as 'God's bride'.[39] Later, Ibn al-Arabi in *Tarjuman al-Ushshaq* and Rumi in *Mathnavi-i Ma'anvi* further elaborated it. Woman as wife symbolises passionate loyalty and loving submission before God in many socio-cultural contexts around the world. Moreover, wedding is employed as a metaphor for spiritual union, which is also reflected in the term urs (literally means wedding) for Sufis' death anniversary celebrations. Death becomes a symbol of ultimate union or waṣl with God,[40] hence, these anniversaries are not just observed but celebrated with joy.

Sufi poetry witnessed the expansion of bridal metaphor in succeeding centuries, when it was employed in varied meanings. The depiction of God as beloved or groom is found in the poetry of Baba Farid of Pakpattan (d. 1271), Shah Ḥusayn of Lahore (d. 1599), Sulṭan Bahu of Jhang (d. 1691), Bhitai and Sachal Sarmast in Sindh (d. 1827), while Prophet Muḥammad (PBUH) is represented as a beloved or groom in Bhitai as well as Ismaili ginan literature wherein in addition to the Prophet, Imams (especially Imam Ali) are portrayed as beloved or groom. Furthermore, the bridal metaphor has also been employed for murshid or spiritual mentor by Sufi poets such as Amir Khursau and Bulle Shah of Qasur (d. 1757), whose mentors were Shaykh Niẓam al-Din and Shah Inayat Qadri (d. 1728 circa) respectively.

In Divine Presence: Khusrau's Poetics of Transcendence

Sufi poetry is considered a perfect vehicle of articulating subtleties and mysteries of divine love as well as of transcendent experience of divine vision and union. In one of his ghazals or love poems, often sung in qawwalis, Amir Khusrau recounts his personal (rather transpersonal) experience of Sufi-mystic transcendence, which he probably had in one of the qawwali sessions. Some select verses of this Indo-Persian ghazal read as follows:[41]

Nami danam che manzil bud shab jae ke man budam
Bahar su raqṣ-i bismil bud shab jae ke man budam

(I wonder what was the state or place where I was last night,
All around me were half-slaughtered lovers, tossing about in agony)

Khuda khud mir-i majlis bud andar lamakaṇ Khusrau
Muḥammad sham-i meḥfil bud shab jae ke man budam

(God himself was the master of ceremonies,
while Khusrau was beyond time and space
Muḥammad was the centre of attraction where I was last night)

This ghazal exquisitely articulates a self-transcendental experience of Amir Khusrau. In retrospect, he recalls his bewilderment as he was unaware of his own altered state or the place he found himself. Here, the trope of manzil in Khusrau's poetry may refer to both spiritual state and physical place. All he could see were the half-slain (bismil) lovers in immense agony. Another verse of the ghazal further informs that the Amir reached or attained lamakaṇ (literally meaning placelessness), i.e., the 'station of no station', or the spaceless realm, referring to Divinity or God. He found himself transported to the heavenly court, where Prophet Muḥammad (PBUH) was its nucleus or focal point. In addition, Khusrau had a direct experience of the Divine Presence there. He was able to establish a direct, (trans) personal and experiential connection with God and the Prophet (PBUH) through sama.

In academic studies, mystic self-transcendence has been theorised by psychologists. Linking self-transcendence with religion and spirituality, Austrian neurologist and psychologist Viktor Frankl views self-transcendence as the hallmark of spirituality. He underscores that spirituality is an integral part of human nature, which separates human beings from other species. To him, humans are by nature meaning-seeking and meaning-making creatures.[42] American psychologist Abraham Maslow defines transcendence as 'the very highest and most inclusive or holistic levels of human consciousness, behaving and relating, as ends rather than means, to oneself, to significant others, to human beings in general, to other species, to nature, and to the cosmos'.[43]

Maslow calls self-transcendence a 'peak experience', and going 'beyond self-actualization'.[44] Frankl and Maslow further argue that self-transcendence is personal and subjective, but could be influenced by cultural and religious contexts. However, transcribing the sublime experience of transcendence is complicated and challenging. Khusrau skilfully articulates his profound account of dissolution of the self in experience through the use of poetic and literary devices.

Despite being confined to an earthly life owing to his fleshly existence, he was spiritually transported from earth to heaven, entering another dimension as if through a portal. There he encountered a transpersonal connection with the Divine and the Prophet (PBUH). It was, undoubtedly, a 'peak experience' for Khusrau, and rather than means, it was an end in itself, the zenith of one's spiritual quest and journey attained through sacred music.

Endnotes

1. For details, see Fadlou Shehadi, *Philosophies of Music in Islam* (Leiden: Brill, 1995).

2. See, for instance, Saiyyid 'Ali Hujwirī, *Kashf al-Maḥjub (Revelation of the Mystery)*, Eng. tr. R.A. Nicholson (Lahore: Suhail Academy, 2005), pp. 418-20.

3. Hujwirī, *Kashf al-Maḥjub,* p. 404.

4. Amnon Shiloah, *Music in the World of Islam: A Socio-cultural Study* (Detroit: Wayne State University Press, 1995), p. 40.

5. Raqṣ in Sufi context cannot be fully translated into English as mere dance due to its sanctity, inner meaning, and the sacred purpose behind it.

6. Shaykh Shihab al-Din 'Umar Suhrawardi, The *Awarifu-l-Ma'arif*, Eng. tr. H. Wilberforce Clarke (Calcutta: Govt. of India Central Printing Office, 1891), pp. 165-68.

7. The human movement in whirling dervish dance associated with the Sufis of Mevlevi Silsilah imitates the movement of heavenly bodies in the universe.

8. Some of its shaykhs such as Khwaja Baha al-Din Naqshband (d. 1389) and Shaykh Aḥmad Sirhindi (d. 1624) did not approve of it.

9. See the view of *Ikhwan al-Ṣafa* as cited in Louis Michon, 'Sacred Music and Dance in Islam', in *Encyclopedia of Spirituality*, ed. S.H. Nasr, Vol. 1 (Lahore: Suhail Academy, 2000), p. 470. The concept of ṣawt-i Sarmadi has a parallel in Hinduism and Buddhism as Anhad Nad, literally meaning the unstruck sound, as well as in Judaism and Christianity as divine melody.

10. Carl W. Ernst, *Sufism: An Introduction to the Mystical Tradition of Islam* (Boston: Shambhala, 1997), p. 44.

11. Hujwiri, *Kashf al-Maḥjub*, p. 414.

12. Amatullah Armstrong, *Sufi Terminology (Al-Qamus Al-Sufi): The Mystical Language of Islam* (Lahore: Ferozsons, 2001), p. 256.

13. Saiyyid Muḥammad Mubarak Alawi Kirmani alias Amir Khurd, *Siyar al-Awliya*, (comp. in 1351-82), ed. Chiranji Lal (Delhi: Muḥibb-i Hind Press, 1302 A.H./1885 A.D.),) p. 505.

14. For details, see Kenneth Avery, *Psychology of Early Sufi Sama: Listening and Altered States* (New York: Taylor & Francis, 2004).

15. Mutiul Imam, 'Abu Esḥaq Sami,' *Encyclopædia Iranica*, Vol. I, Fasc. 3 (1983), p. 280.

16. Idries Shah, *The Way of the Sufi* (London: Jonathan Cape, 1968), p. 127.

17. Scott Kugle, 'Sufi Meditation Manuals from the Mughal Era', in *Faith and Practice in South Asian Sufism*, ed. D. Giordani (Rome: Oriente Moderno, 2014), p. 464.

18. See the anecdote of Shaykh Quṭb al-Din Mawdud in *Nafaḥat al-Uns*, as cited in P.M. Currie, *The Shrine and Cult of Mu'in al-Dīn Chishti of Ajmer* (Delhi: Oxford University Press, 1989), p. 64.

19. Ilahdiyeh ibn Abd al-Raḥim al-Chishti, *Siyar al-Aqṭab* (Lucknow: Munshi Newal Kishore, 1877), p. 101.

20. Chishti, *Siyar al-Aqṭab*, p. 103.

21. Amir Ḥasan Ala Sijzi Dehlavi, *Fawaid al-Fuad*, (malfuẓ of Khwaja Niẓam al-Din Awliya) ed. Khwaja Ḥasan Thani Niẓami Dehlavi (Delhi: Urdu Academy, 1992), p. 322.

22. Amir Khurd, *Siyar al-Awliya'*, p. 279.

23. Dehlavi, *Fawaid al-Fuad*, p. 407.

24. For details, see Tanvir Anjum, *Chishti Sufis in the Sultanate of Delhi, 1190-1400: From Restrained Indifference to Calculated Defiance* (Karachi: Oxford University Press, 2011), pp. 133-35, 167-68, 217; see also Raziuddin Aquil, 'Music and Related Practices in Chishti Sufism: Celebrations and Contestations', *Social Scientist*, Vol. 40, No. 3/4 (March-April 2012), pp. 17-32.

25. For a brief discussion on the treatise, see Carl W. Ernst and Bruce B. Lawrence, *Sufi Martyrs of Love: The Chishti Order in South Asia and Beyond* (New York: Palgrave Macmillan, 2002), pp. 37-38.

26. Sharif Husain Qasemi, 'Fakr-al-Dinzarradi, Mawlana', *Encyclopædia Iranica*, Vol. IX, Fasc. 2 (1999), p. 163; for a detailed study, see Kashshaf Ghani, *Sufi Rituals and Practices: Experiences from South Asia, 1200-1450* (Oxford: Oxford University Press, 2024), pp. 87-116.

27. Julian Baldick, *Mystical Islam: An Introduction to Sufism* (New York: New York University Press, 2012), p. 21.

28. Ernst and Lawrence, *Sufi Martyrs of Love*, p. 43.

29. For details see Sijzi, *Fawaid al-Fuad*, pp. 246-47, and Amīr Khurd, *Siyar al-Awliya*, pp. 541-42.

30. Motilal Jotwani, *Sufis of Sindh* (New Delhi: Ministry of Information and Broadcasting, Govt. of India, 1908), p. 136. Bhitai was well-conversant with the Indian and regional musical traditions, and his poetic masterpiece, *Shah Jo Risalo*, is divided and organised in chapters according to various surs or melodies in which they are sung.

31. Bruno Nettl and et. al. *Excursions in World Music*, ed. 7 (New York and London: Routledge, 2017), p. 43.

32. The naqqar-khana is also called Shah Jehani darwaza, and has two huge drums, believed to be the spoils of war. The present meḥfil-khana was built by Sir Asman Jah in 1888 for the performance of sama. Women are not allowed to enter the sama-khana. Currie, *The Shrine and Cult of Mu'in al-Dīn Chishti of Ajmer*, pp. 104-5, 113, 126.

33. Regula Burckhardt Qureshi, *Sufi Music of India and Pakistan: Sound, Context and Meaning in Qawwali* (Cambridge: Cambridge University Press, 1986), pp. 58-60, 214.

34. Currie observes multiple conditions in the sama assemblies at Ajmer shrine that are conducive to trance, and range from rhythmic stimulation by drum beating, strict

limitation of movement, overcrowding, theatricality and group excitement to strong models for trance states. Currie, *The Shrine and Cult of Mu'in al-Dīn Chishti of Ajmer*, p. 128, n. 30.

35. Scott Kugle,'The Spirituality of *Qawwali*: Lyrics and Ritual in the Sufi Music of South Asia', in *The Wiley Blackwell Companion to Islamic Spirituality*, eds. Vincent J. Cornell and Bruce B. Lawrence (Chichester: John Wiley & Sons, 2022), pp. 454-75.

36. Qureshi, *Sufi Music of India and Pakistan*, p. 83.

37. Omid Safi, ed., *Radical Love: Teachings from the Islamic Mystical Tradition* (New Haven, CT: Yale University Press, 2018), p. xxi.

38. Richard D. Patterson, 'Metaphors of Marriage as Expression of Divine-Human Relations', *Journal of the Evangelical Theological Society*, Vol. 51, No. 4 (Dec 2008), pp. 689-702.

39. Carl W. Ernst, *The Shambhala Guide to Sufism* (Boston, Mass.: Shambhala, 1997), p. 60.

40. For details, see Tanvir Anjum, 'Bridal Symbolism in the Sufi Poetry of Islamicate South Asia: From the Earliest Times to the Fifteenth Century', *Pakistan Journal of History and Culture*, Vol. XXXIV, No. 1 (Jan-June 2013), pp. 1-16.

41. Saiyyid Nur al-Ḥasan Mawdudi Ṣabri Faḍl-i Raḥmani, *Naghmat-i Sama* (*Anwar-i Naghma*), (Badayun: privately published, AH 1353/AD1934-35), p. 228. For versified Urdu translation by Ḥakim Shams al-Salam Abdali, see Shahid Mukhtar, *Amir Khusrau: Shakhṣiyat, afkar wa kheyalat wa fikr-o fun* (Lahore: Shahid Publishers, n.d.), p. 241, and for English translation, see *Amir Khusrau Memorial Volume* (New Delhi: Ministry of Information and Broadcasting, Govt. of India, 1975), p. 73. It is important to note that this ghazal of Khusrau is not found in any of his five poetic collections. It is generally believed that it was composed during the last phase of his life, and thus, could not find place among his poetic collections.

42. P.T.P. Wong, 'Meaning-seeking, Self-transcendence, and Well-being', in A. Batthyany, ed. *Logotherapy and Existential Analysis: Proceedings of the Viktor Frankl Institute*, Vol. 1 (2016), pp. 311-22.

43. Abraham Maslow, *The Farther Reaches of Human Nature* (New York: Penguin, 1971), p. 269.

44. Ibid., p. 282.

Nami daanam che manzil bood shab jay kay man boodam

۲۲۸

کسے مارا علی گوید کسے گوید مرا باقی
عجائب شان میدارم بشانِ خویش حیرانم

	خسرو رح	۵۹

نمی دانم چہ منزل بود شب جائیکہ من بودم
بہر سُو رقصِ بسمل بود شب جائیکہ من بودم
پری پیکر نگارے سرو قدے لالہ رخسارے
سراپا آفتِ دل بود شب جائیکہ من بودم
رقیباں گوش بر آواز او در ناز و من ترساں
سخن گفتن چہ مشکل بود شب جائیکہ من بودم

مرا از آتشِ عشقِ تو دامن سوخت اے خسرو
محمد شمعِ محفل بود شب جائیکہ من بودم

	شاہ تراب علی رح	۶۰

نہ ہوشم بود نے دل بود شب جائیکہ من بودم
نمی دانم چہ محفل بود شب جائیکہ من بودم
رقیبان در برش بودند و من دور از درش ہے ہے

Book: Nagmat-e-Sima
Poet: Amir Khusrau
Publication: Nurul Hasan Maududi Sabri in 1935

Courtesy: Suman Mishra

SONGS OF SUFI BASANT

The Ecstasy of Basant

Hazrat Nizamuddin Auliya, recognised as the greatest Sufi saint of his time, earned immense popularity through his liberal attitude and religious tolerance. Basant, typically a Hindu festival, marks the arrival of spring and transforms his shrine into an ecstatic celebration. The atmosphere turns euphoric as yellow dominates the mood—the shrine bedecked with yellow flowers, devotees dressed in yellow, and qawwals offering traditional yellow mustard flowers. Walking in processions from a designated spot into the shrine they sing Basant songs, recreating the day when Hazrat Amir Khusrau, the saint's beloved disciple (mureed) walked in a similar manner for the pir.

Throughout the day, yellow petals shower the shrine as qawwals perform the songs of spring and Basant. This tradition, initiated during the saint's lifetime in the thirteenth century, continues unbroken. The songs sung at the shrine, now seven centuries old, preserve an oral heritage that bridges generations.

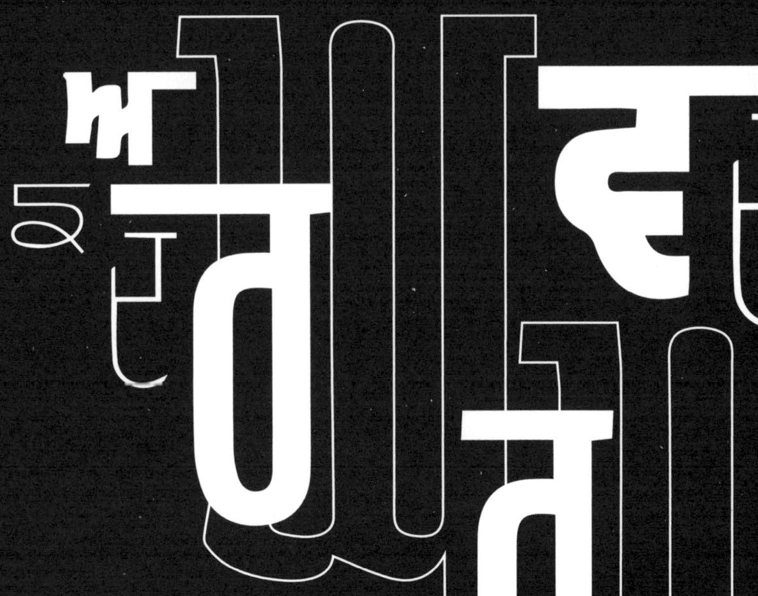

The Yellow Chadar of Basant

Prayers, sometimes spoken and sometimes sung, resonate throughout the day at the shrine, especially during Basant. Through the poetry the qawwals paint a vivid picture of Basant: a fading winter day, fields of vibrant yellow mustard blossoms, the promise of spring in the air, women adorned in elegant attire, birds chirping and singing joyfully, and flowers blooming in abundance.

This journey leads to the sacred threshold of Nizamuddin, where devotees carry a chadar (a beautifully woven decorative cloth) and mustard flowers as offerings to the beloved Pir. Basant stands as one of the most significant and vibrant all-day celebrations at the shrine of Hazrat Nizamuddin Auliya.

The origins of Basant at the Nizamuddin dargah are tied to a poignant story of loss and healing. The story has been handed down through generations, safeguarded and disseminated by the khadims of the dargah. Late Mazhar Nizami, Bhai Haider Nizami, and the esteemed Qawwal Late Meraj Nizami, and his son Qawwal Saqlain Nizami, all of whom maintain profound connections with the dargah of Nizamuddin. Hazrat Nizamuddin Auliya, who had no children of his own, shared a profound bond with his nephew, Khwaja Taqiuddin Nuh. When illness claimed the young man's life, the saint was overcome with grief, and his followers yearned to see him smile again.

One day, Hazrat Amir Khusrau, the saint's favourite disciple, encountered a group of village women dressed in yellow, carrying mustard flowers, and singing and dancing as they headed to the Kalkaji temple. When asked whether they will please their God with singing and dancing, they answered in the affirmative. Inspired by their joyous spirit, Khusrau donned yellow robes, carried mustard flowers, and approached the saint while singing the now-famous *'Sakal Ban Phool Rahi Sarson'*. His playful yet heartfelt gesture succeeded in bringing a smile to the saint's face, marking a moment of joy amid sorrow.

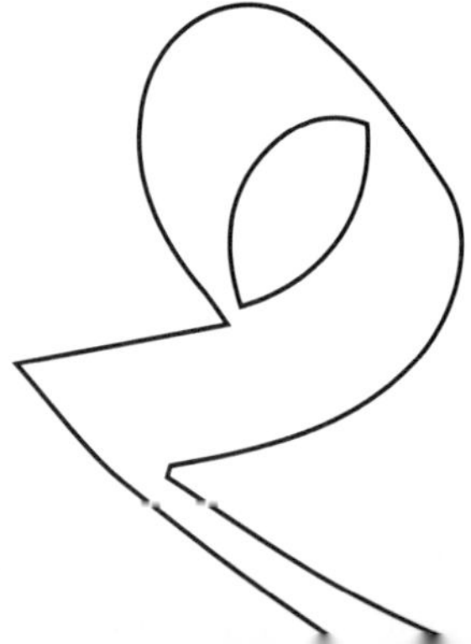

Since that time, the onset of Basant has been celebrated at the dargah with great fervour. Followers dress in yellow, symbolising mustard

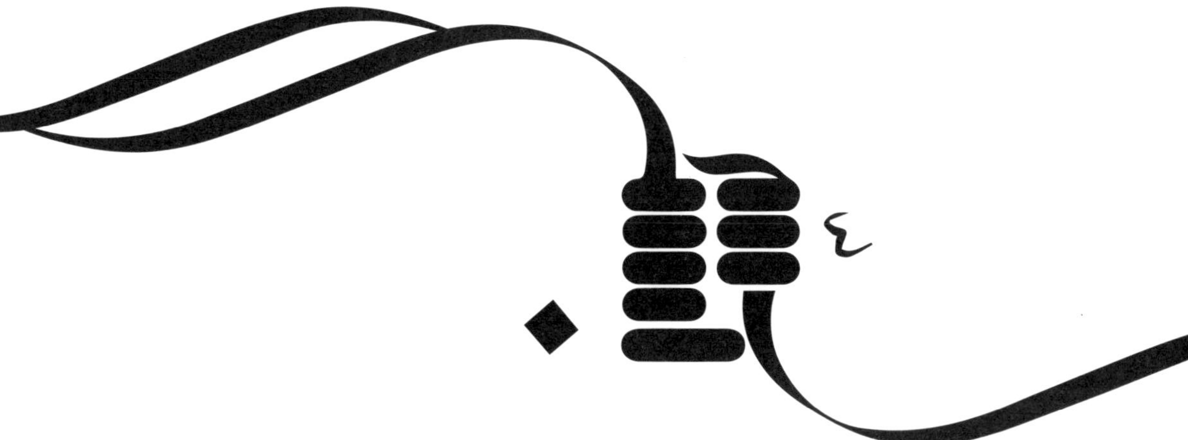

blossoms and the advent of spring, and offer mustard flowers at the shrine. The festival is accompanied by soul-stirring qawwali performances, including renditions of Khusrau's compositions, creating an atmosphere of spiritual upliftment and communal harmony. The Basant festival at the shrine of Hazrat Nizamuddin Auliya is a vibrant and deeply symbolic annual celebration, embodying the harmonious essence of Ganga-Jamuni Tehzeeb.

Photographer: Dinesh Khanna
Pir-e-Tariqat: Late Khawaja Afzal Nizami Syed Bukhari
Qawwali Practitioners: Qawwal Qutubi Brothers, Qawwal Yousuf Nizami and Qawwal Nizami Brothers
Text: Manjari Chaturvedi
Place: Dargah Hazrat Nizamuddin, New Delhi, India
Dargah Hazrat Qutubuddin Bhaktiyar Kaki, Mehrauli, New Delhi, India
Project: The Qawwali Project

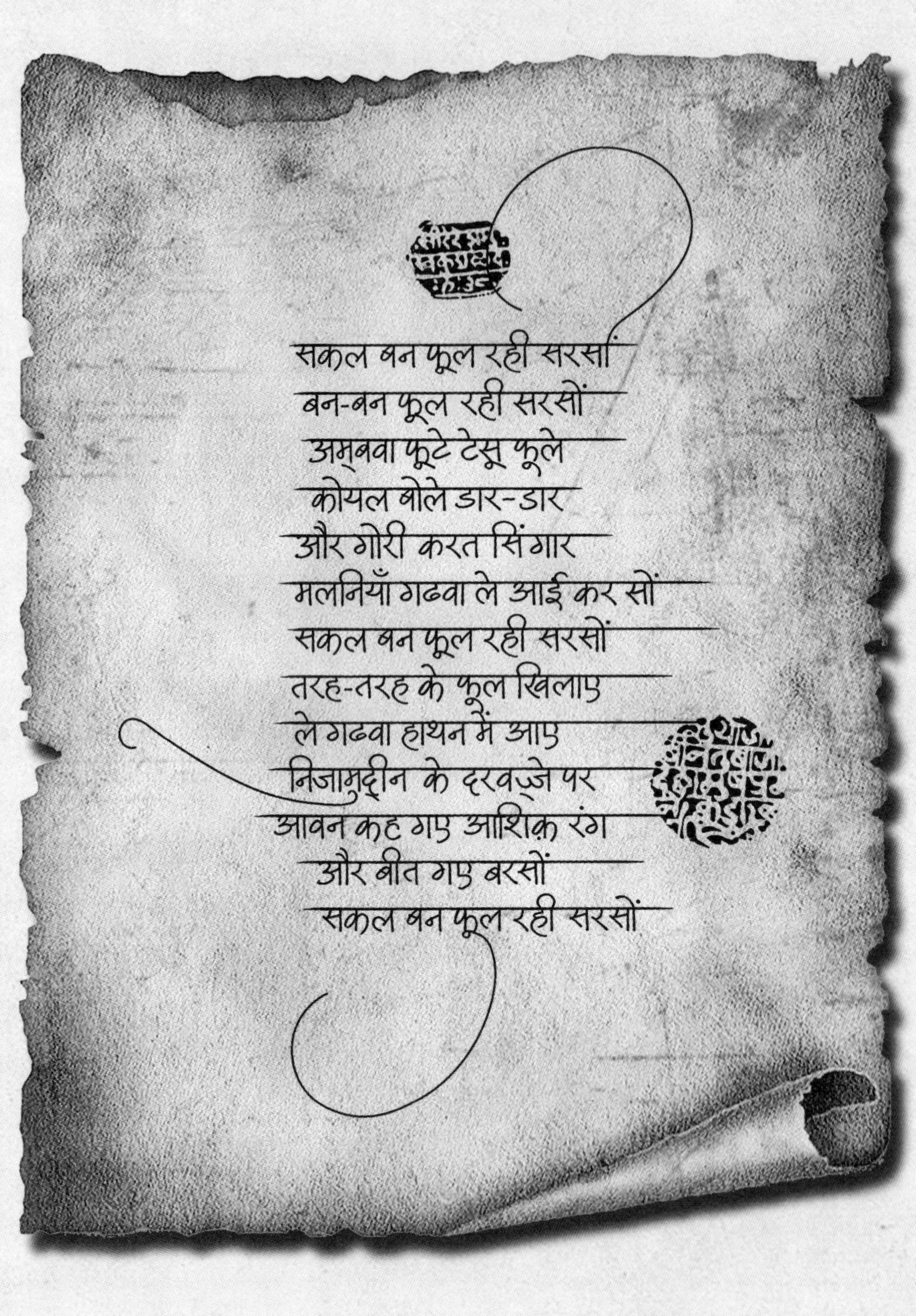

सकल बन फूल रही सरसों
बन-बन फूल रही सरसों
अम्बवा फूटे टेसू फूले
कोयल बोले डार-डार
और गोरी करत सिंगार
मलनियाँ गढवा ले आई कर सों
सकल बन फूल रही सरसों
तरह-तरह के फूल खिलाए
ले गढवा हाथन में आए
निजामुद्दीन के दरवज़्जे पर
आवन कह गए आशिक़ रंग
और बीत गए बरसों
सकल बन फूल रही सरसों

the basant story

QAWWALI: A RIVAYAT

The confluence of cultures

Manjari Chaturvedi

The oral history and the tradition of Qawwali as discussed in a conversation with Late Ustad Meraj Ahmed Nizami of Qawwal Bachche Gharana and Late Ustad Iqbal Ahmed Khan of Dilli Gharana

awwali, as a music form, is an oral tradition passed on from generation to generation without any textbook or a formal format or curriculum of teaching. There is no institutional structure around the training of qawwali and yet the training of qawwals continues unbroken through generations in a seemingly well-specified format. During conversation with a qawwal, it is usual for them to speak of the many generations before them practising qawwali and yet ironically we don't find a single formal research document by qawwals themselves. The question of who has the authority to define the meaning and value of cultural practices, musical structures and the teachings in qawwali is central in documentation. In modern times it carries more significance with commercial Sufi singers gaining more popularity than traditional qawwali singers which also reveals a tension between the spiritual and commercialised realms of qawwali.

In view of the above, the discussion with the two ustads finds relevance in documentation of the form. The perspective gains importance that while academics and researchers may have certain viewpoints based on the available documentation, it is the ustads who are actually transferring information to the next-generation qawwals as oral traditions and not the academic researchers. The ustads are well versed in their art and carry forward their traditions in the truest sense, but may not be academics themselves. Hence we need to also understand what is being passed forward to the next generation qawwals. This essay deals with the intricacies and the stories associated with qawwali as a form. The ustads here highlight the rich diversity and vernacular voices embedded in the tradition of qawwali.

The Origin of Qawwali

Addressing the perennial question of qawwali's origins and its structural evolution in the subcontinent, Ustad Meraj Ahmed Nizami of the Qawwal Bachche Gharana offers a compelling perspective by describing qawwali as rivayati, signifying union. This concept of union reflects the blending of love, traditions, and cultures, creating a confluence of living practices that transcend differences. Thus, qawwali in the Indian subcontinent emerges as a musical expression and a symbol of harmony and interconnectedness, embodying the spirit of Sufism and its universal message of love and unity.

Qawwali, described as a rivayat or confluence, owes its distinct identity to Hazrat Amir Khusrau, who shaped it at the behest of Hazrat Nizamuddin Auliya. While a form of qawwali was initiated nearly a century earlier by Hazrat Khwaja Moinuddin Chisti (RA), it was Amir Khusrau who infused it with life, structure, and unique characteristics, transforming it into the spiritual and musical tradition as we recognise today. Legend says that Hazrat Nizamuddin Auliya emphasised the inclusive essence of qawwali, noting that Hindustan, being a land of diverse religions and rituals, needed a single large umbrella and qawwali emerged as that binding thread to sew the people together. The essence of Sufism is ishq, mohabbat, love. Sufi saint Baba Farid's response once to receiving a pair of scissors beautifully encapsulates this: 'Why give me scissors? I have come here not to divide but to unite; give me a needle and thread to stitch, to sew, to weave and join people.' As we look today, seven hundred years since, Sufism and qawwali and sama music did become that invisible thread to 'sew' people together and till date people of all religions and status throng the Nizamuddin shrine in evenings to listen to qawwali. The hierarchy of class, religion, social status, gender all is forgotten as people sit together on the floor at the shrine and listen to qawwali music, lost in the poetry and emotions. It blurs all divides.

At its core, the meaning of qawwali lies in the word qaul, which means 'to speak' or 'to say'. The qawwal, the one who delivers the qaul, becomes the medium through which the listener is drawn closer to the Almighty. This art of delivering poetry transcends language and understanding, touching the hearts of listeners and inducing a state of spiritual ecstasy. Even those who may not grasp the precise words sway to the qawwali. The power of qawwali lies in its ability to connect the listener to the divine, in accordance with the profound vision of Hazrat Amir Khusrau with the blessings of Hazrat Nizamuddin Auliya. Qawwali as a timeless form continues to be a medium of qurbat (nearness) to the Almighty and is celebrated for its universal appeal and spiritual depth. Hence the instruction to the learner who learns this form, the qawwal, is to aspire for the qurbat so that through his music the listener experiences the nearness to the Almighty.

Ustad Iqbal Ahmed Khan says, qawwali originally came from the Arab region, where it was part of sama or sema (assembly of listeners) rituals, but it underwent a profound transformation when it arrived in Hindustan. It is said that in its early form, in the Arab region, it was performed with minimal instrumentation, typically using only the daff (a hand drum), and even the easily identifiable clapping was not permitted. When Khwaja Moinuddin Chisti, also known as Gareeb Nawaz, arrived in Hindustan to spread Sufism, he encountered the deep-rooted musical traditions of the region. Influenced by the kirtan, the Bhakti Rasgaan, and also the ancient musical heritage of Hindustan, from as early as of the sixth to eighth centuries, he adapted qawwali to align with local sensibilities. He incorporated instruments like the mridang (drums) and kartal (hand cymbals), along with the singing styles of prabandh, druv, and pad (distinct from the later Dhrupad style that emerged during the reign of Raja Man Singh Tomar and Emperor Akbar). These adaptations gave qawwali a new structure and style, blending it seamlessly with the existing traditions of kirtan.

According to oral narrative mentioned by Ustad Iqbal Ahmed, the tradition of qawwali flourished under the stewardship of figures like Mian Hassan Samant, a classical Hindustani singer and a court musician, who left the royal court and became a disciple of Khwaja Moinuddin Chisti. Thus Mian Samant can be said to be the first Sufi qawwal. Further, his brother, Mian Bhola Kalawant, and their subsequent generations continued this legacy. Another notable story is that of Mian Samanti, who was initially mute but miraculously gained his voice after

Hazrat Nizamuddin Auliya placed a chewed betel leaf into his mouth, enabling him to sing and thus further the tradition of qawwali.

These oral narratives with little or no written records and no citation possible, highlight the lineage of qawwali, as well as the pivotal roles that some people played. Ustad Iqbal Ahmed Khan attributes his knowledge of these oral narratives to his own Pir-o-Murshid (spiritual teacher), Late Khwaja Hassan Nizami Sahab. He was the Sajjada-nasheen of both the dargah of Hazrat Nizamuddin Auliya and Hazrat Amir Khusrau, and a descendant of the lineage connected to Hazrat Nizamuddin Auliya and Baba Farid. Hence his insights and oral accounts carry immense historical and spiritual significance for his followers and the qawwali musicians.

Another incident that finds mention amongst the qawwali musicians is of the Dargah Matka Pir (Sufi Saint Sheikh Abu Bakar Tusi Haidri Kalandari urf Matke Shah), a shrine that predates Hazrat Nizamuddin Auliya. At a Mehfil-e-Qawwali where Nizamuddin Auliya himself was present, he experienced the state of wajd (mystical rapture) during the mehfil. This incident speaks about the transcendental power of qawwali as a medium to connect with the divine and also vividly illustrates the enormous effect of qawwali on those present, including the Sufi saint himself.

The contributions of Hazrat Amir Khusrau were pivotal in shaping qawwali as the form we know today. Though he himself was not from a musical lineage, Ustad Iqbal Ahmed says that Khusrau's enormous understanding of mathematics and its integration with music allowed him to innovate and refine the art form. Drawing from his Arabic-Iranian heritage through his Muslim father and the Indian cultural influence of his Hindu mother, Khusrau created a unique synthesis of styles. He introduced new practices, forms, and even instruments, to enrich Hindustani music. His genius gave qawwali a timeless appeal, embedding it in the cultural and spiritual fabric of the Indian subcontinent. This legacy, crafted over 700 years ago, continues to inspire and connect people across generations.

The role of Hazrat Amir Khusrau, particularly his improvisations and contributions to qawwali, such as the qaul, demonstrates his unparalleled genius.

◆

Man Kunto Maula Fa haza Ali'yun Maula

◆

(The Arabic phrase means:
Whoever accepts me as his master, Ali is his master too)

His ability to merge spiritual fervour with musical innovation created a living tradition that resonates across generations even today. This knowledge and these stories are preserved and shared within the musical community as oral traditions. They inspire people in the quest for divine love and understanding. It is interesting how these narratives, passed down through generations, continue to enrich the spiritual and cultural heritage of the Indian subcontinent.

The Asar (Impact) of Poetry in Qawwali

Ustad Meraj Ahmed Nizami mentions that qawwali plays a central role in the Mehfil-e-Sama (assembly of listeners), where its primary purpose is to evoke an overpowering spiritual impact on the listener, leading to a state of kaif or wajd—a spiritual ecstasy also known as haal. This state is marked by intense emotional connection and can even manifest in raqs (spiritual dance). The essence of this experience, called asar (impact), depends on several elements: the rhythmic depth of the performance, the skill of the qawwals, and, most significantly, the presence and guidance of the sahib-e-mehfil (the pir or head of the gathering).

The role of the sahib-e-mehfil was and remains central to the spiritual efficacy of the Mehfil-e-Sama. This figure, often a pir or a spiritual leader, creates the atmosphere necessary for the assembly to achieve wajd—a state of mystical rapture. The sahib-e-mehfil leads the gathering with their spiritual presence, ensuring that the qawwali serves its ultimate purpose of elevating the listeners' souls and fostering a connection with the divine.

Historically, qawwali gatherings formed a complete spiritual circle, as both the qawwals and the attendees of the Mehfil-e-Sama were often Sufis. These gatherings were deeply sacred and exclusive, sometimes known as bandh-e-sama, meaning that only the mureed (followers) of the same pir could participate. This exclusivity ensured a shared spiritual focus and heightened the transformative potential of the experience.

In its poetic essence, to ensure asar, qawwali often explores themes like birha (separation), where the heart grieves in remembrance of Allah (SWT), yearning for divine presence. The tears shed in such moments are symbolic of the soul's longing for the Almighty. This emotional depth is conveyed through the messages embedded in the poetry, which serves as the medium to articulate and evoke spiritual emotions.

Ustad Meraj gives example of Murli Qawwal from Shahjahanpur, a Sufi qawwal celebrated for his exceptional ability to evoke asar. His father and Ustad, Kanhaiya Qawwal, trained him in the art, but Murli's understanding of spiritual ecstasy elevated his performances. His rendition of poetry expressing the longing and separation from the Almighty left listeners in a state of mystical transcendence. One of his celebrated composition was:

O more pardesi balamwa, kaise katey mori raat balamwa,
Kaise kate mori raat balamwa, kaise kate mori raat balamwa

This poetry, steeped in firaq (separation), encapsulates the yearning and pain of being apart from the divine Beloved (balamwa). The theme of separation itself is a recurring motif in qawwali, symbolising the soul's longing for union with the Creator.

In a similar vein, Hazrat Amir Khusrau also captured the mood of firaq (separation), with his heart-rending verses, reflecting the universal human experience of separation and the yearning for divine love.

Jo main jaanti bisrat hai saiyyan ghungta mein aag laga deti,
Inn churiyoo ki laaj piya rakhna, yeh toh pehn layi ab utratt nahi,
Mora bhaag suhaag tumhi sae hai, mai toh tumhi par jubna luta bethi.

In a surge of longing, the poet exclaims: now that I have worn the bangles signifying your love, they will not come off my hands. You are my everything and I surrender my youth to you.

Khadim Hassan Ajmeri writes of similar sentiments of firaq (separation):

Kyun na ashkbar huwa karoon, kyon na beyqaraar raha karoon
Na qaraar aaye tere siva, to tu hi bataa ke mein kya karoon
Mein maroon to tere liye maroon, mein jiyoon to tere liye jiyoon
Tere vaaste meri maut ho, tere vaaste mein jiya karoom

Why must I not be full of tears, why must I not be torn with anxiety,
The only relief for me is you, what should I do without you,
If I die, I die for you, if I live, I live for you

Qawwal and the Pir-o-Murshid (Sufi Master)

Ustad Meraj Ahmed Nizami emphasises the importance of training and initiation of the qawwal into the Sufi thought and the connection of the qawwal with a Sufi master as absolutely essential. The training of a qawwal has to transcend the musical mastery, regardless of the gharana (musical lineage) or khandaan (family lineage). Whether they learn from their father or an esteemed ustad, a qawwal's journey is incomplete without initiation into Sufi thought through a silsila (spiritual order). This initiation must come from an accomplished Sufi, as the essence of qawwali lies not just in technical expertise but in its asar—the impact it has on the listeners. A qawwal must lead the audience into the states of haal (spiritual ecstasy) and wajd (mystical rapture), and this requires a deep spiritual foundation.

Oral tradition says that for a qawwal to elevate their audience to a state of spiritual ecstasy, they themselves must embody the essence of Sufism. Their own direct connection to the divine is what enables them to guide listeners beyond their own comprehension, into realms of mystical experience. Traditionally, qawwals are mureeds (disciples) of Sufi saints and are closely associated with a particular silsila or dargah. This spiritual affiliation roots their art in devotion, ensuring that their musical performances are deeply transformative. The qawwals also add to their names a reference to the shrine or the Sufi saint they associate themselves with. The qawwals who are from the shrine of Nizamuddin, add 'Nizami' to their name, signifying their allegiance.

In the sacred setting of a Mehfil-e-Sama, both the singers and the listeners were often hum-khayal (like-minded) and hum-mijaz (similar in disposition), creating a unified spiritual atmosphere. The presence of the pir was central, as the devotees often saw the beauty of their God reflected in the pir.

This shared devotion magnified the mystical power of the gathering, allowing the qawwali to transcend its musical form and become a vehicle for divine connection. Qawwali as a mystical form of singing can be mysterious with many layers to unearth and its depth can be endless. Amir Khusrau perhaps could do this because he had a great soul connection with his Pir-o-Murshid Khwaja Nizamuddin Auliya.

⬩ ◆ ⬩

Poet: Hazrat Amir Khusrau

⬩ ◆ ⬩

Man tu shudam tu man shudi,
Man tan shudam tu jaan shudi.
Taakas na goyad baad azeen,
Man deegaram tu deegari

(I become you, you become me,
I be the body and you the soul,
So that no one can say, we are separate.)

Musical Components of Qawwali

1. **Raagdari (Melody):** Ustad Iqbal Ahmed Khan says that the universality of musical notes across cultures reflects the shared language of music, transcending geographical and linguistic barriers. In Hindustan, we have 'Sa Re Ga Ma Pa Dha Ni Sa,' while in Western music, the equivalent notes are 'Do, Re, Mi, Fa, So, La, Ti, Do.' In Indian (Hindustani) music, distinctions are often drawn between folk, classical, and semi-classical forms. However, in qawwali, these boundaries blur seamlessly. This genre encapsulates folk elements while simultaneously embracing the sophistication of classical bandish (musical composition). The structure of modern qawwali is attributed to Hazrat Amir Khusrau, whose innovative efforts formalised and musically organised this spiritual art form. The general mausikhi (musical style) can be categorised into three aspects: classical compositions, semi-classical compositions, and mulki (folk) songs. Despite these distinctions, the foundational swar (notes) and naad (sound) remain universal across genres like

qawwali, kirtan, thumri, or ghazal, rooted in the ancient traditions of raag and raagini.

A fascinating oral narrative shared by Pir-o-Murshid Khwaja Hassan Nizami Sahab to Ustad Iqbal Ahmed Khan explores the connection between souls (rooh) and music. In *alam-e-barzakh*—the realm between death and resurrection—all souls are said to have heard Allah's (SWT) voice proclaiming, *'Alastu bi rabbikum'* ('Am I not your Lord?'), to which the souls collectively responded, *'Beshak qalu bala tu hai'* ('Indeed, You are'). Hazrat Nizamuddin Auliya elaborated that each soul heard this divine voice in a specific raag, the one that resonated with its own spiritual essence. He himself is said to have heard it in Raag Poorvi, illustrating the deep connection between music and spirituality.

His favourite disciple, Hazrat Amir Khusrau ingeniously merged the existing raag and raagniya of Hindustani music with the makam and nagma of Arabic music, pioneering the creation of new musical structures that enriched qawwali and Hindustani music alike. His innovative contributions included bandish (compositions) and styles such as qalbana, sawela in brijbhasha, khayal, naqsh-o-gul, dhamal and tirwat, all of which are attributed to his genius.

Dhamal, which is a vibrant style of singing, is closely associated with Sufi practices, especially raqs (spiritual dance), and embodies divine ecstasy and communion. Hazrat Amir Khusrau infused qawwali with a unique sense of taal (rhythm), sur (melody) and a distinctive andaaz (style) of delivering the swar (musical notes). This blend of musical and spiritual elements made qawwali a form of devotional expression and a rich and vibrant musical tradition.

Traditionally, qawwali maintained a strict focus on its spiritual purpose. Elements like sargam (musical notes sung in sequence) and taan (rapid melodic improvisations) were not permitted, as emphasis was placed on takrar (repetition) and simple rhythm to guide listeners into a state of kaif (spiritual ecstasy). The simplicity of this approach ensured that the focus remained on the divine message conveyed through the poetry and the rhythm, avoiding any distraction from intricate musical embellishments. This structured and deeply spiritual approach remains central to the performance of qawwali even today. The sacred origin and purpose of qawwali distinguish it as a devotional practice rather than merely an art (music) form.

2. Takrar (Repetition): Ustad Meraj Nizami emphasises that the two critical poetic components of qawwali are takrar (repetition) and girah lagana (poetic interventions). Takrar is simpler and involves the continuous repetition of a particular phrase or poetic line, which intensifies the spiritual atmosphere and draws the listener deeper into the experience.

The interplay of rhythm, takrar, and the unique style of the qawwals creates the conditions for kaif (spiritual ecstasy). When executed with precision and devotion, qawwali becomes a powerful medium to transcend ordinary consciousness and connect with the divine, fulfilling its ultimate purpose of invoking spiritual ecstasy and closeness to Allah (SWT). Here is an example of takrar:

gar yaar ho baham, koi ho, ho na ho, na ho,
mera yaar ho baham, koi ho, ho na ho, na ho,
mera yaar ho,
bas mera yaar ho,
gar yaar ho,
mera yaar ho,
haan mera yaar ho,
koi ho, ho na ho, na ho.

The above lines by poet Imdad Ali Ulvi, repeatedly say that if my yaar (Beloved) is with me, no one else matters. The repeat of the words creates a meditative state expressing the intensity of ishq.

In qawwali, the poet often evokes a state of extreme devotion with singular focus on the Beloved, where the presence of the divine eclipses all worldly matters. This sentiment, when rendered in Qawwali, often manifests as takrar—the continuous repetition of a specific poetic line or phrase. This repetition anchors the listener's mind to a single thought, heightening the emotional and spiritual resonance until it culminates in kaif, a state of spiritual ecstasy. While repetition in other contexts might seem monotonous, in the structured yet fluid musical framework of qawwali, it becomes transformative, drawing the listener deeper into the spiritual experience.

The impact of this repetition and poetic expression is so otherworldly that it has led to extraordinary spiritual experiences. Hazrat Khwaja Qutbuddin

Bakhtiyar Kaki (RA) is said to have attained union with the Almighty during a qawwali performance. The qawwals were singing a particular section of poetry that moved him so deeply that in the throes of spiritual ecstasy he merged with the divine. The following lines by poet Ahmad Jam were being sung:

• ◆ •

kushtagaan-e-khanjar-e-taslim ra
har zamaan az gaib jaane digar ast

• ◆ •

(Those who are slain by the dagger of surrender;
Receive every moment a new life from the unseen)

This moment clearly explains the spiritual potency of qawwali, where music and poetry become a pathway to transcendence and divine connection.

Ustad Meraj Nizami points out that in the early days, qawwali was not a profession but it was a sacred practice carried out by mureeds (followers) as an expression of devotion and spiritual connection. It was later, during the time of Hazrat Amir Khusrau, that qawwali began evolving into a more organised and formalised tradition. Hazrat Amir Khusrau established the Qawwal Bachche Gharana, a lineage of musicians dedicated to preserving and performing qawwali. Today, most contemporary qawwals trace their roots back to this original gharana. Ustad Meraj Nizami, himself being the direct lineage, is a descendant of this gharana.

3. **Girah Lagana (Poetic Interventions):** Ustad Meraj Ahmed says that while takrar is simpler, girah lagana, on the other hand, is a more intricate art. It involves weaving verses from different poets or even in different languages into the same qawwali composition while maintaining the thematic coherence. This layering adds richness to the performance and keeps the line of thought unified, showcasing the qawwal's mastery over the art form.

Girah is a poetic and musical technique in qawwali that acts as a pivot, allowing a sher (couplet) to unfold its meaning in layers. The qawwals achieve this by weaving another poetic composition into the main verse, interspersing it seamlessly to expand the original thought. This creates depth and complexity while maintaining the consistency of thought. The qawwals then return to the main sher, completing the cycle in a way that feels natural and fluid.

What makes girah particularly captivating is the effortless way it is performed. The listener, entranced by the rhythm and melody of the qawwali, often remains unaware of the intricate poetic mastery at play. The ability to integrate verses from different poets, and sometimes even different languages, while preserving the essence of the original thought, showcases the qawwal's skill and creativity.

This technique enriches the poetic flow and deepens the emotional and spiritual impact of qawwali. It allows the listener to explore the central theme from multiple perspectives, enhancing their experience without breaking the flow of the performance. Girah is the artistic and spiritual ingenuity of qawwals, making qawwali a uniquely immersive and transformative art form. The ability of qawwals to bring forth varied poetic content is commendable as mostly they have no or very little formal education.

An easy example of girah lagana on a very popular qawwali can be understood with the following example. *'Chhap tilak sab cheeni re'* is a very popular peom by Hazrat Amir Khusrau. The original verse written by the poet is:

Chhap tilak sab cheeni ray mosay naina milaikay

Added to the original sher is:

mai dekhat ki dekhat reh gayi,
bairagan kar dini re, mosay naina mila kar

And the example of a girah on this can be the following poetry of Kaamil Shatari:

yaar ki marzi kae tabe, yaar ka dum bhar kae dekh
arz e matlab karke dekha tark e matlab karke dekh,
dekhat dekhat aaisi dekh,
be-irada marne waley ba-irada marke dekh,
sab tamashe kar chuka yeh bhi tamasha karke dekh,
dekhat dekhat aaisi dekh,
mitt jaye dhoka rehjaye ek.

The above poetic lines reflect the emotion of stupendous wonder, a state in which the character has been left by merely the fact that her eyes met with the Beloved's eyes. All subsequent lines elaborate a similar emotion.

4. **Rhythmic Patterns in Qawwali:** Qawwali holds a unique power in its rhythm, where the beat of the performance becomes synonymous with the heartbeat of the listener. This is deeply intertwined with the concept of zikr—the rhythmic remembrance of the divine. The continuous flow of music in qawwali creates a foundation upon which the qawwal emphasises certain phrases, at the same time responding dynamically to the audience's reactions. This interplay between the qawwal and the listeners is a significant feature of qawwali's musicality, where phrases are repeated (takrar) to intensify the spiritual connection and build kaif—a higher state of ecstasy—all the while keeping the same beat intact.

The rhythmic clapping (taali) performed by the chorus is a unique element of qawwali's structure. Alongside the beats of instruments like the dholak or tabla, the taali sustains the rhythm, complementing the main qawwal's performance. The chorus members, typically two to four individuals, provide clapping and also engage in takrar, reinforcing the phrases sung by the lead. Ustad Meraj Ahmed Nizami mentions that, in earlier times, when qawwali was accompanied by the daff, a single hand was initially used to strike the instrument at specific points of poetic or rhythmic emphasis. Over time, both hands were employed to create a fuller sound, enhancing the dynamic energy of the performance.

The Spread of Qawwali

Though primarily associated with Farsi, Arabic, Urdu, Punjabi, and Sindhi, qawwalis also flourished in numerous regional languages and dialects, becoming a powerful medium for spreading Sufism across the Indian subcontinent. These vernacular expressions allowed Sufi teachings to resonate deeply with local communities, transcending linguistic and cultural barriers.

In a discussion on qawwali with the ustads, we easily navigate through Delhi, the Deccan, and Braj, reflecting the vast reach and diversity of qawwali, and to its deep connection with Sufism. This genre of spiritual music has transcended regional boundaries, carried by the mureeds of Hazrat Nizamuddin Auliya as they spread the message of the Nizami silsila across Hindustan. Ustad Iqbal Ahmed Khan says that according to legend, 400 palkis (palanquins) were sent out from Delhi, dispersing this spiritual tradition far and wide.

As a result, qawwali became an integral part of the cultural fabric of Delhi and also other regions spread far and wide, enriched by poetic compositions in multiple languages. From Sindhi and Punjabi to Arabic, Urdu, Bengali, and Purbi dialects like Bhojpuri, Braj, and Awadhi, the versatility and adaptability of qawwali allowed it to resonate with diverse audiences. Each region contributed its unique linguistic and cultural flavour, making qawwali an inclusive and universal spiritual expression.

Though the spread of qawwali was on the seemingly frail feet of regional poetry it was strong-footed enough to survive many centuries. The more the people could understand, the more they clearly participated in their own language, and the wider it spread. Today, each region defines its own poetic tradition associated with qawwali. An example of poetry in Bhojpuri language widely used in qawwali is as follows:

Sagri umar meri maika maeli gayi,
kahan leke jaibe gavanva haye ram,
kahan leke jaibe gavanva haye ram,
Na moh pae ghun dhan na mo pae jubna,
na pehnu aaisa gahenwa haye ram,
Khol ghunghat jab piya mukh dekhe, arey,
ek ho na chalbi bahanba haye ram,
ek ho na chalbi bahanava haye raam.

A woman laments, 'My whole life has been spent in my father's house—now where is this new world that you are ushering me into?' Beyond its literal meaning, these words carry deeper spiritual significance. Just as a bride leaves her familiar home, the seeker transitions from the known world to an unexplored realm of spirituality under the guidance of a Pir-o-Murshid. The metaphor beautifully captures the journey from worldly existence to spiritual awakening.

Two famous Sufi poets who wrote in Brijbhasha, Awadhi and Bhojpuri are Bedam Shah Warsi from Dewa Sharif and Shah Turab Ali Qalandar form Kakori Sharif, both from the region of present-day Uttar Pradesh. Their poetry is sung by all qawwals from India and Pakistan.

Neeki lagat mohe apnay piya ki,
Neeki lagat mohe apnay piya ki aankh raseeli laaj bhari,
aankh raseeli laaj bhari,
Neeki lagat mohe.
Chaen parat naahi mukh daikay bina,
daikh najar bhar jaat mari ray
Kaahay turab darun kaahu say,
kay preet karee ka mein chori karee ray?

(The beauty of the beloved with his intoxicating eyes has put me in a trance. Why should I fear what others have to say? I have simply loved, not done any wrong.)

Basant and Holi are two important festivals that also signify music traditions in qawwali and brought out the celebratory aspect in people. It also ushered in the themes of Krishna and Radha, and the gopis and the dalliance therein, into the purview of qawwali. Ustad Meraj Ahmed Nizami gives example of a qawwali on Holi which is written like a kirtan and when sung it is self-explanatory about the relationship between kirtan and qawwali.

Shyam sundar tohsae khelungi holi re
O tohsae khelungi holi, tohsae khelungi holi
saas nanand puche kahan lagayi itni deri, re deri
mai toh kehdungi, ho li, so ho li piya ki mai toh ho li
piya ki mai toh ho li, piya mai toh ho li, piya ki.
aapne piya, mai toh ho li piya ki

The use of the single word Holi to signify the festival of colours and 'ho li' when used separately as two words to signify belonging to the beloved, the pir, the murshid, is beautiful in this poem. Moreover, Shyam Sundar (the dark lord) here can refer to both the Hindu God Krishna and the Pir-o-Murshid.

Interestingly the poetry written by Kabir in vernacular Hindi is widely used by qawwals and borrowing from various dialects including Braj and Awadhi, it found its way into qawwali woven with other poets who also wrote on the same thought.

⬥ ◆ ⬥

Poet: Amir Khusrau

⬥ ◆ ⬥

Bahut kathin hai dagar panghat ki,
Kaise main bhar laaon madhva se matki

⬥ ◆ ⬥

Poet: Kabir

⬥ ◆ ⬥

Laali more laal ki, jit dekhun tit laal,
Laali dekhan main gayi, main bhi ho gayi laal

The Ustads on the Essence of Qawwali in Modern Times

Ustad Iqbal Ahmed Khan highlights a significant contrast between the essence of qawwali in its original spiritual form and its contemporary popular usage. He distinguishes between 'ilmi qawwali'—music sung as an act of ibaadat (devotion)—and 'filmi qawwali', which caters to entertainment and monetary gains. He laments that the original purpose of qawwali, which was solely for connecting with the Almighty, has often been overshadowed by its commercialised form.

Ustad Meraj Ahmed Nizami echoes this sentiment, emphasising that qawwali has transformed to suit mass appeal but, in doing so, it has strayed from its spiritual roots. He asserts that the popular form of qawwali heard casually on streets or at events cannot induce the state of kaif. He says, qawwali is not mere entertainment or a pastime; it is ibaadat, a prayerful experience designed to elevate the soul towards divine connection. He poignantly describes the changes in qawwali using a verse by Dr Allama Iqbal:

◆

Na Momin Hai Na Momin Ki Ameeri
Raha Sufi, Gyi Roshan Zameeri

◆

(Neither the believer nor his power survives.
The Sufi has outlived his radiant soul)

◆

Khuda Se Phir Wohi Qalb-o-Nazar Mang
Nahin Mumkin Ameeri Be-Faqeeri

◆

(Ask God for the heart and soul of men of the past,
You have to become a fakir, first, to regain the power)

Through this verse, both ustads critique the loss of qawwali's sacred essence and its drift towards materialism and worldly pursuits. True qawwali, as envisioned by the Sufi saints, remains a profound act of devotion and a spiritual journey.[1]

Endnotes

This is excerpted from a conversation moderated by Late Shri Vikram Lall during the seminar 'Understanding Qawwali' in 2014. The legends and incidents are part of the oral narratives and have been reproduced as spoken by the ustads. They may or may not find written historical validation. The complete interview is available on YouTube under The Qawwali Project.

ਲਾਲ ਮੇਰੀ ਪੱਤ ਰਖਿਓ ਭਲਾ
ਝੂਲੇ ਲਾਲਨ
ਸਿੰਧੜੀ ਦਾ, ਸਹਿਵਣ ਦਾ
ਸ਼ਾਬਾਜ਼ ਕ਼ਲੰਦਰ
ਦਮਾ ਦਮ ਮਸਤ ਕ਼ਲੰਦਰ
ਅਲੀ ਦਮ ਦਮ ਦੇ ਅੰਦਰ
ਸਖ਼ੀ ਸ਼ਾਹਬਾਜ਼ ਕ਼ਲੰਦਰ
ਪੀਰਾਂ ਵਿੱਚ ਮੇਰਾ ਪੀਰ
ਸਭ ਦਾ ਵਲੀ ਐ
ਲਕ਼ਬ ਅਸਾਦੂਲਾ ਤੇ ਨਾਮ ਅਲੀ ਐ
ਨਾਮ ਅਲੀ ਸੋਏ ਭਾਗ
ਜਗਾਐ ਝੂਲੇ ਲਾਲਨ
ਸਿੰਧੜੀ ਦਾ, ਸਹਿਵਣ ਦਾ
ਸ਼ਾਬਾਜ਼ ਕ਼ਲੰਦਰ
ਦਮਾ ਦਮ ਮਸਤ ਕ਼ਲੰਦਰ

PUNJAB: THE LIVING HERITAGE

Tracing Qawwali with Ustad Ranjhan Ali

stad Ranjhan Ali is a traditional qawwal from Punjab where this form is notably popular amongst the common people. The qawwal belongs to the Qadiri silsila (order) of the Sufi traditions. Every qawwal prays to the saint before the performance, traditionally held at the dargah, in a way seeking the permission for the performance at the mehfil (assembly). One such impromptu haazri (singing) is shot by the photographer. The dargah where they sing is interestingly decorated at the entrance with bells.

Punjab has been home to many Sufi saints and mystical traditions. Panj peer (or panch pīr), meaning the five saints, were Sufi saints who overlapped in late 12th and early 13th centuries in north western India especially Punjab. The names of panj peer vary from region to region, and from group to group including and excluding. the names based on place and their popularity. The panj peer remains a fluid group of names of Sufi Saints.

The qawwal sings at the shrine and in contrast to the bright colours around him, he is in a sombre mood, lost in praise of the Almighty where he leads with just his voice. His team of musicians wait for their turn to add to the music. While seated on the ground, people lose themselves to music and poetry, yet there is a well-timed rush of activity of giving money to the qawwal as part of their obeisance to the shrine. The performers continue singing undisturbed, an age-old tradition followed equally by men and women at every shrine.

Qawwali under the Trees

The qawwals practise casually under a shade of the old banyan tree next to their house in the premises of the Qadiri shrine. Even a practice session by them becomes a sort of mehfil for people to stop by, sit and listen.

The qawwals sit cross-legged on the ground usually in two rows with the lead singer, side singers and harmonium players in the front row, and the chorus and percussionists in the back row. The interesting addition to this party is the presence of the young woman in this rural Punjab traditional setting. In the past, women were generally excluded from traditional qawwali music, since they were prohibited from singing in the presence of men. Even now, qawwali is mostly kept as a fiercely androcentric tradition.

Dance in the Moment

The qawwals chant some specific words and lines repeatedly and hypnotically, coupled with frenzied clapping of hands in the rhythm which transports the audiences to a trance-like state. Impromptu dance is common in Punjab traditions, the turbaned Sahib-e-Mehfil (the host or the head of shrine) leads first and then the people start dancing to the music.

Lost in Poetry

This unusual decor with modern-day balloons adds to the colour of a mehfil, with the serenity of the moment intact. The qawwal uses his voice modulation with an intensity that brinks on spiritual ecstasy. The popular repertoire for qawwals in Punjab is a Kafi (a poem), the language used is Punjabi, Seraiki or Sindhi with the local dialects. The mystical, spiritual poetry of Baba Farid, Sultan Bahu, Shah Hussain and Bulleh Shah are popular in such assemblies of music. The Beloved takes the shape of Jogi, of Ranjha, of the one who holds the keys to the hearts of the followers.

The poetry is so powerful that it can lead to a profound state of ecstasy for the listeners while the qawwals are at times lost in their own music. One of the singers of this qawwali team has a speech condition and he stutters and stammers when he is speaking in normal life. The moment he sings, however, his voice soars right up to the skies, without any restraint. There is no speech impediment when he sings, for then he raises his voice for the Almighty. He is flawless, he is the chosen one to open his heart and sing, in love. He is the qawwal.

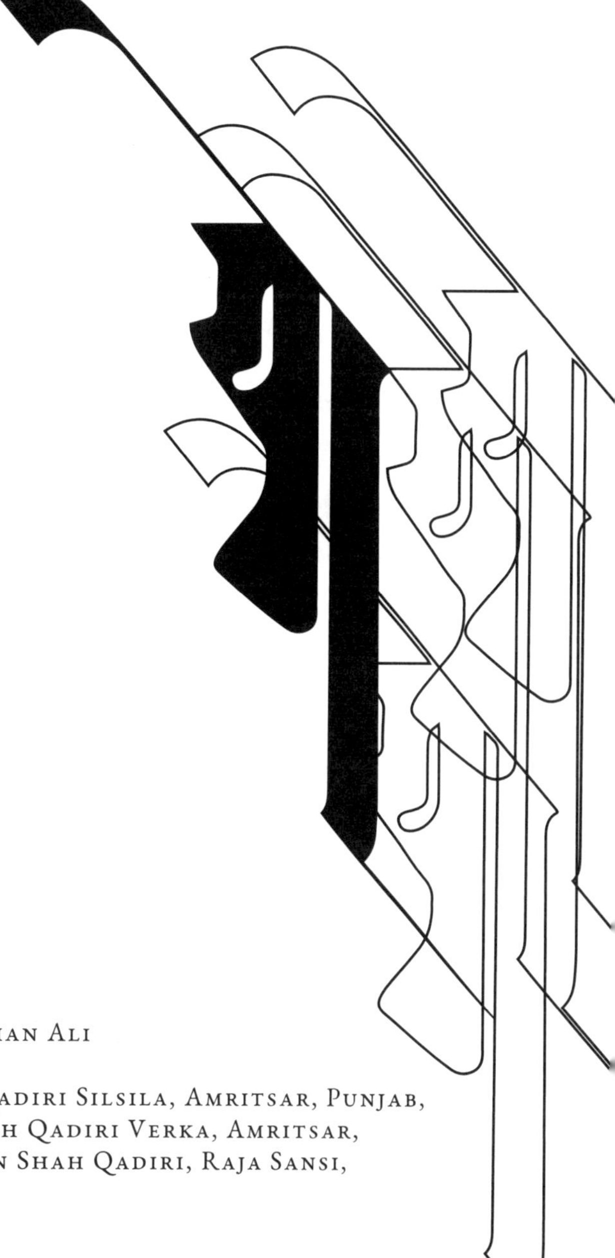

Photographer: Dinesh Khanna
Qawwali Practitioner: Qawwal Ustad Ranjhan Ali
Text: Manjari Chaturvedi
Place: Dargah Hazrat Bannnay Shah, Qadiri Silsila, Amritsar, Punjab, India. Dargah Nihal Shah-Sundar Shah Qadiri Verka, Amritsar, Punjab, India. Dargah Hazrat Hussain Shah Qadiri, Raja Sansi, Amritsar, Punjab, India
Project: The Qawwali Project

ਦਰਬਾਰ
ਗਾਲੀ
ਨਾ ਕਰੋ

the punjab story

ਪੰਜਾਬ ਦੀ ਕਹਾਣੀ

يا محمد
يا الله

Dama Dam Mast Qalandar: Unravelling a Sufi Qawwali

Kumkum Srivastava

ama Dam Mast Qalandar is one of the most recognizable Sufi songs in the world, with a rich history spanning centuries. Originating in the thirteenth century as a devotional poem to Lal Shahbaz Qalandar, a revered Sufi saint, the song has undergone many transformations over time. From its roots in Sufi mysticism to its modern-day adaptations in popular music, *'Dama Dam Mast Qalandar'* has evolved into a cultural phenomenon, transcending geographical and spiritual boundaries.

This essay delves into the fascinating history of *'Dama Dam Mast Qalandar'*, exploring its origins, cultural significance, and the factors contributing to its enduring popularity. I shall examine the song's transformation from a sacred Sufi hymn to a profane, secular anthem, and how this shift reflects broader changes in societal values, cultural norms, and the role of music in shaping identity and community.

Through a critical analysis of the song's lyrics, historical context, and cultural adaptations, this essay aims to provide a nuanced understanding of *'Dama Dam Mast Qalandar'* as a cultural icon, a symbol of spiritual devotion, and a reflection of the complex, ever-changing dynamics between tradition and modernity.

'Dama Dam Mast Qalandar' is an evident example of the presence of folk, bearing a transnational nature. The inclusive, secular note in this litany made it a 'number' that is refreshing, energetic, universal and permanent. It is liberating, emerging beyond groups, factions, boundaries, identifying connections that would otherwise go unseen, unnoticed. Ever since it has been sung, since the thirteenth century, the audience has swayed and danced to its lyrics and beats. A spontaneous connection between the singer and the listeners gets created

and the listening turns participatory. The song gets transformed into a cultural behaviour that is communicated to the group through the mode of performance that is ritualistic, verbal, and expressive; personal joy is shared by the audience and becomes 'public joy', the singer of the song, inadvertently becomes a mystic. The mysticism inherent in the song has touched the chord of every human heart irrespective of borderlines, political or religious.

In the song, we can perceive the unending pursuit of the divine. Passionate and ecstatic, spiritual and entrancing, this song acts as a uniquely valuable bridge between the East and the West reflecting the most accessible, liberal and pluralistic aspects of Islam. The song acts as a strong, cultural symbol that advocates national and ethnic pride. The song is the quest for absolute truth. E. Underhill remarks that it epitomises the organic process which involves the perfect consummation of the love of God, it is the art of establishing his conscious relation with the Absolute.

'Dama Dam Mast Qalandar' has played a significant role in promoting communal harmony and Hindu-Muslim Unity in several ways.

1. **Shared cultural heritage:** It is part of the shared cultural heritage of the Indian subcontinent. Its religious ties are loose enough so that, despite differences, people from various faiths can come together to celebrate their common heritage.

2. **Universal message of love:** The song lyrics, rooted in Sufi philosophy, emphasise the importance of love, compassion, and devotion. This message of love and unity resonates for people across spiritual boundaries, fostering a sense of shared humanity and love.

3. **Interfaith celebrations:** This is often sung during interfaith celebrations, such as the urs festival at the shrine of Lal Shahbaz Qalandar in Sehwan, Pakistan, and the qawwali sessions held at Sufi shrines throughout the Indian subcontinent. These festivals attract devotees from various faiths, promoting unity and communal harmony.

4. **Crossover Appeal:** The song's catchy melody and energetic rhythm have made it a crossover hit, appealing to people from diverse musical and cultural backgrounds. This has helped break down cultural and religious barriers.

4. **Transcendence:** Repetitive and rhythmic nature of the lyrics creates a state of spiritual ecstasy, encouraging listeners to transcend their worldly concerns and connect with the divine.

5. **Unity and Oneness:** This song emphasises the concept of unity (tawhid) in Sufism, suggesting that all paths lead to the same ultimate truth.

6. **Celebration of Life:** The lively rhythm and upbeat tone promote a sense of joy and reflection, feeding the belief that spiritual experiences can bring happiness and fulfilment.

7. **Mysticism:** The words invoke mystical imagery, representing the journey of the soul towards enlightenment and the search for divine love.

Overarching Themes in the Song

1. **Continuous Divine Presence:** Every breath ('Dama Dam') is a reminder of the constant presence of divine love, suggesting that spirituality is not confined to rituals but is an ongoing experience.

2. **Mystical Ecstasy:** The state of being 'mast' captures the essence of Sufi mysticism—a state of spiritual intoxication where worldly concerns fade away in the overwhelming presence of the divine.

3. **Devotional Homage:** By invoking revered figures such as Ali and Lal Shahbaz Qalandar, the song pays tribute to those who embody spiritual ideals, urging devotees to follow their example of selflessness, courage, and surrender.

4. **Unity and Universal Love:** Although rooted in a specific cultural and spiritual context, the song's themes of love, protection, and ecstatic devotion have resonated widely. Its call for spiritual unity invites listeners from diverse backgrounds to share in the celebration of divine mystery.

Understanding *'Dama Dam Mast Qalandar'*

'Dama Dam' literally means 'with every breath' or 'moment by moment'. This phrase sets the tone for the song, implying that the divine or mystical presence infuses every moment of life.

'Mast' means 'intoxicated or ecstatic' in a spiritual sense. It is not about literal intoxication but about being overwhelmed by the love and presence of the divine.

'Qalandar' refers to a type of wandering Sufi mystic and is particularly associated with Lal Shahbaz Qalandar, a saint revered for his spiritual insight and defiance of conventional norms.

'Dama Dam Mast Qalandar' celebrates the mystic's freedom from worldly constraints and his complete immersion in divine love.

Ali in *'Ali da Pehla Number'* refers to Hazrat Ali (RA), a central figure in Sufi and Islamic mysticism, symbolising courage, piety, and spiritual authority.

'Da Pehla Number' translates roughly as 'is the number one' or 'first in rank'. This line honours Hazrat Ali's (RA) esteemed status, suggesting that among all spiritual guides or divine manifestations, he holds the foremost position. It reinforces the idea that true spiritual leadership and guidance are paramount.

'Lal Meri Pat Rakhio Bala Jhule Lalan'. 'Lal' is a term of endearment and can refer to the beloved saint or the divine itself (sometimes evoking the image of Lal Shahbaz Qalandar or symbolising the red (or 'lively') essence of passion. 'Meri Pat Rakhio' can be understood as a supplication, 'please protect me' or 'watch over me'. 'Bala' often intensifies the plea, sometimes interpreted as 'O Dear' or 'my beloved'. Jhule Lal was a Sindhi Hindu deity, a contemporary of Shahbaz Qalandar.

In this verse, the devotee is asking the divine or the revered mystic for protection and guidance, expressing complete surrender and trust in the higher power.

Repetitive Structure

The song's repeated lines—especially *'Dama Dam Mast Qalandar'*—serve a dual purpose. They reinforce the idea that the divine presence is constant and they help the listener enter a meditative, trance-like state.

The rhythmic repetition is a common feature in Sufi music, intended to dissolve the ego and transport the listener into a state of ecstatic union with the divine.

A Note on Variations

Because *'Dama Dam Mast Qalandar'* is a folk and devotional song, many artists have addressed verses, rearranged the order, or altered certain words to reflect local traditions or personal interpretations. Some renditions include additional verses that elaborate on the miracles or compassionate nature of Lal Shahbaz Qalandar. Other versions might incorporate regional languages or reference, deepening the cultural context of the song.

The song is not just a collection of words but a spiritual journey, overlapping all religious boundaries. It is the inherent characteristic of any folk song that it can bind people together and thus resonate with its global, local, national or international audience. Deeply connected to the social process, a folk song cannot exist on its own and needs to work within the context of society and community, simultaneously maintaining standard cultural values while doing so. In this song, we can perceive an unending pursuit for the divine that is omnipresent in all elemental forms. A loving impulse for the divine restricts the moralising strain to some extent and there is a sense of immersion in the love and power of the divine whose presence inside the hearts is in the form of love. Passionate and ecstatic, spiritual and entrancing, this song acts as a uniquely valuable bridge between East and West, reflecting the most accessible, liberal and pluralistic aspects of Islam. The song also acts as a strong cultural symbol that advocates national and ethnic pride.

Written and sung in honour of Sufi mystic saint Hazrat Lal Shahbaz Qalandar (Usman Marwandi), every word of his name used in the song has a meaning. He was known as Hazrat (Holiness). Lal refers to the red robes he wore. Shahbaz (Shah = King and Baz = Falcon, king of falcons) in Iranian mythology represents the godly figure who led them to victory. Finally, Qalandar means a Sufi saint, poet, mystic, nobleman. He settled in Sehwan (Sindh, now in Pakistan) and tried bringing peace between Hindus and Muslims.

⬩ ◆ ⬩

O, laal meri pat rakhio bala Jhule Laalan,
Sindri da Sehwan da, Sakhi Shahbaz Qalandar,
Dama dam mast qalandar,
Ali dam dam de andar

⬩ ◆ ⬩

(O the red robed one, may I always have your benign protection, Jhulelal [as he was affectionately called]. O master, friend and Sire of Sind and Sehwan, the red-robed God-intoxicated Qalandar, the Lord in every breath of mine, glory be to you.)

• ◆ •

Char Charaag tere balan hamesha,
Panjwa mein baaran aayi, bala, Jhule Laalan.

• ◆ •

(Your shrine is always lit with four lamps, and here I come to light a fifth lamp in your honour. Here, I come with fifth, O master, friend and Sire of Sind and Sehwan [or Serwan]).

• ◆ •

Hind Sind (Ghanan Ghanan) peera teri naubat vaaje,
naal vaje ghadiyaal, bala, Jhule Laalan,
O naal vaje ghadiyaal bala Jhule Laalan.

• ◆ •

(Let your heroic name ring out in Hind Sind [or let the gongs toll]. Let the kettledrum resound for your glory day and night by the ghadiayal [the watchman]).

• ◆ •

Hardam peera teri khair hove,
Naam-e-Ali Beda paar laga, Jhule Laalan,
O naam-e-Ali, O naam-e-Ali beda paar laga Jhule Laalan.

• ◆ •

(O Lord, may you prevail every time, everywhere, I pray of your well-being. In the name of Ali, I pray to you to help my boat cross in safety [in the river of life]).

• ◆ •

Uchara rauza peera tera,
heth wage dariya bhala Jhule Laalan.

• ◆ •

(On the hilltop is your shrine,
and below flows the river.)

• ◆ •

Maavan nu peera bachde denda,
behnan nu denda e veer mila, Jhule Laalan.

• ◆ •

(Oh Lord, you bestow children to childless women,
and you unite brothers with their sisters.)

This Sufi anthem of Hindu and Muslim unity, this manaqabat dedicated to Lal Shahbaz Qalandar, the litany, prayer petition or an appeal to Jhulelal has become the most popular qawwali sung at almost every shrine in the subcontinent. The song's raw emotionality and appeal transcends border.

Who wrote these words, who were Lal Shahbaz and Jhulelal? Where is Sehwan. Why are their names, one Sufi, the other a Hindu, mentioned in the same song. These are questions that need to be addressed.

Lal Shahbaz and Jhulelal were contemporaries, who belonged to the same region, and also to the same cultural and spiritual milieu. The song seeks both their spiritual blessings and protection. By invoking the names of these two revered figures the song's lyrics aim to create a sense of spiritual connection and communal binding among the listeners. The mention of both these mentors in the same song is also proof of the beautiful blend of Sufi and Sindhi traditions. Some legends suggest that they were friends and spiritual companions.

A contentious and controversial issue is the authorship of this song. It is believed that folk songs have no single author, words are added over time and it becomes everyone's song. If we delve into the lyrics of the song, explain its meaning and significance, we shall find that it transcends religious differences, allowing people to interpret it in their own way. It is believed that this litany was written by Amir Khusrau in the twelfth century and a few lines were added by Sharfuddin Bu Ali Shah Qalandar of Panipat in the thirteenth century.

The song's lyrics based on traditional Sufi poetry and folklore makes us believe that it evolved over time through oral traditions. However, some lines have been credited to Abdulla Shah Qadiri (Bulleh Shah, 1680-1758) who was a Sufi poet and mystic in eighteenth-century Punjab. Some have attributed the lyrics to the Sindhi Sufi Poet, Shah Abdul Latif Bhittal (1689-1752).

This brings us to explore the history of the main personalities who are mentioned in the song, that is, Lal Shahbaz Qalandar and Jhule Lal.

Jhule Lal: Life and Legacy

Jhule Lal is a revered deity in Sindhi culture, particularly among Hindus. He is considered an incarnation of Lord Varuna, the Hindu god of water bodies. According to a legend, Jhule Lal was born in the tenth century in Sindh (Pakistan) during the rule of a tyrannical Muslim ruler Mirak Shah who ordered Hindus to convert to Islam, or face death or leave Sindh. Faced with persecution, the Sindhi Hindus prayed to Lord Varuna for forty days, after which their prayers were answered with the birth of Jhule Lal, also called Udero Lal.

Another story about Jhule Lal is that before his birth a divine voice (aakashvani) announced his arrival. It is believed that an old, bearded man riding a Pallu fish (a type of fish found in the Indus) proclaimed the birth of Jhule Lal symbolising the divine origin and significance of the blessed child and his mission. Pallu fish is considered a sacred symbol among Sindhis, representing fertility, prosperity and spiritual growth. Both the stories highlight Jhule Lal's importance as a saviour born to protect the Sindhis and promote harmony.

Lal Shahbaz Qalandar: Life and Legacy

The other revered name mentioned in the song *'Dama Dam Mast Qalandar'* is Lal Shahbaz Qalandar. In the rich tapestry of South Asian Sufism, Lal Shahbaz Qalandar (1177-1274) stands as a colossus whose legacy transcends time, religion and geography. A mystic poet, philosopher, and spiritual revolutionary, he epitomised the Sufi ideals of divine love, human unity and resistance to dogma.

His shrine in Sehwan Sharif, Pakistan, remains a vibrant symbol of cultural synthesis and spiritual resilience, drawing millions annually.

Born Syed Usman Shah Marwandi in Marwand (modern Afghanistan), Lal Shahbaz Qalandar hailed from a lineage of Sufis. His father, Syed Ibrahim Kabiruddin, was a revered dervish who fostered in him an early passion for spirituality. The epithet 'Lal' (red) refers to his crimson attire, while 'Shahbaz' (royal falcon) symbolises his soaring spiritual quest and detachment from worldly ties.

In his youth, he traversed the Islamic world, studying in Baghdad and Samarkand before settling in Sindh (now Pakistan) during the thirteenth century—a region ripe for Sufi missionary work and political upheaval under the Delhi Sultanate. His travels included encounters with contemporaries like Baha-ud-din Zakariya and Baba Farid, thus enriching his syncretic philosophy.

Lal Shahbaz Qalandar's teachings revolved around *Wahdat al-Wujud* (Unity of Being), emphasising that all creation reflects the divine. Rejecting sectarianism, he worked with Hindus and Muslims alike. Legend recounts him converting a Hindu temple into a khanqah while preserving its sanctity, symbolising interfaith harmony.

He challenged societal hierarchies, advocating for the marginalised—women, lower castes, and the poor. His defiance of orthodoxy, such as altering ascetically to transcend ego, underscored his belief in love as the path to God.

Sehwan: The Revered Land of This Litany

Sehwan Sharif's history is primarily marked by its association with the Sufi saint Lal Shahbaz Qalandar. The city's history also includes its conquest by Mohammad bin Qasim who captured the Sehwan fort in 713 and by Mahmud Ghazni in 1026. This fort predates the common era with legends attributing its construction to Alexander the Great. A folk tale suggests that the settlement was upended by Lal Shahbaz in the thirteenth century thus leading to its current name 'Ulti Basti' (inverted village). Sehwan has a long history of dynastic struggles between the Summas, the Arghuns and the Tarkhans.

Sehwan has a historical connection with Shaivism. Evidence suggests that the region originally known as Sivistan was inhabited by the Sivi tribe in the Vedic period and later became a centre of Shaivism. During the early seventh century a Chinese traveller Xuanzang documented over 235 Shiva temples in upper Sindh, including a large one in Sehwan. Sehwan was home to the Pashupata sect, a branch of Shaivism. The *Shiva Purana* mentions the Indus as a place for holy ascetics to purify themselves.

There is a striking similarity between the dressing of contemporary faqirs and Shaivite yogis as both wear patched robes and have matted hair. The shrine's dhamaal ceremony, a meditative dancing session, is believed to have evolved from Shaivite practices and the Sufi Qalandarriya order traditions introduced by Lal Shahbaz Qalandar. Frembegen has used the term 'figures of ambiguity' in the Sufi tradition in Sindh and Punjab suggesting an openness of the tradition, an acceptance of people from all faiths and background.

In his book *Tarikh-e-Tamadan-e-Sindh*, Molai Shaidai says that Sehwan was built by the Sewi Aryas, hence called Sewistan. Others suggest that this town dates back to the period of Prophet Shees, son of Adam, hence, Sheestan, Sewistan, and eventually Sehwan.

QALANDAR SUFI ORDER

The Qalandariyya is a distinctive Sufi sect renowned for its antinomian practices, asceticism, and rejection of societal norms. Emerging in the medieval Islamic world, qalandars (from the Persian, meaning 'wanderer' or 'free spirit') challenged orthodox religiosity through radical spiritual expression.

The Qalandariyya emerged in twenfth-century Persia and Central Asia, influenced by the earlier Sufi mystics like Bayazid Bistami (d. 848) and Hallaj (d. 922). The term qalandar may derive from the Arabic kalandar (vagabond) or Persian kalantar (elder), reflecting their itinerant lifestyle. They coalesced as a movement under figures like Jamal al-Din Savi (d. 1232), who institutionalised practices like celibacy and mendicancy (Karamustafa, 1994). The Mongol invasions (in the thirteenth century) further catalysed their spread, as disillusioned seekers embraced their radical detachment.

From Persia, the Qalandariyya spread to Anatolia, India and the Balkans. In South Asia, they integrated with local bhakti traditions, facilitating Islam's syncretic growth (Rizvi, 1978). The Delhi Sultanate (1206-1526) saw both persecution and patronage: historian Ziya al-Din Barani criticised their 'immorality', while poets like Amir Khusrau celebrated their sincerity. Ottoman Qalandars, such as the Bektashis, influenced Janissary culture (Le Gall, 2005).

Qalandar Practices

Qalandars prioritised inner spiritual awakening (haqiqa) over exoteric rituals (sharia), though they remained within Islam's broader framework. Key practices included:

1. **Asceticism:** Renunciation of material wealth, family and social status.

2. **Antinomianism:** Public defiance of norms, e.g., shaving hair and beards, wearing iron chains or animal skins (Schimmel, 1975).

3. **Music and Dance:** Engage in ecstatic rituals (sama) with instruments like the daf, tambourine, etc, akin to the meditative whirling of the dervishes, the followers of Mevlana Rumi of the Mevlevi order.

4. **Use of Intoxicants:** Symbolic consumption of wine or hashish to transcend ego (controversial among orthodox scholars).

Their motto, 'be darveshi, be qalandari' (to be a dervish is to be a qalandar), encapsulated their ethos of radical freedom.

Societal Impact and Legacy

1. **Cultural Influence:** Qalandars inspired Sufi poetry (Rumi, Hafez) and qawwali music. Their aphorisms permeate Punjabi and Sindhi folklore.

2. **Social Critique:** They condemned hypocrisy among elites, advocating for egalitarianism. Their shrines became hubs for marginalised communities.

3. **Modern Perception:** Today, qalandars are venerated at festivals like the urs of Lal Shahbaz, though some view them as eccentric. Contemporary orders, like the Malang in Pakistan, continue their traditions (Werbner, 2003).

The Qalandariyya represents Sufism's radical edge, challenging orthodoxy while enriching Islamic spirituality. Their legacy endures in cultural practices, shrine rituals, and the enduring appeal of mystical rebellion.

'Dama Dam Mast Qalandar': Tracing Its Path in Modern Times

The song serves as both a spiritual invocation and a celebration of the Sufi path, inviting its listeners to experience love, unity, and ecstatic devotion. Hence, the singer of the song inadvertently becomes a mystic and represents the sacred mysticism through the music.

The song has featured in various Pakistani and Hindi (Bollywood) films, further increasing its popularity and reach. This has helped spread the message of unity and devotion to a wider audience. Though newer renditions may add to the experience with modern styles and dance, the deeper meaning and essence remain intact. The youth may be drawn to the song's spiritual significance and may even find inspiration and meaning in its lyrics and message.

Emile Durkheim's concept of the sacred and profane can be applied to explain the changes in lyrics, the space and the responses of the musicians, singers, and audience wherever *'Dama Dam Mast Qalandar'* is rendered. In its original context, *'Dama Dam Mast Qalandar'* was a devotional Sufi poem, sung in reverence to Lal Shahbaz Qalandar and Jhule Lal. The lyrics were considered sacred, conveying spiritual themes and emotions. As the song was adapted and secularised, the lyrics underwent changes, and the context shifted from the sacred to the profane. The song became a popular, entertaining piece, stripped of its original spiritual significance.

Using Durkheim's understanding we can analyse the changes in lyrics and various responses. The original sacred lyrics were modified, and the spiritual context was lost, the song became a mundane ordinary song. Additionally, the song's meaning and significance shifted from spiritual to secular, focusing on entertainment and cultural identity. The song's performance changed from a ritualistic, devotional act to a staged performance, emphasising entertainment over spiritual expression, thus losing its authenticity.

The space where *'Dama Dam Mast Qalandar'* is rendered has also undergone a significant transformation. Originally, the song was sung at the shrine of Lal Shahbaz Qalandar, a sacred space for Sufi devotees. Today, the song is often performed in concert halls, festivals and other secular spaces, where the focus is on entertainment rather than spiritual devotion. The song has been commodified.

The audience for *'Dama Dam Mast Qalandar'* has also changed from devotees to 'concertgoers'. Originally the song was sung for the Sufi saints or the Sindhi Hindu's deity Jhule Lal, who sought spiritual connection and meaning. Today, this song is performed for a broader audience, who may appreciate the music and cultural significance without necessarily seeking spiritual connection, and are detached and non-participatory.

The musicians and singers also sing lyrics different from the original. However, some may appreciate the song's cultural significance, recognising its importance in Indo-Pak and Sufi cultural heritage. A majority of responses might focus on the song's commercial value, as also its melody and energetic performance, thus transforming a sacred devotional poem to a profane secular song.

This mixed idiom of local and classical vocabulary in *'Dama Dam Mast Qalandar'* creates a new universal Sufi language of love, bringing out the intense longing to be one with the divine. The song and its music touch inner spaces in every listener, transporting them into a dimension beyond this material world. The devotees' seeking can transform him from just a singer or listener to a qalandar, a free spirit, unattached, a renouncer, a wandering dervish, 'beqaid', 'beparweh', and 'beyond the law'.

Bibliography

- Karumustafa, A.T. (1994). *God's Unruly Friends: Dervish Groups in the Islamic Later Middle Period*. Oneworld.

- Schimmel, A. (1975). *Mystical Dimensions of Islam.* University of North Carolina Press

- Trimingham, J.S. (1971). *The Sufi Orders in Islam.* Oxford University Press

- Rizvi, S.A.A. (1978). *A History of Sufism in India*. Munshiram Manoharlal

- Le Gall, D. (2005). *A Culture of Sufism: Naqshbandis in the Ottoman World*. SUNY Press

- Werbner, P. (2003). *Pilgrims of Love: The Anthropology of a Global Sufi*. Hurst and Co

- Srivastava, Kumkum (2009). *The Wandering Sufis*. Aryan Books

- Digby, Simon (1997). *The Encyclopaedia of Islam*, Ashmolean Museum, Oxford

- Carl W. Ernst (2017). *It's Not Just Academic: Essays on Sufism and Islamic Studies*, Sage

- Molai, Shaidai (2000). *Tarikh-e-Tamaddun Sindh*, Sindh Adabi Board, Hyderabad

- Frembegen, J.W. (2006). *The Friends of God: Sufi Saints In Islam, Popular Poster Art from Pakistan*, Oxford University Press

- M. Bolvin, M.A. Cook, J. Levesque (2018). *Discovering Sindh's Past*, Oxford University Press

- Raza Rumi (2017). 'The Meaning of Sehwan', *The Friday Times*

- Raza Rumi (2018). *Being Pakistani – Society, Culture and The Arts*, HarperCollins, India

AJMER SHARIF

The Rhythm of Love

Reema Abbasi

◆

Poet: Khwaja Muinuddin Chishti

◆

'Listen to the voice from the incoming waves; it is loud.
But when the tide goes out, the voice becomes silent'

◆

Poet: Shah Abdul Latif Bhittai
(mystic and poet)

◆

'Let us go and visit the dwelling place of these ascetics,
who have consumed their ego completely'

The Ajmer Sharif shrine, central to the human geography of Sufi belief in South Asia, is lodged in a bend of an Ajmer hill; Muinuddin Chishti spent forty-six years of his life here. India was a more spiritually favourable refuge than the politically volatile environs he had left behind. But strife was a constant backdrop to his life; even his first love happened amid tumult in Rajasthan as a war raged between Jaichand and Prithviraj Chauhan.

His wife, Bibi Ummatullah, who was a former Rajput princess, listened to devotional music that challenged the clergy. Not long after their marriage, their hut turned into a caravanserai for the hungry, the homeless, and the weary traveller. Bibi established a communal kitchen, and the couple devoted themselves to providing solace without prejudice—a lifestyle that became their creed.

Khwaja was a vehicle of catharsis for tired souls, and he understood the healing powers in dance, song and verse. These pursuits eventually transformed into organised gatherings that harked back to pre-Islamic times and to the dance of rapture.

Sufi Islam dawned in South Asia with Muinuddin and his Chishti order; its philosophy a barricade to clerical ascendance. Some Sufi scholars maintain that Khwaja Muinuddin introduced qawwali to attract more people to remote Ajmer as most pilgrims would turn to the strains of bhajans in Pushkar. The reasons aside, it was at this time, when the couple ran a kitchen for solace and succour, that qawwali was born—one of the unique aspects of the Chishti Sufi order.

Music set the order apart from the other three schools or orders: Suhrawardi, Qadiri, Naqshbandi. Layered with connotations, the inclusive essence of qawwali has survived epochs and their vagaries. Muinuddin united Iranian customs with native Indian devotional traditions. Sama, atmosphere, and qawwali are structured on qaul, 'saying' in Arabic, and the narrator is a 'qawwal', or sayer.

Qawwali is still a male-dominated practice, which is rendered by descendants of various qawwal gharanas (lineages) who often trace their geneses to Amir Khusrau. Abundantly infused with Persian, the qawwali recital follows a sequence, which is essentially a litany of the hierarchy of revered figures in Islam, often turning to the languages of this region, such as Urdu, Hindi, Punjabi, Purbi, Sindhi and others. The haal, a state of ecstasy or trance, is the ultimate reward for a qawwal and his art. Every Chishtiya shrine rings out loud with the power of this art form on Thursday nights, as does the week of Gharib Nawaz's urs.

At Ajmer Sharif, rituals evolved under the Mughal, Rajput, and Maratha rules, creating a syncretic ethos. For example, baridari, key custody, is derived from Meccan practices whereas haft chauki, seven clans, merges a composition of the Mughals with temple traditions. Dalbadal, a canopy for dignitaries, along with torchbearers and macebearers in resplendent robes are some features from Mughal courts. Aside from ceremonial attributes, many Persian terms from Mughal darbars are alive in the shrine complex—ghulam gardish, a passage for the keepers, farrashas, long handwoven peacock feather dusters, and bangla, fastening a rose-woven netting over the cenotaph, and many others.

Lyaqat Moini, a scholar at Aligarh Muslim University, records in *The Dargah of Khwaja Gharib- un- Nawaz of Ajmer*, that, in the eighteenth century, Maratha and Rajput customs arrived with kesaria bhat, sweetened saffron rice, which is still prepared in the two Mughal cauldrons. In his counter-narrative to P.M. Currie's tome on Ajmer, Moini also serves up the most relevant aspect of this pluralistic sanctuary—non-Muslims occupy significant offices and they have a fixed share in the communal feast.

THE RECITALS OF REVERENCE

Before the primary ceremonies begin, passages to the gates are thick with devotees. At sunrise and noon, the main doorway to the sanctum closes and black curtain covers the small back door for the khidmat service. An hour before first light, the main silver door of the sanctum is opened by the custodian with the key; an elder recites the azaan, devotional greetings ensue, keepers enter and the door shuts behind them.

By the back door, senior khuddam (keepers) in black and green robes pour in to rinse the tomb in sandalwood, saffron and rosewater; oil lamps and candles dance in the four corner niches. A chosen server removes the sej, a finely knit floral mantel. It is placed in a basket and covered with a special cloth, then carried to Bibi Hafiza Jamal, where, after the ghusl, her father's flowers are laid on her grave. Two custodians enter the inner fence around Muinuddin's tomb, and sweep towards the smaller doorway by the footstone; petals are gathered in containers and distributed among the visitors. Once the cleaning rituals conclude, the same keeper recites holy verses as a drape is spread over Khwaja; a fresh sej sprinkled with ittar (perfume). The darbar (term used for the Khwaja's shrine) is then declared open for homage. At noon, the ritual is repeated with a difference: the area seen as the saint's chest is coated with sandalwood paste before it is washed and new drapes are placed; the sanctum key is then handed to the custodian in charge for the next twenty-four hours.

Roshni, the Ceremony of Illumination

As the sun slides behind the dome, another set of cleansing customs are set in motion fifteen minutes before Maghrib, sunset prayers. Roshni, the ceremony of illumination in Muinuddin's sacred chamber, is the most ancient custom. Unique to the Chishti Sufi order, it is also carried out in reverential progression. Incense sticks and oud, aloe wood, are arranged in a holder and placed in the centre of the western railing to symbolise Maghrib, both dusk and west.

Four large shamadans facing the incense burner stand tall on each side, with four keepers turned towards the tomb to lift these stands above their heads. Outside, in the central portico, three khuddam emerge from an enclosure near the communal kitchen, carrying candles. As they begin their walk to the shrine, drums resound from the platforms above the gates, adding undeniable power to the ceremony. The keepers cross the Sandal Mosque, enter the sanctum, and male pilgrims gather inside the chamber.

Candle bearers step towards the candle stands. The first in line lights the one in his hand and another passes candles to the remaining keepers. The candle maker fixes a few in the silver holders of the tomb's posts. The first keeper to enter lights all four candles, the warden beside a post sets off a narration of odes to Khwaja, most likely compiled by Hamiduddin Nagauri. As the reading ends, lamp stands are carried to all four sides. The entourage then lights a candle at the saint's daughter's enclosure, and the Roshni comes to a close.

Karka, War Song

Oh ye Muinuddin, truly lord protector, who graces fortunes.
You have lit the Chishti lamp the world over
Oh ye Muinuddin, truly lord protector who graces fortunes.
The spiteful came with brutal trickery
Their fifty-two attempts vanquished,
They scattered in the air at thy orders
You the pillar for here and hereafter
The saint of India, the Light and Beloved of God, a door to Divinity
Such a master of masters, your shrine has a splendour its own.
It brightens the four ends of the universe.

The pillar of virtue,
Cast a glance, bestow gnosis upon me.
The great emperor, hazrat-e-Chishti
Oh Muinuddin, Khwaja, the tower of compassion.

Karka, originally an ancient Rajput war song, is a reminder to battle evil with grace. At 10 p.m., this ceremony, pitched on the above verse, completes the sanctum's journey through the day.

Three keepers, in brief intervals, purify the area outside the inner fence. Pilgrims file in two rows by the eastern door, but no one is allowed in. The khuddams emerge and dust bowed heads with farrashas as they walk towards the Sandal Mosque to place flowers and their dusters in a specific vessel.

Everyone rises when Karka is underway, and the shrine qawwals, descendants of families employed by the Mughals, belt out cantos in the saint's honour. After the last keeper leaves, the ghariali, timekeeper, pronounces the passage of six gharis. In ancient times, one ghari lasted twenty-four minutes. The door is bolted amid bowed heads. The Karka stanza is in Bhojpuri, and is said to have been penned by either Shaikh Mitha, a devotee, or Roora Mithu, a musician in the court of Jahangir.

On Thursday nights, the eastern Courtyard of Light, Ehaata Noorani, becomes the stage for qawwali, performed in the presence of the dewan. After the night prayer, he arrives in regalia, escorted by torchbearers. The qawwals launch into 'qaul' and other devotional verses, followed by a distribution of special sweets for the occasion; the recital ends with the Karka.

Another custom, naubat, at sunrise and at sunset, pierces through the complex and the bazaar, marking the distribution of a barley dish to pilgrims, tourists and the dervishes as an early breakfast and then again as supper.

Chhati Sharif, The Sixth

The sixth of each month of the Muslim lunar calendar is honoured as Chhati Sharif to commemorate Muinuddin's departure for his Divine Beloved—wisaal in Sufi terms. A reading from the Islamic scriptures begins at 9 a.m., then a keeper delivers the spiritual lineage of the Chishti order with verses from the ancestors of the present custodians. Blessings are sent to every devotee in attendance, and jaggery, sweetmeats, and batasha are presented as bequests of a sanctified day.

Fanfare at the shrine marks the urs of celebrated saints throughout the year. One such occasion is the urs of Muinuddin's spiritual mentor, Usman Harooni. The Jannati Darwaza opens in his honour, for Bibi Hafiza Jamal and for Hisamuddin, offsprings of the Khwaja buried in his grounds. Qawwalis, langar and sweets for visitors continue throughout their days.

Rasm-e-Basant, Holi, Diwali

Basant was introduced in Chishti customs by Amir Khusrau, the renowned mystic poet and Nizamuddin Auliya's caliph. At Muinuddin's shrine, Basant means colour and fervour without the recital of rang. On Holi, devotees gather at the Buland Darwaza chanting verses for the Khwaja and smear gulaal on its steps. Similarly, the shrine glitters with diyas on Diwali, with the main communal kitchen serving elaborate vegetarian fare.

Urs

The most evocative rite of devotion begins at Qutub Minar's Hauz-i-Shamsi. This is where Baba Farid carried buckets of sand to build his spiritual mentor Qutubuddin Bakhtyar Kaki's early grave. Today, Charris from Kaki's shrine are handed to the procession making its way to Ajmer Sharif. A fortnight before Muinuddin Chishti's death anniversary, this tradition at the venerated venue heralds the beginning of their journey. The custom preserves Kaki's memory and ardour; he had walked with a flag to Ajmer with his followers. A caravan of dervishes and devotees sets out on foot from Qutubuddin Bakhtiyar Kaki, the saint whose funeral prayers were led by Iltutmish.

Five days prior to the urs, the nishan, flag, is hoisted at the Buland Darwaza and devotees fill the Sehan Chiragh. Finally, the Qalandar caravan carrying flags shuffles in, and is received by the khuddam and musicians at the gate.

Among them, the Walking Iron Man stands out as a portrait of passion. Eagle-eyed and reed thin, he, oblivious to the material world, walks with 60 kg of iron fastened to his wrists, waist and ankles every year.

On this day, the smaller door at the foot-end, jhijri, remains closed. As the moon of the sixth day brightens the skies, drums roll to announce the onset of the anniversary celebrations. The qawwals arrive at sunset, settle in the front porch, and recite the couplets below:

◆ ◆ ◆

'Bar tui mehfil shahana mubarak zindabad'

◆ ◆ ◆

(Hail, the grandest gathering, long live this
grandest gathering)

◆ ◆ ◆

Ilaahii ta abad aastaan-e-yaar rahe,
ye aasraa hai gariibon kaa barqaraar rahe

◆ ◆ ◆

(O Lord, grant eternity to this sacred abode
May the sanctuary of the poor and weary, never cease)

During the urs days, the tomb is cleansed twice in the night and the ghusl of the central cenotaph is carried out in the dark hours. Before the visitors are allowed in, the khuddam (keepers) conduct the cleaning while reciting sacred verses. The second service is after midnight, in the presence of the dewan (chief caretaker of the shrine), the seven representatives of the keepers, and the key custodian. Once they leave, the shrine is closed till sunrise. These scenes echo with mystical energy, however intangible.

Qawwali strains from the Celebration Hall flow through the compound for all six days. The dewan arrives with the same pomp and circumstance at the Punjshamba (fifth evening of the urs); the two macebearers maintain order and carry out various duties.

The shrine qawwals inaugurate the gathering, and troupes from within and outside India follow. Persian and Bhojpuri verses, eulogies to the saints, are also read in chorus in various areas of the complex. After midnight, the dewan departs for the sanctum and returns by 3 a.m., which is the last rite of the day.

The Jannati Darwaza is not locked for all six days of the urs; multitudes gather to await their turn to make the seven rounds.

The Roshni also plays out in Begami Courtyard; the entire complex is bathed in lights, oil lamps and candles. The communal breakfast is prepared by anderkotis, residents of the fort, and its cost is borne by one whose circle of prayer, or the fulfilment of a wish, is complete. The final ceremony of Qul, invocation, falls on the fifth night; the music gathers a feverish pace with qawwalis, songs, drumrolls. On the sixth morning, the Khwaja's sanctum is closed to the public. Keepers in customary garb and turbans go in with flowers, incense and sweets. They recite the spiritual lineage of the Chishti order, and the faryad, a plea, along with other rites of dedication, repentance and blessing. At the Gathering Hall, the qawwals begin sama at 11a.m., ending in Rang. Finally, Badhawa, a presentation of praise, is sung with synced clapping without any instruments.

Both universes be sacrificed
at your behest, O Khwaja
my rounds of the dome in deep devotion
the splendour cascades from the balcony above, you survey the world

Cannons fire at nearby hills; drumbeats mark the end of the urs and the Jannati Darwaza is sealed. Everything halts in orchestrated harmony. Interestingly, the rituals, enshrined in the age-old order of practices, have been performed in their original form for centuries.

And each practice, guided by reason and kindness, has a singular message—no one can halt another's path. This defines the life and legacy of a man in a mud hut.

Endnotes

Excerpted from Reema Abbasi, *Ajmer Sharif: Awakening of Sufism in South Asia*, Niyogi Books

Sing a Prayer,
Sing a Melody,
Sing My Tears,
Sing My Heart,
Sing for My Pir

he Chishti silsila, or Sufi order, established by Khwaja Moinuddin Chishti, is the most widespread and influential Sufi order in the Indian subcontinent. This Persian mystic, philosopher, and religious scholar laid the foundation of the Chistiya order in Ajmer during the early thirteenth century. Known as 'Khwaja Garib Nawaz' (benefactor of the poorest), he is deeply loved by people across social strata. His shrine in Ajmer, Rajasthan, draws thousands of visitors every day, regardless of gender, religion, or social status. A common belief holds that only those called by the Khwaja's grace will visit the shrine—many find themselves arriving at precisely the destined moment in their lives, despite previous attempts.

The experience of qawwali in the shrine can be overwhelming for the uninitiated. At first, and to an outsider, the rituals might seem like a daily festival or carnival of colours and smells – the chaos with narrow lanes of countless stalls selling flowers, especially rose, incense, sweets, chadars, prayer threads, devotional Islamic symbols and photos of the shrine and the pir. All of this, brightly lit at night, make for a festive and glitzy affair which may at first seem out of place for a devotional spiritual music session. After navigating the narrow lanes, one arrives at the shrine which usually has a wide courtyard where everyone congregates. Here is where you encounter the qawwal and his music as a prayer for the master, the pir, and ultimately for the Almighty as a musical offering.

The powerful presence of the tomb of the saint is central to the whole setting. Pilgrims are found in various stages of prayer, seeking, crying, scribbling requests for the saint on torn scraps of paper, tying and opening threads for fulfilment of wishes, prostrating themselves in prayer, or simply sitting and basking in the kinship that is naturally created between the followers of the same order, 'lovers of the Pir' as they call themselves.

Main toh diwani, Khwaja ki diwani,
Diwani, main toh diwani,
Main diwani, main diwani, main diwani,
Diwani, diwani, diwani, diwani, diwani,
Khwaja ki diwani

Photographer: Dinesh Khanna
Qawwali Practitioner: Not Known
Text: Manjari Chaturvedi
Place: Dargah Ajmer Sharif, Ajmer, Rajasthan, India
Project: The Qawwali Project

the ajmer
story

अरज सुन लीजो मोरी
ख्वाजा मोइनउददी अजमेरी
नजर-ए-करम फरमाओ मोपे
विनती करत हूँ तिहारी

Qawwali and Sufi Literature in Awadh Region

Yousuf Saeed

n India, the growth of qawwali or other musical and poetic forms among Sufis was a prerequisite not only for their spiritual salvation but also as a medium to attract the local populace who were already entrenched in the use of pietistic music, as has been acknowledged by saints like Moinuddin Chishti who encouraged the use of music. Undoubtedly, music and poetry in local dialects were probably the most important vehicles for the popularity and expansion of Islam via the Chishti Sufi order in South Asia in general and the Awadh region in particular.[1]

Although the region of Lucknow and Awadh is traditionally associated with musical forms such as thumri, dadra, tappa, mujra, kathak, and other forms of classical arts and courtesan culture, mostly patronised by the aristocratic nawabs and provincial taluqdars, qawwali has also been nurtured here abundantly. The devotional arts of the Shias, such as the recitation of marsias and nauhas, associated with the memory of the battle of Karbala, were also developed significantly in the region.[2] While the history and richness of Awadh's musical past has been well documented by many authors,[3] what has not been explored in detail is the practice of qawwali and Sufi music or literature that thrived in the region in equal terms.

For instance, one does not hear of the Lucknow region producing any qawwali 'maestros' and grooming schools, at least in the nineteenth and twentieth centuries, just as one finds them in the nearby Rohilkhand region, Delhi, Punjab, or Hyderabad. The mystic culture of Awadh did not come into limelight probably because its patronage was limited mainly in the popular and rural domain rather than the ruling elite which largely followed the Shia theology, although one may find exceptions, such as in Rampur. This write-up surveys the spaces and institutions that nurtured qawwali and Sufi music in Lucknow and its environs, knowing that more research work is still required to ascertain its larger impact.

Arrival of Islam and Sufis in Awadh

Islam and Muslims had arrived in the Awadh region much before the typical nawabi era of the eighteenth and nineteenth centuries that saw the pinnacle of the Indo-Muslim cultural practices in Lucknow. In fact, some local residents believe that pre-Islamic prophets (mentioned in the Quran and the Bible) like Hazrat Yaqub (Jacob), Hazrat Shees, and Hazrat Nooh (Noah) are actually buried in Ayodhya—a fact that has been mentioned by several medieval commentators including the Mughal courtier Abul Fazl in *Ain-e Akbari*, although unconfirmed by historians.

Ayodhya in any case has been a place of great spiritual importance for Hindus and Buddhists since millennia. Muslims and Islam may have arrived in the Awadh region in the last quarter of the twelfth century when Mohammad Ghauri established his rule over Delhi and north India after defeating the local rulers. Though he returned to Central Asia after handing over the rule to Qutbuddin, this is the first time when governors were appointed by a central government for local regions under their control. Thus, Bakhtiyar Khalji was sent to govern the Awadh region, although he did not sustain his rule for long due to constant changes within the government. For several reasons, the Awadh region, which constituted not only the town of Ayodhya but also Kara, Qannauj, Dalmau, Sandila, Bahraich and Jaunpur, was considered very strategic for all kings and dynasties of Delhi. Hence, almost all famous rulers, such as the Tughlaqs, the Sayyads, the Mughals, and even the British made visits here and ensured strong governance which benefited their own rule at the central level.

Many scholars and Sufis came to settle in various locations of Awadh along with the Muslim rulers. One of the earliest-known Muslim saints in the region was a warrior named Salar Masud Ghazi who came with the army of Mehmud of Ghazna at the age of sixteen, and was martyred in a battle with the local Hindu rulers in Bahraich in AD 1032. He was buried at Bahraich and his shrine is a centre of pilgrimage for thousands of Hindus and Muslims every year, especially due to its supposed healing powers. Since Ghazi was unmarried before he died, an annual memorial at his shrine, just outside the Bahraich town, is supposed to celebrate his post-mortem wedding with one Zohra Bibi.[4] Even today, many young unmarried women dressed like a bride visit the shrine for Ghazi's blessings and recite traditional poetry. Even a khadim or caretaker of the shrine sings verses in the local dialect.

Miyan ka pujan chala sevakia garh Bahraich naagari
Chhod chhad ke baal bachche taj ke ghar aur baakri,
Miyan ka pujan...[5]

(To worship Miyan, the devotee embarks on a
pilgrimage to Bahraich town Leaving his children and
giving up his home and wife to worship Miyan...)

There are also popular music videos and audiocassettes available outside the shrine, featuring devotional songs in praise of the warrior-saint.[6] However, it is not known as to which formal Sufi order Salar Masud belonged and what were his mystic inclinations.

In a cemetery in Ayodhya town, one can find so many ancient tombs of Sufi saints and Muslim figures that it is called Khurd Mecca (Little Mecca).[7] Among other early Sufis to have arrived in Awadh was one Qazi Qidwat ud-Din, who came from Central Asia at the behest of Usman Haruni (the Sufi master of Moinuddin Chishti who settled in Ajmer).[8] Considered an ancestor of the famed Qidwais of Lucknow, Qazi Qidwat died in 1208 and was buried in the complex of the now-demolished Babri mosque. Many of these early Sufis were scholars of Islam, philosophy and mysticism, and some also practised the listening of sermons, sama or poetry for their mystic or devotional experiences.

Some information about their lives can be gleaned from the malfuzat or hagiographical accounts available in old manuscripts. Shaikh Badruddin Wa'iz, an orator par excellence from Ayodhya, lived in the period of Alauddin Khalji (thirteenth-fourteenth centuries). His spirited sermon gatherings were attended by all, and often witnessed the audience faint with tears.[9] The early Sufis may not have strictly followed the doctrine of any one particular Sufi order such as Chishti, Qadiri, Suhrwardi, Qalandari, or Naqshbandi that came into India, although the Chishti silsila was definitely one of the more popular orders whose members were appointed by their shaikhs in small and large towns of Awadh region.

Syed Ashraf Jahangir Samnani, buried in Kichhaucha, a small town near Lucknow, came from Samnan in Iran where he was born in 1308 in a ruling family. He was a Sufi of both the Chishti as well as Qadiri orders, and naturally listened to sama and qawwali. Before coming to Awadh region he had already stayed for some years in Uchch town (now in Pakistan, near Multan) and Bengal. It is said that when his time of death came, at the ripe age of 120 years, Ashraf Jahangir asked for a mehfil of sama to be arranged, and died trembling like an injured bird (murgh-e bismil) while listening to a particular verse of poet Sa'di.[10] Even today, his shrine gets thousands of devotees for its supposed healing powers, especially during his urs when qawwalis are performed.[11]

Chishti Sufi Linkages between Delhi and Awadh

Many disciples of Chishti saint Nizamuddin Auliya of Delhi (or others in his lineage) were appointed the spiritual heirs in Awadh, Qazi Mohiuddin Kashani being one of the important ones. He left his courtly job of a qazi (judge) in Awadh during Alauddin Khalji's reign to follow the mystic path taught by Nizamuddin Auliya—often disappearing into forests with his book of prayers to meditate. Similarly, Nasiruddin Chiragh Dehlavi, the most famous disciple of Nizamuddin Auliya, was born in Ayodhya around 1274, and his descendants have connections with Awadh till today. There are many others such as Shaikh Shamsuddin Awadhi, Jalaluddin Awadhi (d. 1337), Jamaluddin Awadhi, Qiwamuddin Awadhi, and Kamaluddin, who were either direct or hereditary disciples of Nizamuddin Auliya, and practised the listening of sama and qawwali in their spiritual experiences.[12]

Another disciple of Nizamuddin Auliya based in Awadh was Maulana Alauddin Neli (d. 1360), popular for giving powerful wa'z or sermons about mysticism. His Friday sermons were even attended by the famous Arab traveller Ibn Batuta (born 1304) who described these as full of ecstasy with regard to the listeners. During one of Neli's sermons, when a particular ayat (passage) of Quran was recited, a restless listener in the mosque reacted with a loud scream. When the passage was repeated during the session, the person screamed with ecstasy again and ultimately died on the spot. Ibn Batuta claims to have attended his funeral too.[13] One can find many other accounts about the early Sufis of Awadh where their deep interest in poetry and music is apparent.

For instance, Syed Ali of Jaunpur (1423-1500) was never particular about any specific song or style of music for sama. 'I can get *wajd* (ecstasy) with any ghazal or verse being recited,' he would say.[14] Similarly, Shaikh Adhan Jaunpuri (born 1452) lived for over a hundred years and used to get so mesmerised by listening to qawwali that he had to be controlled by over ten people even in his old age.[15] Shaikh Adhan may have also been an important courtier for the Mughal ruler Babur in Delhi since he is said to have organised mehfils of sama in the latter's court, along with another courtier, Shaikh Dhoran. Moreover, Adhan's disciple, Shaikh Banjhu, a 'very sweet singer' from Jaunpur, got employed with Akbar and was rewarded suitably for his music performances.[16]

Lucknow's most prominent Sufi shrine today (near the present Medical College) is that of Hazrat Shah Mina Chishti (d. 1479) who was the son of another Sufi Shaikh Qiwamuddin and a disciple of Shaikh Sarang. Being initiated into not only Chishtiya but also Qadiria, Suhrwardiya and Qalandaria, Shah Mina is also attributed with many miracles which he is supposed to have conducted since his childhood.[17] Mehfils of qawwali and sama are still held at his shrine which is also famous for its healing powers. But it is difficult to say if such an institution nurtured any robust schools or gharanas of qawwali in the town. Among other Sufis of this region, Alauddin Husaini Awadhi (died circa 1560) was not only a Persian poet par excellence but also an expert in Hindustani music. He is buried in the Khurd Mecca cemetery of Ayodhya.[18] Many other Sufi shrines of Awadh from the medieval period have remained centres that promote qawwali during the urs ceremonies.

The Emergence of Lucknow and Its Musical Heritage

When nawab Asaf-ud-Daula shifted his capital from Faizabad to Lucknow in 1775, he and the later nawabs nurtured all kinds of cultural and literary activities and talent in the new capital. The convergence of great artists and musicians from nearby areas in Lucknow allowed the growth of rich traditions of music and performative arts. Husain Shah Sharqi, the ruler of nearby Jaunpur (r. 1458-1479) had already played an important role in the evolution of several forms of classical music, especially khayal (slow and elaborate rendition of vocal music). According to some, Sharqi's court had benefitted and influenced from the experiments in music carried out by composers like Amir Khusrau in Delhi via the blending of Indian and Central Asian musical forms and instruments.[19]

There was also a constant give and take between the musicians and patrons of Delhi and Awadh. With the decline of the Mughal Empire in the eighteenth century, many of the talented musicians and artists started migrating to Awadh. Hence, Lucknow slowly became a platform where the best talent of north India was gathering and entertaining the nawabs and courtiers with their fine art. However, while we know about the nawabs' patronage and special interest in classical dance and vocal music, instruments like sitar and tabla,[20] and the Shi'a-oriented devotional arts, there is very little information available about how much the Awadh's court patronised qawwali.

Among the unique institutions of Lucknow that did support Sufi ideology and qawwali, albeit indirectly, is one known as Firangi Mahal. Although Firangi Mahal (literally meaning a 'foreigner's palace' which was indeed inhabited in Lucknow by a European trader in the seventeenth century) refers to one of the earliest Muslim families migrating into Awadh from the Afghanistan region, it is more popular as a madrasa or educational institution that this family of great scholars established centuries ago.[21] Mullah Nizamuddin, a prominent member of this family from the seventeenth century, compiled an elaborate syllabus for the study of Arabic and Persian that is still taught in some madrasas of India, and known as the *Dars-e Nizami* (Nizam's syllabus). Besides being authors of hundreds of books (and exegesis of older works) on philosophy, jurisprudence, religion, literature and mysticism, the members of the Firangi Mahal family were also Sufis themselves.[22] Many family members not only composed mystical poetry but also listened to Sufi sama and qawwali. According to Maulana Azad, several members of Firangi Mahal were well versed in music.[23]

One of the last well-known Sufis and scholars of the family was Maulana Abdul Bari (d. 1926), also known as Bari Miyan, whose urs (death anniversary) is still celebrated at the Bagh or cemetery where most luminaries of Firangi Mahal are buried. The late scholar Salim Kidwai of Lucknow (whose father and grandfather were mureed or disciples of Bari Miyan) remembered attending Firangi Mahal's qawwali performances in his childhood with his father. According to him, 'until the mid seventies, any qawwal worth his qaul would have paid tribute at the urs'. Until recently, the last surviving good qawwals such as Murli performed at the Bagh in Firangi Mahal.[24] The urs is still held but it no longer has the same cultural significance it earlier had. This obviously has to do with the decline of Firangi Mahal both in terms of spiritual authority as well as the physical decline of its building into a ruin/slum.[25]

Saints and Qawwali in Lucknow's Vicinity

While many Sufi saints lived and practised their mysticism in the Awadh region throughout the last one millennium, very few may have matched the popularity of Haji Waris Ali Shah of the nineteenth century. Waris Ali was born in Dewa town of Barabanki district (near Lucknow) around 1809 and travelled extensively, all over the country as well as other parts of the world, especially on his pilgrimages to Mecca, as a barefoot fakir wearing an ihram (two unstitched pieces of white cloth worn by Hajj pilgrims) throughout his life. Waris Ali was fond of listening to poetry and sama, and one of his most favourite disciple was Avghat Shah Warsi, a poet from Bachhraon (near Moradabad) who composed mystic poetry, especially dohas (couplets) in Awadhi, Braj and Urdu languages, for his Sufi master.[26] Some of Avghat Shah's poetry is still sung by qawwals, such as Meraj Nizami of Delhi who featured at least one such verse in his collection – a song in Braj in praise of Prophet Muhammad (PBUH).[27] Contemporary qawwals like Noorul Hasan from Dewa sharif sang Awadhi compositions like *'Sayyan sajeele tore naina raseele'* (O stylish beloved, your eyes are intoxicating).[28]

The mystics at the shrine of Haji Waris Ali still follow the tradition of wearing a light yellow-coloured ihram or unstitched cloth, attending ceremonies like qawwali mehfils. Most followers of Haji Waris, including qawwals, use Warsi as their title, and are spread out outside the Awadh region too – as far as Hyderabad (Telangana), Karachi (Pakistan) and even some Western countries. A well-known follower of the saint was poet Bedam Shah Warsi (d. 1936) whose poetry is regularly performed by qawwals in India and Pakistan. At least seven of Bedam Shah's poems are documented by Meraj Ahmed Qawwal for the purpose of qawwali performance.[29] For instance, this verse describing the Chishti saints celebrating the festival of Holi in Braj dialect:

⬩◆⬩

Ganj-e-Shakar ke lal Nizamuddin, Chisht nagar mein phaag rachayo,
Khaja Moinudeen aur Qutub ke prem ke rang ki raini chadhayo,

⬩◆⬩

(Nizamuddin, the favourite of Baba Farid,
plays the Holi in the town of Chisht,
Fills the water fountain with the colour of love
for Khwaja Moinuddin and Qutbuddin Ka'ki)

There are many other poets of the region such as Aarzoo Lakhnavi, Behzad Lakhnavi, Shakeel Badayuni, Majnun Lakhnavi, Nadir Kakorvi and others whose devotional verses are part of the qawwals' repertoire.[30] Several rural areas on the outskirts of Lucknow nurtured literature and performative traditions related to devotional Islam and Sufism that carry strong bonds of pluralism. One of them is Kakori, a small historic town outside Lucknow that has been famous for its scholars, poets and Sufis. One of its poets, Mohsin Kakorvi (d. 1905), not only wrote na'tiya qaseedas (long poems in praise of Prophet Muhammad, (PBUH), but also syncretic Urdu songs like *'Simt-e Kashi se chala janib-e Mathura badal'* (a cloud from Kashi sailed towards Mathura...) that is full of devotion for Lord Krishna.

Kakori is also famous for Sufis Shah Muhammad Kazim Qalandar and Shah Turab Ali Qalandar whose poetry is full of mystic philosophy bearing Indian symbols of bhakti and references to Lord Krishna.[31] These mystic poets were also well versed in music and their poetry is filled with shanta rasa (the emotion of tranquillity),[32] one of the nine rasas of Indian aesthetics. Poet Hasrat Mohani, born in 1875 at Unnao near Lucknow, was also a great admirer of Krishna and wrote several Urdu verses celebrating the romantic lore of Krishna and Radha as Sufi symbols of love.[33]

Qawwali and Sufi Saints in Rohilkhand

While exploring qawwali and Sufi literature in Awadh, one cannot ignore the nearby, smaller provincial centres such as Rohilkhand which comprise towns like Rampur, Bareilly, Badaun and others, and had their own unique centres of Sufi culture, especially the shrines of several important saints. Nizamuddin Auliya himself was born in Badaun in 1238; the tomb of his father, Syed Ahmad Bukhari, in the town is still visited by a large number of devotees. Many poets from Badaun (such as Fani Badayuni and Babu Haya Badayuni) wrote mystical and romantic poetry that is used by qawwals. Bareilly is known for the Islamic scholar Ahmed Raza Khan (b. 1856), whose followers have over the years inculcated a more syncretic and pantheistic Islam, involving 'innovations' or local religio-cultural practices, especially the listening of sama. Another Sufi, Shah Niyaz Barelvi (d. 1834), wrote hundreds of devotional and mystic poems in Persian and Urdu, that are sung by qawwals all over South Asia. For instance, the following is one of his Urdu ghazals that has been sung by the famous Pakistani vocalist Abida Parveen:[34]

• ◆ •

Ishq mein tere koh-e gham sar pe liya jo ho so ho,
Aish-o nishat-e zindagi chhod diya jo ho so ho

• ◆ •

(In your love, I took a mountain of woes on my head,
let whatever happens, happen.
I abandoned the luxuries and pleasures of life,
let whatever happens, happen)

While many of Shah Niyaz Barelvi's poems sung by qawwals such as his maquebats (praise) for personalities like Imam Ali (Raziallahu Ta'ala), saint Abdul Qadir Jeelani, Khwaja Moinuddin Chishti, and saint Nizamuddin Auliya are written in Persian, some are also in Hindi or its local Bhojpuri dialect, such as the following verse:

• ◆ •

Rooth gaye mose pritam pyare, kaho ri mein kaise mana'un re
Birha ki aag jarawat jiyara, un bin kaise bujhaun re[35]

• ◆ •

(My pretty beloved is angry with me,
how do I please him now,
The fire of separation burns my heart,
how do I put it out without him)

The region is named Rohilkhand after the Rohilla pathans who came from Afghanistan and settled there in the eighteenth century. Rampur was probably one of the strongest and culturally richest provincial regions after Lucknow, whose nawabs patronised music and literary traditions so much so that an entire gharana or school of classical music known as Rampur-Sahaswan gharana evolved, its many well-known exponents active even today. While Nisar Husain Khan, Ghulam Mustafa Khan, Hafeez Ahmed Khan of this gharana regaled the audiences with their finest renditions of khayal and tarana throughout the twentieth century, its most famous maestro was Rashid Khan—one the greatest khayal and tarana singers of India.

Besides the practice of classical music forms, the Rohilkhand region had a rich tradition of qawwali performance and learning, with many famous qawwal families active even in the twentieth century. While Rampur still has north India's finest qawwals, such as Mohammad Ahmed Warsi (whose father performed in the court of the erstwhile nawab of Rampur), one of the best qawwals of the twentieth century was undoubtedly Jafar Husain of Badaun. Jafar Husain started learning singing from his uncle Ustad Mushtaq Ali Khan at the age of four before becoming the pupil of Mehdi Hasan of Agra gharana.[36]

Jafar Husain also performed at the shrine of Hazrat Alauddin Sabir at Kaliyar sharif (now in Uttarakhand) where he formed his qawwali group. The biggest reason for this region nurturing the qawwali tradition is the presence of a large number of tombs of different saints where sama is practised. Besides the Sufi shrines, qawwali was/is also performed in this region at public venues such as during annual melas or fetes, which originally started as cattle fairs. Such venues promoted qawwali and poetry sessions in other nearby towns as well, such as in Aligarh, where the twentieth century's famed qawwals like Habib Painter had a great following. Habib Painter's qawwali had an emphasis on powerful lyrics rather than music and instrumentation; he often wrote his own poetry and also used verses from bhakti poets like Mirabai and Kabir.

What could be the reasons behind qawwali thriving much more in the Rohilkhand region of north India than in Awadh, at least in the nineteenth and twentieth centuries? One of the reasons is certainly the Rampur nawabs' preferences for Shi'a-related liturgical music and the classical entertainment forms. But another factor could be the presence of a large number of Rohilla pathans who migrated from Afghanistan into the Rampur-Bareilly region and brought with them their own rustic musical forms, especially a song type known as chahar bayt, literally meaning a quartet or 'four lines'. Although chahar bayt sounds very little like other Indo-Muslim musical forms such as qawwali, ghazal or any classical vocal form, the qawwali of Rohilkhand region, it seems, may have been influenced slightly by this high-energy singing style of the pathans, especially in the delivery of its lyrics. The dafs (a large-sized frame drums) are the main instruments of chahar bayt singing that are not only played by a couple of group members, but also used to improvise the dance-like actions of the singers. A solo recitation of the main poem in moderate or slow tempo is interspersed by vigorous repetitions or refrains of the first line. There is no clapping involved, but the singers do raise or wave their hands towards the audience to stress on certain words. A direct and frank addressing of the lyrics to the audience and the refrains in a chorus are at least some of the elements that can be found common between qawwali and chahar bayt.

Contemporary Situation of Qawwali in Awadh

Despite Lucknow's meagre heritage of contemporary qawwali, one cannot ignore the few qawwals from the town that did perform in the twentieth century. Artists such as Agghan Qawwal, Asif Ali, Faruq, Patrick Qawwal, Raju and Sarvar Husain performed both at the shrines as well as concerts. The town of Kakori itself boasted of many qawwals in the twentieth century, such as Ali Waris, Azimullah, Jaffar Husain, Kalaam, Mohammad Umar, Nusrat, and Rais,[37] whereas M. Zahir Khan came from the town of Malihabad, and Murli qawwal from Shahjahanpur. Interestingly, Murli's father was called Kanhai Qawwal and his son performs with the name Raju, even though they are Muslim. Much of their repertoire carries lyrics in local Bhojpuri or Awadhi dialect. Sadly, many of these qawwals could not find larger popularity, probably because they were not promoted either by the recording industry or the film industry in Bombay, which incidentally brought many other qawwals such as Ismail Azad, Jani Babu, or Shankar-Shambhu into the limelight.

One important qawwali group hailing from Lucknow, whose live concert recording was released in 1983 by the Gramophone Company of India Ltd. (EMI), is Afsar Husain Khan and party. Afsar's rustic and seasoned voice reveals the traditional style of qawwali that was common in north India in much of the early part of the twentieth century. He not only sings a traditional Basant composition (normally performed at Chishti shrines) but also several contemporary Urdu compositions such as Bedam Shah Warsi's

'*Bekhud kiye dete hain*' or one of Jigar Moradabadi's popular ghazals, '*Yeh hai maikada yaha rind hai*'.[38]

Interestingly, for north India's music industry, the popular and folk music in Bhojpuri and Awadhi dialects has been a major market, which grew with the arrival of audiocassettes in the 1970s and '80s.[39] Thousands of new qawwalis and Islamic devotional songs in the local dialects were produced through cassettes by upcoming artists in the region. Companies like the T-Series combed through rural areas in Awadh to find promising artists and encouraged them to record albums. Singer Sharif Parwaz of Kanpur sang this devotional qawwali in Bhojpuri, a longing to go to Madina if Allah (SWT) gave some money:

⬩ ◆ ⬩

Pyare Nabi ka rauja, ankhiyan se rahi rahi chumbe,
Aapan jiyara bichaide
Jaibe Madina hum jaroor jab Allah paisa daide

⬩ ◆ ⬩

(The tomb of the Beloved Prophet,
I keep kissing with my eyes,
Let me lay my soul for you,
I will definitely visit Madina if Allah gave some money)[40]

There are many other local artists who recorded Islamic devotional songs in Awadhi dialect. A popular woman artist, Rani Disco Qawwala of Jaunpur, sings a Bhojpuri qawwali: '*Taiba bulaila hamke Arbi sawariya*' (Invite me to Madina, O my Arab Beloved).[41]

A question that one may ask is whether the qawwali of Awadh region (or north-central India) is any different from, say, the qawwali style of Punjab region or Pakistan where it is equally (or probably more) active. One of the important differences is that Punjabi or Pakistani qawwals are characterised by a vigorous and powerful folksy style of singing in which rhythm and vocal intonation play a significant role (for instance, in the case of the late Nusrat Fateh Ali Khan or Abida Parveen), whereas the qawwals of Awadh/Uttar Pradesh or Delhi often give more stress on the lyrics to inspire the Sufis in their spiritual quest. For instance, Jaffar Hussain qawwal of Badaun uses a subtle and comparatively slow style of singing Urdu poetry without using too much vocal dramatics. The repertoire of north India's qawwals features nuances of Urdu/Persian poetry and literary idiom, often combining the bhakti of Krishna-Radha and other local lore, whereas Punjabi musicians use their own regional legends like Bulleh Shah, Heer-Ranjha and others.

Lucknow, which evolved as one of the most important centres for the promotion of music and devotional arts in north India between the eighteenth and twentieth centuries, is sadly losing much of its cultural sheen today. Besides thumri and kathak which still survive, there is hardly any other form whose practitioners can still be proud of their current state of the arts. According to the late Naushad, one of Lucknow's best-known stalwarts in the field of Indian cinema, 'Lucknow's *gayeki* gharana (vocal music school) could not survive the way other gharanas such as those from Gwalior or Kirana, even though the city produced great maestros of music in the past.' One of the reasons for this, according to Naushad, is that the writers who compiled history did not think of documenting the lives of musicians and other traditional performers, assuming them to be of 'low' strata of the society.[42]

Naushad himself worked hard through several decades to become one of the greatest music composers of Indian cinema, often using devotional and mystic music in his scores. Naushad also introduced a lot of folk tunes from Awadh and Uttar Pradesh into film songs, some of which, in fact, he heard from the local qawwals.[43] While the still surviving qawwals in Awadh, especially those connected with the Sufi shrines like Dewa Sharif, try hard to make a living, they do remember music directors like Naushad with nostalgia for the old times that may seem difficult to come back now.[44]

Endnotes

1. Jafri, S.Z.H. 'Sufi Traditions and Popular Literature: Chishti Ideology, the Awadhi Dialect and Local Practices,' in Surinder Singh, I.D. Gaur (eds), *Popular Literature and Pre-modern Societies in South Asia*, New Delhi: Pearson Longman, 2008, pp. 271-280.

2. Trivedi, Madhu. *The Making of the Awadh Culture*, Delhi: Primus, 2010.

3. Sharar, Abdul Halim. *Lucknow: The Last Phase of an Oriental Culture* [titled *Guzashta Lakhnau* in Urdu], edited and translated from Urdu by E.S. Harcourt and Fakhir Hussain, Delhi: Oxford University Press, 1994.

4. Schwerin, Kerrin G.V. 'Saint Worship in Indian Islam: The Legend of the Martyr Salar Masud Ghazi,' in Imtiaz Ahmad (ed.), *Ritual and Religion among Muslims in India.* Delhi: Manohar, 1981, pp 143-161.

5. Azeez, Rashid. *Rohilkhand mein Lok Geet* [Urdu], Delhi: Adabistan Zaar (Hind), 2011, p. 418.

6. See for instance a video CD titled *Ghazi ka Karam* (Blessings of the Warrior-Saint), artists: Neha Mehmood Khan, Asif Saidpur, produced by Golden Eye Films, no date. (Purchased in 2008).

7. Rajalakshmi, T.K. 'Ayodhya, a picture of diversity,' *Frontline*, Vol. 20-Issue 22, October 25-November 07, 2003.

8. Kamal, Razi Ahmed. *Mukhtasar Tarikh Mashai'kh-e Awadh*, Delhi: Alhasanat Books, 2006, p. 30.

9. Ibid, Kamal, Razi Ahmed, p. 33

10. Samnani, Makhdum Ashraf. *Lataif-e-Ashrafi* [Urdu], Vol. 2, pp. 406-12. Quoted by Razi Ahmed Kamal.

11. Ashrafi, Syed Ali. 'Athwin sadi hijri ke sahib-e karamat buzurg: Syed Ashraf Jahangir Samnani,' *Naya Daur*, Oct-Nov. 1994, Awadh number part 2, Lucknow: Department of Information and Public Relations (DIPR), pp. 132-35.

12. Kamal, Razi Ahmed, pp. 41-55.

13. Hasani, Abdulhayi. *Nuzhatul Khawatir* (Vol. 2), quoted by Razi Ahmed Kamal, 2006, pp. 61-62.

14. Dehlvi, Abdulhaq Muhaddis. *Akhbar al-Akhyar* [translated from Persian into Urdu by Subhan Mehmud, Mohd. Fazil, and Moinuddin Na'imi], Delhi: Farid Book Depot (no date), p. 481.

15. Ibid.

16. Brahaspati, Kailash Chandra. *Muslman aur Bhartiya Sangeet*, Delhi: Rajkamal, 1974. (Quoting Athar Abbas Rizvi and Abdul Qadir Badayuni).

17. Ernst, Carl W. and Lawrence, Bruce B. *Sufi Martyrs of Love: The Chishti Order in South Asia and Beyond*, New York: Palgrave Macmillan, 2002, pp. 54-57.

18. Kamal, Razi Ahmed, pp. 89-90.

19. Brahaspati, 1974.

20. Miner, Allyn. *Sitar and Sarod in the 18th and 19th Centuries*, Delhi: Motilal, 1997.

21. Robinson, Francis. 'The ulama of the firangi mahal and their adab' in B. Metcalf (ed.), *Moral Conduct and Authority in South Asia*, Berkeley, 1984.

22. Ansari, M. Waliul Haq. 'Firangi mahal ki ilmi, adabi, aur siyasi khidmat' [Urdu], *Naya Daur*, Feb-March 1994, Awadh number, Lucknow: DIPR, pp. 40-52.

23. Azad, Abul Kalaam. *Ghubar-e Khatir* [Urdu], edited by Malik Ram, Delhi: Sahitya Akademi, 1967.

24. Video clips of Murli and other qawwals mostly performing at the Bagh in Firangi Mahal, Lucknow, can be seen on YouTube. See http://youtube.com/watch?v=FynmVQ9Bs9E

25. The author would like to thank Salim Kidwai for providing help in this matter.

26. Warsi, Anis Ahmed (compiled). Avghat Shah Warsi's *Faizan-e Warsi* [Also known as *Zamzama-e Qawwali*], Delhi: S.A. Publications, 2006.

27. Qawwal, Meraj Ahmed. *Surood-e Ruhani, Qawwali ke Rang*, Delhi, 1998, p. 342.

28. https://www.youtube.com/watch?v=lF3B1iC6rkM

29. Meraj Ahmed (see the table of contents of the said book for the mention of Bedam Shah's lyrics).

30. Hussaini, Anwar Kamal. *Mehfil-e Qawwali* [Urdu], Delhi: Farid Book Depot, 2004

31. Tariq, Shamim. *Sufia ki She'ri Basirat mein Shri Krishn* [Urdu], Delhi: Educational Publishing House, 2009.

32. Tariq, Shamim. Sufia ka Bhakti Raag, Kitab Numa [Urdu], New Delhi: Maktaba Jamia, 2003, p. 118.

33. Tariq, Shamim. 2009.

34. Parveen, Abida. *Raqs-e Bismil*, Music Today (audiocassette), New Delhi, 2000.

35. Meraj Ahmed, 1998, p.375.

36. https://www.youtube.com/watch?v=Tuzr4uHTR_8

37. Qureshi, Regula B. *Sufi Music of India and Pakistan: Sound, Context and Meaning in Qawwali*, Chicago: University of Chicago Press, 1995, p. 261.

38. *In Concert: The Famous Qawwal of Lucknow*, Afsar Husain Khan with Kafeel

Husain Khan, EMI, ECSD 2922, 1983. (Features 6 songs)

39. Manual, Peter, *Cassette Culture: Popular Music and Technology in North India*, Chicago: University of Chicago Press, 1993.

40. Kanpuri, Sharif Parwaz, *Allah Paisa Daide*, audiocassette, T-Series, NOIDA, c. 2005 (Lyrics by Akmal Kanpuri, music by Master Munna).

41. https://www.youtube.com/watch?v=rSu1nA8U1Po

42. Naushad, 'Lakhnau ki gayeki, Lakhnau ka kathak' [Urdu], *Naya Daur*, Feb-March 1994, Awadh number, Lucknow: DIPR, Uttar Pradesh, pp. 20-23.

43. Saeed, Yousuf, *Qawwali in Bombay Cinema* (forthcoming).

44. Abbas, Shirin. 'Naushad passes away in Mumbai; from Barabanki, qawwal mourning,' *Indian Express*, Lucknow, 6 May 2006.

QAWWALI AT DEWA SHARIF

Barabanki, Home to Qawwali History: Shahenshah-e-Awadh

ewa, a town in the Barabanki district of Uttar Pradesh, India, is renowned for the shrine of Haji Waris Ali Shah and is reverently known as Dewa Sharif. Haji Waris Ali Shah was initiated in the traditional Chishtiya Sufi order. Subsequently, as founder of the Warsi order of Sufism, he brought a more liberal interpretation to the traditional Sufi order, allowing followers to maintain their respective religious practices while following his spiritual guidance. The region became a stronghold of qawwali tradition, producing many celebrated performers. Among his disciples (*mureeds*), Bedam Shah Warsi emerged as a distinguished Sufi poet whose compositions continue to resonate through performances at the shrine and all over the world today.

Let the Mela Begin

The Dewa mela is observed on dates according to Islamic calendar. It is attended by nearly a million people. Both Muslims and Hindus, transcending religious boundaries, gather for this spiritual occasion. The qawwals sing all night in mehfils where spiritual poetry of Sufi saints is sung, filling the air with mystical resonance.

Qawwali, traditionally performed by artists from minority communities, holds deep cultural significance in its association with shrines. It instils a larger sense of belonging, and hence these qawwals reside near the shrine grounds, performing daily and often accompanying in special rituals, such as when notable visitors present their chadar. Their livelihood depends on the age-old tradition of monetary offerings from shrine visitors—a practice that yields unpredictable and often meagre income. This economic uncertainty has forced many qawwals to seek alternative vocations, threatening the continuity of this ancient musical tradition. Without successful practitioners to carry forward the art, qawwali faces the risk of losing its authentic voice and spiritual essence in these sacred spaces.

Pages of History

Qawwali compositions are treasured for their philosophical and lyrical value. The traditional repertoire spans multiple languages—Persian, Arabic, Punjabi, Awadhi, and Brajbhasa—along with various local dialects. Each qawwal maintains personal written records of these songs, keeping them handy during performances and preserving them for future generations. These traditions and writings celebrate the syncretic values embedded in the cultural ethos, and have always challenged notions of religious and social barriers and thus have created occasions to shape unity in our country.

Holi at Dewa

The vibrant Holi celebrations at Dewa Sharif are a result of the spirit of 'Ganga-Jamuni Tehzeeb'. Here, a festival widely perceived as Hindu, transcends religious boundaries to become a celebration of unity, devotion, and shared joy. Dewa Sharif is the torchbearer of the message of 'mohabbat', of love and fraternity. The pilgrims who come to celebrate Holi, amongst the performances of qawwalis and poetry, are from all faiths.

Photographer: Mustafa Quraishi
Qawwali Practitioners: Qawwal Shakeel Warsi, Qawwal Sohail Warsi, Qawwal Ghulam Waris
Text: Manjari Chaturvedi
Place: Dargah Haji Waris Ali Shah, Dewa Sharif, Barabanki, Uttar Pradesh, India
Project: The Qawwali Project

dewa sharif

Qawwali: The Shared Sacred

Qawwal Dhruv Sangari
(BILAL CHISHTY)

Ibteda: The beginning

◆

'Khayaal aaya Rabb ko, ke dekhunga khud ko
toh Khud mein se Khud ek tasveer dhaali
jo dekha toh khud ho gaya uss pe shaida
voh tasveer apne mukabil sajaa li'

◆

(In the beginning the Creator was alone.
Wishing to be known for his creation to be seen and appreciated. He, from his divine light manifested the perfect being.)

This naat sharif written by Adeeb Raipuri was somewhere in the subconscious mind, a memory of my childhood and it mesmerised me in the early 1990s when I heard it live by Sabri Brothers qawwals, at a concert in Delhi. As a twelve-year-old, late one winter night in Delhi, when I heard the strains of a mellifluous sonic flux in the distance, I decided to explore further. Back then there was little traffic and no large highways sprawling across the city. Besides me, there was the cool winter breeze, the bright moonlight, and my future calling out to me. I found myself walking to the shrine of Hazrat Nizamuddin Auliya and his ardent dervish Khwaja Amir Khusrau.

Walking down barren streets, drawn towards the distant yet compelling sound, crossing roads and railway tracks along the way, I arrived at a hitherto unfamiliar quarter of the city. Confused about the epicentre of the musical vibration, I approached a gentleman brewing tea in the bylane where I stood.

He smiled and pointed at an imposing gate covered in calligraphy and floral motifs. 'Go in through there, it seems Khwaja Nizamuddin Auliya himself has beckoned you.'

I did not quite know what to expect, but knew somehow that I was supposed to be there. Taking off my shoes at the gate, I stepped across the doorway and started walking down a marble corridor. Walking past an ancient stepwell and tiny winding avenues full of small shops selling flowers, incense, chadors with shiny borders and sacred verses, cassette tapes and even books, I entered into a rather regal courtyard with an ornately domed shrine surrounded by perforated latticework at its centre. As my senses absorbed the calming perfume of roses and sandalwood incense, my eyes met the musicians sitting cross-legged on the chequered floor facing the sanctum. I instantly recognised them to be qawwals. The lead vocalist who would go on to become one of my first teachers was reciting the following lines when I arrived.

◆

Mujhe aap ne bulaya,
yeh karam nahin toh kya hai

◆

(You called me to your doorstep,
if that is not divine grace what is?)

I was sold. Despite having been a student of Indian classical music for several years, at that tender age, I had no understanding of the melodic nuances or what was being conveyed. I could only hear the music. But with the passage of time, a deep illumination began occurring within. As I internalised the repetitive rhythm, the improvisation, the poetry, the sheer sonority of the form, I found myself spontaneously understanding what was being said almost viscerally, even without being formally trained in its technical aspects. The music was speaking directly to me. I realised that something greater than myself was calling me from across the vast vibratory ocean of Sufi musical expression. Qawwali as a complete form in itself appealed to me. Navigating its sonic waves my classically trained ear gradually shed its purist bias and I found myself unable to resist the rather distinctive vocal register of the qawwal. The notion that this is what I was meant to do crystallised within me.

Whenever asked whether I wanted to be a doctor, engineer or pilot, much to the chagrin of my family, my reply was, I wanted to be a qawwal. They responded with the stock phrase: 'Qawwals live in ghettos and tenements. How will you make a living?' Meeting my hero, ideal, guru and the emperor of qawwali, Ustad Nusrat Fateh Ali Khan Sahab, a couple of years later, answered all my questions and prayers and my rebelliously casual retort became a serious goal. It was the time spent and learnings gained at his feet and those of his esteemed younger brother Ustad Farrukh Fateh Ali Khan that really moulded my life, thought and music. Its pursuit is what I have endeavoured to do ever since. Qawwali captivated me and after repeated requests and trials, I persuaded Ustad Meraj Ahmed Nizami (Meraj Baba) to start teaching me the intricacies of his art.

Being accepted into the Chishty silsila (spiritual order) and given ijazat (permission) by my Sufi Master Syed Najmul Hasan Chishty to perform a haziri (formal offering) at Ajmer Sharif shrine as a qawwal with my ensemble to spontaneous acclamation, was for me no less than an artist winning a Grammy. To my teachers I forever remain indebted. In the Sufi courtyard there is something for everyone, no one goes away empty handed and neither did I. The shared symbology, composite structure and fluid nature of qawwali had taken me under its waves and I emerged as a qawwal.

⬩ ◆ ⬩

Khwaja Nizam ast, o Nizami manam

⬩ ◆ ⬩

(Khwaja Nizamuddin shows the way,
I follow his path)

A Note on Sama

⬩ ◆ ⬩

Daani-e-Sama Che bood,
Saut-e-Bala Shonidan
Az Khweshtan buridan,
Ba Wasl-e-Haq Rasidan

⬩ ◆ ⬩

(Do you know what Sama is?
It is the hearing of the call of the Beloved.
To be cut off from one's temporal self
and be subsumed by the eternal)

The word sama has Arabic roots and literally means to hear. To the Sufis, sama is the auditory experience of music as prescribed in the traditions set down by the elders. When asked about the validity of sama in Sufi piety, the great ninth-century Islamic scholar and mystic, Junayd Baghdadi, replied, 'That music which takes one closer to the remembrance of the divine is valid, that which takes one away from it is indeed forbidden.'[1]

Two divergent views about the nature and quality of sama emerged over time. Natural Sama and formal sama, both found their place in different Sufi milieus. For instance, Imam Ghazali, who answered the challenge to the religious legality of sama by positing the question, 'What of the music produced by the chirping of birds', narrates a well-known anecdote in his writings on the beggar who, upon hearing the singing of a slave girl in her master's home on the banks of the Tigris, received her music as if it were divine revelation (Ilham) sent to resolve his deep internal spiritual struggle.[2]

The other more complex and deliberate sama bound by ritual, space, time, purpose and audience slowly became part of the dargah system where trained musicians facilitated their honed listeners in experiencing altered states (wajd or haal), the emotions of contraction and expansion (Halat-e-Qabz-wa-Bast) and other forms of inner ecstasy (kaifiyat) as a means of finding solace (sukoon), healing (shifa), spiritual rejuvenation (kushadgi) and revive their connection (nisbat) with the teacher (pir-o-murshid).

Qawwali as Sama

Potent, grand and possessing the power to transcend, qawwali with its compelling rhythms and melodies have for centuries celebrated the oneness of the divine, of love and of music. Chishty Sufi sama or qawwali is the physical and musical manifestation of the devotional tradition of Islam in South Asia, and qawwali is its main vehicle of outreach. The practice of qawwali as Sufi sama was first introduced to India during the era of Hazrat Muinuddin Chishty popularly known as Khwaja Gharib Nawaz. It is said that the first mehfils or gatherings of sama in India took place at his khanqah in Ajmer and he initiated its daily offering along with a community kitchen (langar) by the permission of his master Syed Uthman e Harwani, who was himself a prolific poet and scholar.[3]

The antecedents of qawwali itself lie in pre-Islamic Arabia. The qawwal much like their South Asian counterparts, the kathakaar and kathavaachak, was a storyteller.[4] It was a rudimentary form of musical narration practised by bards and dancing minstrels. Themes ranged from folk tales and fables to myths and romances. Adopted by the Sufis, the form gained great influence and eventually travelled to the Indian subcontinent with them. Its ever-expanding repertoire and structure eventually came to include hundreds of sub-genres from both the Indic as well as the Persian traditions such as Qaulbana, Manqabat, Taranah, Naqsh-o-Nigar, Sohela, Ghazal and Geet, to name a few.

Performed widely at Sufi shrines as part of urs (anniversary of passing) gatherings, Milad [birth of the Holy Prophet (PBUH)] and other important days in the Islamic calendar such as Eid-e-Ghadeer, qawwali is said to have reached its zenith during the age of the early Chishty Sufi saints Khwaja Moinuddin Chishty, Khwaja Qutubuddin Bakhtiyar Kaki, Baba Fariduddin Ganjshakar, Hazrat Nizamuddin Auliya and Hazrat Alauddin Sabir Kaliyari. It was the beloved disciple of Nizamuddin Auliya—courtier, chronicler, author, poet laureate, musicologist and renaissance figure of thirteenth-century India—Khwaja Amir Khusrau who imbued qawwali with the love and devotion of his master and gave it eternal fame.

In the world of Sufi music, veiled meanings within canonical verse and mystic poem may be uncovered with merely a shift of emphasis or turn of phrase, but their true essence is only revealed to those who know the secrets of the path. Not just for the seeker or saalik, but for the uninitiated too there is enough to ponder and indeed yearn for. The qawwal is essentially following a method that is constantly transgressing and breaking its own patterns in order to delve into the heart of the listener rather than engage their logical mind. Perhaps similar to modern Western jazz exponents or to the medieval wandering minstrels of Central Asia and the spiritual archetypes, they were trying to break and remake the complete experience of creating and assimilating. Qawwali or Sufi sama is a technique designed to break open the fragile ego that envelops the mind and reach the very depths of the soul.

Qawwali as a medium is engineered to congregate and assemble the self-understanding of its audiences, in the context of how they view their past, their ancestral traditions, innate faith and ultimately their journey back to the divine. No wonder then that artists like John Coltrane likened it to gospel music and called it the jazz of the East.

Aahang-e-Khusravi: Stylistic Creations and Contribution of Hazrat Amir Khusrau Dehlavi

◆ ◆ ◆

Poet: Amir Khusrau

◆ ◆ ◆

Turk e Hindostani'am,
Man Hindavi goyam cho aab

(I am a Turk of Indian origin,
I speak Hindi like flowing water)

By the medieval era several hybrid forms thriving in shared cultural registers came into existence. On one end of this confluence was dhrupad, having absorbed into its framework songs from almost every form and genres and developed the penchant for sankirna ragas (blended modes). On the other end of this hybrid spectrum lay relatively newer and exciting forms such as qawwali, khusravi khayal and ghazal. Based on the Indo-Persian tradition of the blending modes, poetic metaphors and sacred symbolism along with the practice of experimenting on root ragas and their derivatives by the process of Asl-ul-faraa (root of the fabric) as used by Amir Khusrau, we see the true emergence of a syncretic sonic tradition.

One of the hallmarks of Khusrau's innovative approach was the ease with which he could emote in Hindavi while using the meter and grammar of Persian. Though not found in any of his divans or collections, when asked about his vernacular poetry, he used to say, 'I did pen a few words in Hindavi, but only for the enjoyment of my friends and fellow poets.' However, the poetic structures and linguistic crossovers he had left behind in oral culture provided future generations with a map or blueprint so that they may carry forward his legacy and eventually led to the creation of languages such as Rektha and Urdu.

Significantly, Khusrau, neither born into a family of musicians or scholars nor taught by anyone, fostered his genius through self-training. Having chosen not to teach his own children music (except possibly one son, Ruknuddin), he chose twelve disciples from among hereditary master musicians of varying genres and called them Qawwal Bachche, training them to accomplish the task of preserving and nurturing his stylistic interpretations and innovations collectively known as Aahang-e-Khusravi. Today the Dilli Qawwal Bachche and Dilli Gharana are two schools that have best preserved and passed down this tradition seena-ba-seena (generationally) in the oral system of ustad-shagird (master-disciple transmission).

In its earliest days, qawwali consisted of two main components. Firstly, the Arabic qaul which had been part of Sufi practices since the earliest days was a sort of musical storytelling form that initially found prominence in Iraq and possibly other parts of Arabia. Along with instruments such as duhl (dhol), tabl (tabla) seh-tar (sitar) and ruhbaab (rabab), it found its way to the Indian subcontinent with both wandering minstrels and royal bards. Secondly, forms such as taranah and tilallanah, their roots lying in the folk music of Iran and the Yalali singers of the Arab landmass, which had gradually Indianised themselves through exchanges with their native counterparts such as the Tenaka singers.[5]

Thus, qawwali, originally conceived by Khusrau for the auditory pleasure of his pir, his guru, came to represent the culture or adab of a mili-juli tehzeeb (composite heritage) where compositions were created in a totally new way, using words from Hindavi and Farsi and setting the rhymes to rhythm and scale, that is, specific talas and ragas while basing the aesthetics and mood on Indian wisdom traditions such as rasa, where a range of emotions could be felt and expressed through various artistic mediums.

It is noteworthy that just as the Turks and Persians were finding themselves attracted to the Purbi, Hindavi and Braj culture of Hindustan, so too in turn were the professional music-and-dance-based communities such as the Natt, Kalavant and others being inspired by various facets of Central Asian culture. Gaining knowledge and proficiency in the meter of the ghazal and playing the rabab, they started using Persian poetry to compose melodies for their performances which were then presented to a wide audience with ghazal as their medium of melodic expression. In an interesting way it may have been that the meter of ghazal was first adopted in India as a form of folk music and only later as a literary form by the likes of Amir Khusrau and others.[6]

In his writings, Hazrat Amir Khusrau mentions some of his favourite musicians at the royal court. One of them is a female Uzbek harp player and vocalist known as Turmati Khatun.[7] He also speaks of his preferred vocal pitch and range indicating a preference for thin, high, soprano voices, which can easily glide all the scales and can switch ragas and modes with ease.[8] Interestingly, the rhythmic drumming, clapping and high-pitched vocals qawwali artists often utilise, have their roots in a wide range of folk traditions ranging from kirtaniyas (Hindu devotional singers) to the music of the kinnar (transgender) community as well as the chanting of the jogis (mendicants), all of whom are frequently mentioned in Sufi texts and considered as fellow seekers by the Chishty order.

By the late medieval era both the secular and devotional forms of courtly music came to be dominated by the Dhupad style of gayaki and layakari. Simultaneously, qawwali, ghazal and geet had advanced themselves and gained popularity among people at large through the efforts of Sufi saints. Faqirullah, the medieval commentator and musicologist, compares Indian musical tradition to a river with mingling waters, and explains it as a coming together of Lafz-e-Taazi, Tarz-e-Parsi and Khayal-e-Hindavi: Arabic word, Persian style and Indian thought.[9]

Gulshan e Chisht: The Syncretic Sama of the Chishty Garden

Ma'ra Dar Roz-e-Mithaaq Nida-e-Alast
Barbakht Dar Aahang-e-Purbi be-gosh rasidah bood

According to Hazrat Nizamuddin Auliya, the great saint of Delhi, 'each soul on the day of creation heard the call of the divine in a unique frequency'. Sultan-ul-Mashayakh himself reported that he heard it in Raga Purbi.[10] While the legendary sama of Hazrat Amir Khusrau and his disciples such as Khwaja Mubashir and Miyan Samanti would be almost impossible to recreate, a wonderful anecdote gives us a hint as to how it may have been.

Once, Khwaja Nizamuddin was travelling towards Mehrauli to visit the mazaar or resting place of Khwaja Qutubuddin Bakhtiyar Kaki, accompanied by his brother Syed Moosa, Amir Khusrau, Hasan Sanjari and others. Along the way they came to rest in a field and saw a farmer working a wooden wheel to extract water from a well. As he laboured, in order to fortify his efforts he loudly repeated the phrase *Baara laiyyo, Ram manaiyyo* (may this water be extracted to please lord Rama). Upon hearing this, Hazrat Nizamuddin asked Amir Khusrau about the meaning of the words being repeated by the man, and when he understood it, he uttered a cry of Allah (SWT) and, getting up, began to whirl ecstatically. Witnessing this amazing scene, all the dervishes began to sing the phrase together. Khusrau immediately recited a Quranic verse:

◆ ◆ ◆

Ala Ba'dhikrullahi Tatmainn'al' Quloob

◆ ◆ ◆

(Verily in the remembrance of Allah (SWT)
do hearts find rest)

The khadim (server) of Khwaja Nizamuddin, Khwaja Iqbal, was then asked to return to the khanqah and bring back the qawwals upon whose arrival the shaikh asked for these two verses to be sung together. Soon a composition emerged in his favourite Raga Purbi and the mehfil carried on for many hours, being interrupted only for namaz and langar. It is said that this sama went on for three days and three nights.[11]

Some examples of this type of interplay between sacred symbols and modes of expression are qawwalis like *'Mori maili gudariya dho de, Ganjshakar le Lal'* (Wash my muddy blanket, O beloved of Farid), invoking both the favourite disciples and successors of the legendary Sufi saint Baba Farid, his nephew Alauddin Sabir Kaliyari and Nizamuddin Auliya. The kalaam is recited by the qawwals to this day on the annual Ghusl ceremony for the birthday of Hazrat Nizamuddin Auliya. Or Khusrau's poignant bidaai geet (farewell song) that still brings brides and their families to tears: *'Kahey ko byaahi bides ri lakhi baabul morey'* (Why did you marry me abroad, O dear father). Not to be missed is *'Zehaal e Miskeen makun taghaful, doraey naina banaaey batiyaan'* (Do not ignore this miserable one's state, with your beguiling gaze and flattering words)—an incredible blending of colloquial Hindi and Persian. The popular sohela *'Chhap tilak sab chheeniray, mosay naina milaaike'* (The beloved has stolen all sense of self from me, with just a glance). The stately sehra by Bedam Shah *'Ganj Shakar ke laal Nizamuddin, Chisht nagar mein phaag rachaayo'* (The beloved of Farid, Nizamuddin, has set up a grand celebration of colours in the city of the master of Moinuddin). I mention these songs because we see in them the emergence of a third space, one beyond creed, caste and ethnic identity. Where a Radha can learn the deepest secrets of Sufism from her Lord Krishna and Pir Nizamuddin can wear a peacock feather crown and play Holi with Amir Khusrau.

◆ ◆ ◆

Poet: Bedam Shah Warsi

◆ ◆ ◆

Khelo re Chishtiyon Holi khelo

(Come gather, O Chishtys, play Holi)

Mehfil-e-Sama

◆ ◆ ◆

Poet: Hazrat Nizamuddin Auliya

◆ ◆ ◆

Ba lehn e Dawood hamnavaa shau
Ba naala o dard aashnaa shau

(With the voice of David, to the Beloved,
Convey my lament of the pain of separation)

Although little inference can be made as to how devotional Sufi musical offerings were performed in bygone ages, some scholars have speculated that in the beginning the forms known as khayal and qawwali that I have mentioned above often used to be sung together, using elements from both folk and classical streams. Typically, a Mehfil-e-Sama would open with a qaul/qaulbana with complex rhythmic interchanges and heavy use of raga-based ornamentation not dissimilar to the structure of Dhrupad music. Qaul would then give way to tarana, a composition using monosyllabic utterances, mimicking string and percussion, with hidden meanings as its refrain, followed by canonical verses, sacred chants or mystical poetry. Following this, the qawwals would pick up a lilting ghazal often accompanied by mazaamir (instruments) such as the chhang, daff, tabla, dhol, sarangi, been, rabab, kemanche or other regional varieties. A celebratory 'rang' (containing the *khatam ul khwajegan* or repetition of the names of Sufi saints), or a dhamaal (accompanied by raqs or dancing) in the regions of Sindh, Punjab or Multan, brought the ceremony to a close. Over time as the Sufi silsilas became formalised, Hamdiya-Naatiya kalaam or Nasheed poetry in praise of God, the angels and the Prophet came to gain prominence.

Today most qawwali offerings begin with a hamd invoking the Almighty and is followed by a naat for Huzoor Muhammad Sahab, the Prophet (PBUH) and founder of the Islamic faith. Next comes a qaul in praise of Hazrat Ali (RA), the Prophet's son-in-law and spiritual successor. Together with Bibi Fatima and their progeny Imam Hasan and Imam Hussain, they form what is known as the Panjetan or the five purified ones. Faith upon their intercession on the day of reckoning, as well as a deep spiritual connection with and obedience to the teachings of the Buzurgaan-e-Deen (ancestors and elders) is a core part of Sufi beliefs.

While qawwali denotes a specific set of musical performance styles and genres, sama is the ritual of spiritual audition or deep listening. The practice of listening to Sufi music or sama involves introspection, reflection, divine remembrance that must be approached with discipline, control, decorum and purity of both outer body and intention so that a sense of riqqat (attenuation) is achieved.

To the Sufi, sama is a means of spiritual advancement and vital nourishment for the soul. Listeners yearn for union with the divine beloved, immersing themselves in the vibratory experience of the music as the samakhwaan attempts to alter their inner states with an intense but gradual expansion. As the wise elders say: 'Sama happens when Sama happens. Its acceptance by those whom it invokes is apparent to all present, when at some hidden moment, the energy of the space changes ever so subtly.

A Note on the Qawwal

I am not a Sufi, it is a very big thing to be a Sufi.
I am nothing more than a humble qawwal.
My job is to help the Sufi on their path towards the divine.

Singer: Ustad Nusrat Fateh Ali Khan

The khanqahi qawwal is a repository of the collective memory of the Sufi world. A conduit between the apparent and unseen. Humble yet powerful, skilfully weaving melody, rhythm and verse to both interpret and represent the timeless verses of prophets, saints, lost lovers and wandering minstrels. Memorising vast tomes of kalaams (poems, songs, compositions) in various languages such as Farsi, Punjabi and Hindavi. To know their inner and apparent meanings, to be aware of their context and using the appropriate form and the emphasis and resonance for each occasion. To be ritually purified, make intention and obey the decorum of the gathering, taking cognisance of the state of those in attendance. Tread cautiously with deep awareness, connected to the presence of the murshid (master), the sahib-e-mazaar (saint), their nisbat (affinity), and the mahaul (vibratory frequencies) of the space of offering.

⬩ ◆ ⬩

Ba adab ba naseeb,
be adab be naseeb

⬩ ◆ ⬩

(With respect comes good fortune,
with disrespect comes misfortune)

'Qawwal kaun hai' (who is a qawwal), my teachers used to ask. I learnt to respond with the answer they had taught us—Qawwal *ba adab, ba qaul aur apni nisbat ka ghulam hota hai.* (Subservient to the words of the elders, obedient and committed to their duty and a slave to their spiritual masters.) It was always stressed that as practitioners of a devotional art form, we were not allowed to be publicly swayed or moved by our own renditions or the emotive content of the poetry. That was reserved for the listeners. Just like those distributing langar do not partake of it themselves, the one offering sama to one's listeners should not slip into a state of ecstatic joy and disrupt the flow while doing one's task as that might negatively affect those experiencing altered states and inner travel while listening to them, and even prove to be fatal.

Intehaa: The penultimate

◆

Nigah jis pe ho teri hai uska kya kehna,
Teri nazar hai khuda ki nazar Gharib Nawaz

◆

(What to say of the fortunate one upon whom your
blessed gaze comes to rest,
For is not your gaze, O beloved Moinuddin,
the gaze of the divine.)

What is qawwali except a retelling of the state of separation between the lover and the Beloved and the imploring by the lover to the Beloved for the bestowal of that one gaze (nigah) that shall fulfil the lover's life's desire and purpose? For is not the gaze of the master, the gaze of God?

A qawwal is never the one to be moved to tears by his own rendition, instead he becomes a pillar of poise and reserve, hiding his own innermost feelings behind the veil of musical ingenuity and playfulness. There is no 'me' in the qawwal's offerings, just a holding of others, of 'you'. Their discipline is obedience to the occasion and commitment to their task to tune, honour and heal the hearts and souls they encounter.

A qawwal is not just a musician or singer, he must have the memory of a great storyteller, the sensitivity of a poet and deep understanding of human emotion and its conscious and unconscious expressions. He should be observing people in each gathering with great care, inviting them to sit and to deeply listen and, if seeing them moved by a verse or a melodic fragment, he should encourage their inner attunement and strive to help achieve a possible emotional breakthrough with patience and love.

Inshallah, it is this naaqis (worthless) qawwal's hope that both the qawwal and their ancient art form, the qawwali, shall enjoy a real and not a 'reel' revival once more, in the not-too-distant future!

Endnotes

1. Yazdani, K.: *Sufism and Philosophy*, pp. 110–115, 1987
2. Avery, Kenneth: *A Psychology of Early Sufi Sama,* Routledge, 2004
3. Chishty, Syed Najmul Hasan: *Sama,* Al Quran Company, 2010
4. Ahmad, Najma Parveen: *Hindustani Music,* Manohar Publishers and Distributors, 1984
5. Sarmadee, S.: *Tarjuma-e-Maankutuhal-o-Risala-e-Rag Darpan,* pp. 34–35, IGNCA, 1996
6. Sarmadee, S.: *Amir Khusrau,* pp. 34–39, Publications Division, 1975
7. Khusrau, Amir: *Ejaaz-e-khusravi,* Munshi Nawal Kishor, 1876
8. Deewan Nihayatul Kamaal: Internet Archive, Matba Qaiser e Hind, Delhi, 1913
9. Sarmadee, S.: *Tarjuma-e-Maankutuhal-o-Risala-e-Rag Darpan,* IGNCA
10. Khwaja Amir Hasan Ala Sijzi: *Fawaid ul Fawaid,* Khwaja Hasan Sani Nizami
11. Hardev, Rajkumar: *Chahal Roza* (Urdu version: *Nizami Bansari Khwaja Hasan Nizami*), p. 73–75, Liberty Art Press, 1990

QAWWALI AT SAFIPUR SILSILA

Safipur is a small sleepy town in Unnao district of Uttar Pradesh, India. The original name of this town was Saipur. The town's name Safipur comes from the name of the Muslim Sufi Saint, popularly known as Hazrat Maqdoom Shah Safi. Qawwali mehfils are held regularly under the patronage of the family in the premises of the shrine.

The Sufi traditions of the Awadh region were all interconnected through the *nisbat* (connection) of the prominent Sufi saints Maqdoom Shaikh Saad, Maqdoom Shahmina of Old Lucknow, Maqdoom Khairabadi of Khairabad, Sheikh Sarang of Majhgawan Sharif. Till date, qawwals continue to sing at all these shrines interchangeably.

Mehfil-e-Sama

Mehfil-e-Sama, or the assembly for listening, is considered important at the dargah and hence qawwali becomes a medium where believers create a link to religious ecstasy and to God through the performer. During the Mehfil-e-Sama, along with the lead qawwal, there is a chorus of four or five men who repeat key verses and follow him. They follow his mood with their eyes on him and simultaneously aid the percussion by the rhythmic clapping of hands, all this taking the audience on a journey of spiritual ecstasy. As the lead qawwal takes the poetry to a different tangent, another refrain is picked up by the chorus. This fluid interplay of refrains, coupled with the lead qawwal's improvisation, creates a captivating and entrancing atmosphere. The goal is to bind the audience in a mystical state, drawing them deeper into the spiritual and emotional journey of the performance.

◆

Poet: Rasheed Ahmed Khalili
urf Jaggan Miya Safipur

◆

Saiyan Sajilay torey naina rasilay
Palkan aut rakhun saajan ko, manwa wa ka pyaar re
Saajan mora, main saajan ki, ab kou jeet na haar, re
Saiyan Sajilay torey naina rasilay

Qawwali is increasingly becoming a decentred art form and is no longer limited to being part of religious institutions and the khanqahs. And yet, qawwals continue to owe strict allegiance to the khanqah or the dargah. They respect the direct descendants of the Sufi master or his chosen disciples, who become the custodians of the tradition, the Sajjada-Nashin as they are formally known at the shrines. The kissing of the hand defines certain hierarchies among the age-old Islamic traditions that are still followed in the Khanqahs.

◆

Poet: Khaleel Miya Safipuri

◆

Balam tori chitwan per main wari
Mad-bhare naina saanwli surat, humka lagat pyari pyari
In ankhiyan per in nainan per, Khaleel piya balihari
Balam tori chitwan per main wari

Photographer: Mustafa Quraishi
Qawwali Practitioners: Qawwal Mohammad Imran, Qawwal Gufran Aslami Khairabadi, Qawwal Qamar Warsi, Qawwal Ali Waris
Text: Manjari Chaturvedi
Place: Dargah Hazrat Maqdoom Shah Safi, Safipur, Unnao, Uttar Pradesh, India
Project: The Qawwali Project

safipur
silsila

KIRAN

Anthropology of Qawwali

Vinay Kumar Srivastava &
Rachna Atri Saksena

Qawwali, a form of devotional ritual deeply rooted in the Sufi religious tradition of South Asia, traces its origins to the spiritual practices of eighth-century Persia. In the Indian subcontinent, qawwali performances initially took place at Sufi shrines, where the spiritual ambience enriched the devotional experience. The royal patronage of Sufi orders further facilitated the spread of qawwali beyond sacred spaces, allowing it to be performed in courts and public gatherings. During the British colonial period, qawwali adapted to new socio-political contexts, surviving through the support of zamindars and affluent patrons within the jajmani system, marking its transition towards entertainment alongside its spiritual role (Bhattacharjee and Alam, 2012).

A study of qawwali within its cultural context necessitates an exploration of the multifaceted dimensions that constitute culture—social, religious, and performativity. This approach not only illuminates the devotional elements of qawwali but also reveals the intricate relationships between performers, audiences, and the spiritual experiences it engenders. By focusing on qawwals—the professional performers of qawwali music—their roles not only as musicians but as spiritual mediators who transmit divine messages through their music, we situate qawwali within the broader framework of cultural anthropology, with particular emphasis on the interplay between the 'Great Tradition' and the 'Little Tradition' in both historical and contemporary contexts.

Through this lens, we examine the intricate processes that have shaped the evolution of qawwali tradition, its role within Sufi rituals, and the significance of qawwals as both performers and cultural custodians. Qawwali emerges as a multidimensional cultural system, interwoven with class structures, gender dynamics, age hierarchies, and even therapeutic practices. This exploration draws on concepts from cultural anthropology and ethnomusicology to analyse qawwali's evolution, its enduring cultural impact, and its engagement with contemporary digital spaces.

Rooted deeply in Sufi mysticism, qawwali is more than a form of devotional music; it is a vital component of spiritual and cultural identity in South Asia. An interdisciplinary approach—incorporating insights from anthropology, sociology, and medical humanities—offers a comprehensive understanding of qawwali's cultural hybridity, the social stratification within its audiences, the gender dynamics at play, and its therapeutic potential in promoting mental and emotional well-being.

The significance of qawwali is in its functions as a dynamic medium for forging social bonds, shaping religious experiences, and facilitating emotional resonance across diverse communities. Its transformative power lies not only in its melodic and rhythmic intricacies, more so in its capacity to bridge the sacred and the secular, the traditional and the contemporary.

In the Indian subcontinent, Sufi shrines became the primary venues for qawwali performances. Here, the music became an integral part of the sama (listening) ritual, which involved both the performer and the audience engaging in an emotional, meditative experience. The performance of qawwali at these shrines was seen as a devotional practice that could lead to a mystical connection with the divine.

As a living tradition, it faces several challenges, particularly in adapting to modernity and maintaining its cultural relevance. To ensure its survival, we must examine both its cultural dynamism and the evolving forces that shape its practice. This work seeks to integrate the anthropological perspective on qawwali, exploring the academic works done on this tradition, and analyses how contemporary interpretations, performance settings, and economic realities impact its sustainability.

An Anthropological Gaze on Qawwali as a Sacred Tradition

At its core, qawwali is a religious ritual. The term 'Qawwali' comes from the Arabic term 'qawl', meaning 'speech' or 'utterance'. It refers to a poetic form of expression that combines poetry and spirituality. The purpose of qawwali is to facilitate sama, or a state of spiritual listening, where the audience is able to transcend the mundane world and enter into a deeper state of consciousness. The music creates a collective effervescence that draws the listeners into a communal experience of religious fervour, where the boundaries between the individual and the divine become blurred.

The performance space itself—whether it be a shrine, a religious gathering, or a private setting—plays a critical role in shaping the sacredness of the qawwali experience. In Sufi shrines, the atmosphere is charged with a sense of divinity, where the qawwals channel their voices and instruments to connect with the spiritual world. The ritual of qawwali is thus not only an artistic performance but a deeply immersive act of worship, with the words of the songs (often composed in praise of Prophet Muhammad (PBUH), Sufi saints, or divine love) taking precedence over the music itself. The lyrics of qawwali are powerful carriers of meaning, where each word is intended to invoke divine presence, reflecting the belief that the spiritual experience is as much about the listener's inner transformation as it is about the external performance.

As an anthropologist, I view qawwali not merely through its musicological elements but as a rich cultural phenomenon shaped by tradition and social dynamics. Anthropology's focus on culture, tradition, and societal structures provides a comprehensive framework to study qawwali—not just as a religious practice but as a vital part of the performers' lives and the communities they come from. This approach helps us understand how qawwali integrates into the broader cultural, social, and economic fabric of South Asia, particularly for those who depend on it as a means of livelihood.

Qawwali can be studied using key ideas from anthropology to understand its ritualistic nature. Emile Durkheim's distinction between the sacred and the profane is highly relevant to qawwali. Sacred rituals, for Durkheim, are those that foster social solidarity and collective effervescence—emotional experiences that unite a community. Qawwali, particularly when performed in Sufi shrines, embodies these characteristics. It creates a collective emotional experience that binds the performers and the audience together, facilitating a sense of shared religious devotion. In contrast, when qawwali is performed in a secular or commercial setting, such as a music festival or a concert, the sacred essence of the performance is often diluted, and the focus shifts to entertainment and individual enjoyment.

Victor Turner's concept of liminality and communitas—a state of equality and togetherness that arises in the liminal phase of a ritual—can be applied to qawwali performances. Qawwali performances are like spiritual ceremonies. They create a special, almost magical atmosphere where people feel connected to the divine. The lyrics are full of symbols about love, longing, and the mystical journey, helping people connect deeply with the spiritual message. The way qawwali is performed matters—singers, musicians, and the audience all play a role, making the experience meaningful. Besides being a religious act, qawwali brings people together, strengthening community ties and cultural identity. While it's a sacred practice, qawwali is also enjoyed publicly, blending the spiritual with everyday life.

Clifford Geertz's approach to interpretive anthropology emphasises understanding cultural practices as part of a 'web of meaning'. For Geertz, every cultural expression (including music) is embedded in a larger system of symbols that convey meaning. To fully understand qawwali, it's helpful to see it from both the inside (as practised by devotees) and the outside (as an observer or scholar).

During a qawwali performance, especially in the shrine setting, the hierarchical distinctions between the performer and the audience can temporarily disappear. Both performers and listeners enter a state of liminality, where they are united in a shared spiritual and emotional experience. This communal aspect of qawwali reinforces social solidarity and strengthens the collective identity of the community.

Qawwali's significance lies in the broader cultural and religious meanings attached to the performance. The experience of listening to qawwali is therefore an interpretive act, where the audience derives personal and communal meanings from the lyrics, the music, and the context in which it is performed.

One of the key insights drawn from qawwali, as viewed through the work of Indian sociologist Yogesh Atal, is the concept of sandwich culture—a framework that describes the convergence of various cultural elements. Qawwali, as a hybrid cultural practice, is shaped by a complex set of religious, musical, and social influences. These elements come together to create a form that resists easy categorisation and challenges the idea of a singular, homogeneous tradition.

I like to use the metaphoric concept of the 'cosmic sponge' in relation to qawwali that describes its remarkable ability to absorb and integrate diverse cultural, religious, and spiritual influences while retaining its core essence. The metaphor highlights the dynamic, adaptable nature of qawwali as it evolves over time, remaining highly relevant to various communities and audiences around the world.

Qawwali has the capacity to absorb elements from different religious traditions—such as Hinduism and Sufism—along with a variety of cultural and linguistic influences. By doing so, qawwali adapts and reshapes itself, incorporating new meanings and forms while staying grounded in its original spiritual and musical structure. This process of absorption makes qawwali a unique and inclusive tradition, able to bridge gaps between various faiths and cultural practices. It resonates with a wide range of listeners, regardless of their religious or cultural backgrounds.

Qawwali remains highly vital and alive, continuously evolving without losing its essential character. This adaptability is crucial to its global appeal. Whether in traditional Sufi shrines or modern settings, qawwali's ability to transform and embrace new contexts ensures its continued relevance. It can be performed in various settings, even in unconventional contexts like Hindu festivals or secular gatherings, without losing its spiritual essence.

In a world where cultures often collide and diverge, qawwali serves as a powerful example of how a cultural form can unite people through its adaptability. Its 'cosmic sponge' quality ensures that it remains an enduring and transformative force, capable of transcending time, geography, and religion while keeping its deep-rooted spiritual core intact.

One of the most striking anthropological insights about qawwali is its adaptive structure. Even as qawwali faces criticism for its commercialisation, the tradition has continued to thrive and adapt, blending the sacred and the secular in new ways. This adaptability is crucial for its survival, as it shows how cultural forms can evolve while still retaining their core values.

An important observation has been that qawwali is not just about music—the words are paramount. The lyrics convey profound spiritual messages and cultural teachings, often taking precedence over the musical elements themselves. This insight invites anthropologists and ethnomusicologists to think beyond the sounds and rhythms of qawwali, focusing instead on the deeper symbolic and meaning-making functions of music.

Qawwali's therapeutic potential, explored by scholars like Adam Nayyar, blends music and spirituality to promote emotional and psychological healing. When performed in shrine settings, it offers symbolic healing by creating transcendent experiences that aid mental health recovery, fostering emotional well-being and mental nourishment through its immersive, transformative nature.

The anthropological perspective on qawwali significantly enriches ethnomusicology. Scholars like Qureshi, Johnston, Neville, and Holland have examined not only its musical structure and spiritual significance but also its cultural context. Holland's distinction between traditional qawwali singers (embedded in religious lineages like Nizamuddin) and secular performers raises critical questions about identity, authenticity, and cultural appropriation.

Anthropological methods provide a holistic understanding of qawwali, focusing on social roles, ritual contexts, and performance dynamics. The interaction between performers and audiences in shrine settings contrasts sharply with commercial performances, where qawwali can become commodified. Additionally, the global rise of artists like Nusrat Fateh Ali Khan has sparked debates on cultural authenticity in a globalised world.

The interaction between scholars (like Holland and Qureshi) and key informants (such as Miraj Ahmed Nizami) can be analysed using anthropological theories of power and knowledge. The question of who has the authority to define the meaning and value of cultural practices is central in anthropological research. In Holland's work, the interviews with traditional qawwali singers reveal a tension between the spiritual and commercialised realms of qawwali. These interviews illuminate how knowledge and tradition are negotiated and contested. Anthropologists often examine the power dynamics between the researcher and the researched, questioning how knowledge is constructed and who gets to speak for a particular tradition.

The scholarly work of Regula Burkhardt Qureshi, who studied the Sufi music of India and Pakistan, represents one of the earliest attempts to understand the structure and context of qawwali. Her ethnographic approach provides valuable insights into the traditional practices of qawwals, particularly in the context of Sufi shrines. Sherilee Johnston's work on the qawwals of Hyderabad and James Neville's study of qawwali at the Taj Baba shrine further explore the distinctions between shrine-based and non-shrine-based qawwali performances. Christopher Holland's research revisits Qureshi's work and expands on the question of how traditional qawwals view the commercialisation of the tradition and the incorporation of qawwali into secular spaces.

Qawwali as a Cultural System, its Context and Perspectives

Qawwali can be viewed as part of a broader religious and cultural ritual; it is a form of worship, an act of devotion that occurs in a specific setting—often at Sufi shrines. The ritualistic function of qawwali is central to its significance within the Sufi tradition. Anthropology pays close attention to how rituals help reinforce social norms, beliefs, and collective identities. In this case, Qawwali plays a transformative role, serving as a conduit between the human and the divine. The audience's participation or lack thereof can be seen as an integral part of the ritual experience. The anthropological notion of 'communitas' (from Victor Turner) would suggest that the performance of qawwali, with its communal audience, creates a sense of collective identity and shared transcendence. This communal aspect is a hallmark of many religious rituals in anthropological studies.

An essential tenet of anthropological theory is the recognition that cultural practices are not monolithic. Instead, they are marked by contestations and multiple perspectives that exist within a society. When analysing qawwali as a cultural system, it is critical to acknowledge the diverse interpretations and meanings attached to it, shaped by factors such as gender, age, and class.

The study of qawwali provides an opportunity to explore how music serves not only as an art form but also as a cultural practice deeply embedded in religious, social, and historical contexts. Qawwali is analysed as a living tradition—constantly evolving, adapting to new settings, and interacting with various external forces, including commercialisation. The core of the anthropological perspective lies in understanding cultural transmission, ritualistic functions, and how practices like qawwali maintain their relevance across generations.

One of the central themes in this narrative is the tension between traditional and modern performances of qawwali. This tension is embodied in the distinction between shrine-based and non-shrine performances, a concept introduced by Qureshi and later explored by other researchers like Sherilee Johnston and James Neville. Traditional qawwali performances at shrines are seen as deeply rooted in religious and mystical experience, focusing on the spiritual and communal dimensions of the music. On the other hand, the commercialisation and broader performance contexts, such as concerts or festivals, are often viewed with scepticism by traditional practitioners who perceive a certain vulgarisation of the art form. This highlights the anthropological idea that cultural expressions, like qawwali, are not static but interact with their social environment, absorbing and sometimes resisting external influences.

The Performers: Qawwals and Their Social Role

Qawwali remains a flexible, syncretic tradition that evolves with social, religious, and political changes. While commercialisation, especially in Bollywood, has impacted the 'Great Tradition', the 'Little Tradition' often remains untouched. To ensure its survival, it's crucial to address the economic challenges faced by qawwals, integrate qawwali into mainstream performances, and document the lives of lesser-known performers, preserving both its artistic and cultural integrity.

Through ethnographic fieldwork, anthropologists can document the lives of qawwali performers, capturing their struggles, aspirations, and the evolving nature of their art. Such studies are essential for preserving the tradition and ensuring its continued vitality. Moreover, examining the economic realities of qawwali performers—many of whom face financial hardship—can inform meaningful interventions that support their work and secure qawwali's future as both an art form and a spiritual practice.

The role of the qawwal in society is central to understanding qawwali traditions. Qawwals are highly skilled musicians who perform qawwali, often with a deep knowledge of both music and Sufi mysticism. They are trained in a lineage system, typically passing down their craft through family traditions or through mentorship from senior qawwals.

The qawwal's relationship with the audience is dynamic and reciprocal. In the shrine setting, the qawwal is not merely a performer but a spiritual guide who facilitates the communal experience of devotion. The qawwal's ability to evoke the sacred through their music and lyrics is seen as an act of piety, and their performance is often considered a form of worship in itself.

In modern contexts, however, the role of the qawwal has evolved. With the rise of qawwali as a commercialised genre in popular media, performers such as Nusrat Fateh Ali Khan gained global fame, performing for both sacred and secular audiences. While this has expanded the reach of qawwali, it has also raised questions about the authenticity of the tradition and the role of commercialisation in altering its spiritual essence.

The Performance, the Bodies, and the Infinite

Qawwali, viewed through an anthropological lens, transcends its role as musical expression to become an embodied practice intertwined with cultural, spiritual, and social identities. Its dynamic structure—marked by intricate vocal techniques, rhythmic patterns, and instruments like the harmonium and tabla—serves not just as art but as a ritual that shapes and reflects communal life.

Singing, listening, and even dancing within qawwali performances are active, embodied engagements. Performers channel spiritual devotion through their voices and bodies, while audiences respond with emotional and spiritual intensity. This mutual interaction creates a feedback loop where the performance is co-constructed by both performers and listeners. The performer's emotional state often mirrors the audience's response, fostering a shared, dynamic experience.

The practice of sadka—voluntary offerings made by the audience—illustrates qawwali's spiritual economy. These offerings are not mere transactions but symbolic gifts, reflecting respect, gratitude, and belief in the spiritual blessings conferred through the performance. This practice highlights qawwali's role in Sufi shrines, where music connects the divine with the human.

Repetition is central to qawwali's structure, serving as a ritual tool that induces transcendence. The repetitive chanting of verses fosters a meditative state, guiding listeners beyond intellectual understanding towards direct, experiential connection with the divine. This process dissolves social barriers—gender, age, class—emphasising the Sufi belief in the inherent equality of all beings under God.

Qawwali and the Qawwals in Contemporary Times

The transformation of qawwali—particularly its commercialisation and secularisation—presents a fascinating case study of cultural adaptation in a connected world. Within cinema, popular culture, and digital media, qawwali has become increasingly popular outside of traditional religious contexts. Famous qawwali performances in Bollywood films and international music festivals have introduced this once-sacred tradition to a global audience.

While these performances have led to the worldwide recognition of qawwali, they have also sparked debates about the loss of its original spiritual and ritualistic function. Critics argue that the performance of qawwali in secular settings, divorced from its religious roots, strips away its sacred meaning. However, others see the global spread of qawwali as a form of cultural preservation, allowing the tradition to survive in a rapidly changing world.

Qawwali, as a form of devotional music, can be situated within the broader framework of cultural anthropology through the lens of the 'Great Tradition' and 'Little Tradition' concepts. The 'Great Tradition' refers to the formal, often elite religious and philosophical systems, while the 'Little Tradition' involves local, folk practices and beliefs.

Historically, qawwali emerged from the 'Little Tradition', evolving within Sufi shrines where local musical traditions blended with Islamic mysticism. It has been a means of expressing spiritual devotion, reflecting local customs, and providing communal healing. Over time, however, qawwali became incorporated into the 'Great Tradition' as it gained recognition beyond the shrine settings, transcending regional boundaries and attracting a more global audience.

In contemporary contexts, qawwali continues to embody this interplay, while it maintains its roots in the 'Little Tradition' through its performance at Sufi shrines and its connection to folk culture. It has also been adapted for mainstream audiences, with artists like Nusrat Fateh Ali Khan bringing it into the global spotlight. This blending of the 'Great' and 'Little' traditions highlights qawwali's dynamic role in both preserving cultural heritage and adapting to modern, globalised contexts. Thus, qawwali exemplifies the fusion of local and global religious practices, offering a unique lens through which to explore the relationship between the 'Great Tradition' and 'Little Tradition' in both historical and contemporary cultural anthropology.

The anthropology of qawwali reveals a complex interplay between music, spirituality, and social dynamics. As a form of Sufi devotion, qawwali has been a powerful tool for fostering collective consciousness and spiritual connection. However, its journey through commercialisation and secularisation in modern times has raised important questions about the preservation of cultural traditions in a globalised world. Anthropology, by examining the role of qawwali in both sacred and secular contexts, offers valuable insights into how this powerful tradition continues to evolve while maintaining its deep cultural and spiritual significance.

Cultural Hybridity: Tradition Meets Globalisation

At its core, qawwali embodies the fusion of diverse cultural influences—local, regional, and global. It intertwines Sufi mysticism, popular religious rituals, and even commercial performances, reflecting the hybrid nature of cultural practices. This hybridity challenges notions of cultural purity, offering a dynamic understanding of identity that acknowledges how traditions evolve while preserving foundational elements.

Through cultural anthropology, qawwali provides a rich context to explore human behaviour within social frameworks. Themes such as ritual, performance, identity, tradition, and cultural change illuminate how music functions as a vital form of cultural expression.

In qawwali, repetitive rhythms and emotionally charged lyrics are more than aesthetic elements—they are conduits for spiritual ecstasy. Audience reactions—swaying, clapping, shedding tears—are active, meaning-making components that blur the line between performer and listener. This interaction fosters a communal experience that reinforces both individual and collective identities.

The shrine setting acts as a symbolic space where the sacred and the social intersect. Here, performance transcends entertainment to become a ritual act that strengthens the community's connection to the divine, the saint being honoured, as also the community listening to the performance. This sacred space is dynamic, where cultural meanings are continually performed, negotiated, and redefined.

The commercialisation of qawwali has sparked debates among scholars and practitioners. Traditional qawwals often express discomfort with non-shrine performances designed for entertainment rather than spiritual experience. Qawwali, deeply rooted in Sufi shrine contexts, is seen not just as music but as a conduit for spiritual connection.

Figures like Nusrat Fateh Ali Khan, though pivotal in globalising qawwali, have been critiqued by traditionalists for appropriating the style without its religious roots. These performers, often detached from specific shrines or religious lineages, are viewed as 'singers' adopting qawwali's style without embodying its sacred and communal essence.

A key distinction emerges: the difference between a 'singer' and a 'qawwali singer'. A qawwali singer, rooted in spiritual and communal practices, holds a sacred role that transcends mere performance. Miraj Ahmed Nizam emphasises that learning to sing qawwali does not grant one the right to perform it in sacred spaces.

This tension manifests in real-world contexts. For example, during a qawwali performance at Hindu College's Mecca festival, the young audience showed little interest in the spiritual or musical depth, focusing instead on the spectacle. This shift highlights the challenge of preserving qawwali's spiritual essence in an era where it's often commodified as entertainment.

One striking aspect of qawwali performances is the varied experiences of participants. Some may be so moved that they engage in spontaneous dancing or emotional outbursts, behaviours often seen as disruptive but accepted as part of spiritual intoxication within the qawwali context.

Such differentiated experiences reflect the subjective nature of cultural practices. Anthropology challenges the notion of uniformity in ritual responses, highlighting how personal and cultural factors shape individual engagements.

Ultimately, qawwali is more than a genre; it is a living tradition embodying art, spirituality, and community. Its study reveals how cultural practices are performed, experienced, and transformed across generations. How do performers navigate the emotional and spiritual demands of their role? How do audiences interpret and internalise the music? Ethnographic methods—participant observation, interviews, and performance analysis—unveil the layered meanings embedded in qawwali.

Conclusion: Revisiting Social Change and Cultural Evolution

By applying an anthropological lens to the study of qawwali and its intersection with Sufism, music, and cultural transformation, we gain insight into how ritual, tradition, identity, and power function within cultural practices. Anthropology helps us understand how such a complex tradition not only survives but adapts in the face of changing social conditions, drawing attention to issues of authenticity, performance, and cultural evolution. Moreover, the role of the audience, the preservation of traditions, and the cultural significance of music in fostering community and spirituality are all core elements of anthropological inquiry in this context. The discussion on how qawwali is evolving in response to globalisation and commercialisation speaks to broader themes of social change. These shifts are not merely about the music but also reflect wider social transformations. For example, the increasing popularity of qawwali outside the religious context challenges the boundaries between sacred and secular, raising questions about how religion and culture intersect in modern societies. The behaviour of the students at the college festival, prioritising dancing over the deeper, more contemplative aspects of qawwali, exemplifies how modernity and globalisation influence cultural practices. Anthropology examines how traditional practices are reshaped in response to new social realities, such as tourism, media, and global celebrity culture.

Qawwali emerges as a complex and multifaceted cultural system that cannot be understood through a single framework. It is a dynamic practice that reflects the contested nature of cultural identity, shaped by gender, age, class, and spiritual experience. By examining qawwali through the perspectives of cyber-ethnography, differentiated experiences, social stratification, and symbolic healing, this article contributes to a deeper understanding of how cultural practices evolve and thrive in both traditional and modern contexts. The study of qawwali, therefore, offers valuable insights into the ways that music, religion, and culture intersect to form unique spaces of cultural expression and spiritual healing. Qawwali's evolution from a deeply spiritual, devotional practice to a widely commercialised and globalised music form reflects the dynamic nature of culture and tradition. While some may lament the secularisation and commercialisation of qawwali, it is undeniable that these changes have allowed the music to thrive in new contexts, reaching audiences that might otherwise have remained outside its influence.

As qawwali continues to evolve, it remains a testament to the power of music to transcend religious, cultural, and geographical boundaries, serving as both a form of spiritual expression and a dynamic global cultural phenomenon. Through its transformative journey, qawwali has demonstrated the resilience of cultural traditions and their ability to adapt to the forces of modernity while maintaining their core identity. Its continued relevance, both within the South Asian diaspora and in the global music scene, underscores its enduring capacity to unite people from different backgrounds, providing a shared space for spiritual and emotional connection. As we look to the future, it is clear that qawwali will continue to evolve, finding new expressions and meanings while remaining deeply rooted in its Sufi origins.

In conclusion, the study of qawwali from an anthropological perspective offers valuable insights into both the art form and the communities that preserve it. As we work to preserve qawwali, it is essential that we understand its spiritual roots and the sacred spaces in which it thrives, while also addressing the economic and cultural challenges posed by commercialisation and modernity. Through a balanced approach that integrates traditional and modern elements, qawwali can continue to inspire and unite, transcending boundaries while remaining true to its origins.

Anthropology, with its emphasis on understanding cultures and traditions in various context, can provide crucial understanding for ensuring that qawwali remains a vibrant, living tradition, capable of adapting to the future without losing its essence. By continuing to support research, fieldwork, and education, we can help safeguard this cherished art form for generations to come. In sum, qawwali is a dynamic cultural system that reflects the complexities of society, spirituality, and individual experience. Its ability to transcend the boundaries of music and religion makes it a unique form of art. As a practice deeply embedded in both sociocultural structures and spiritual practices, qawwali offers valuable insights into the contestations of gender, age, and class. The expanding use of cyber-ethnography provides new avenues for studying this music in the digital age, ensuring its continued relevance across diverse contexts. Finally, the therapeutic effects of qawwali merit further holistic research, as they reveal the profound impact this music can have on both mind and body, offering a symbolic form of healing that has existed for centuries.

نفیس

Bibliography

- Farrell, G. (2016). *The Art of Qawwali: A Study of the Sacred Music of the Sufi Mystics.* Routledge. This book provides a detailed exploration of Qawwali, including its evolution, musical forms, and cultural significance in Sufi practices, supporting the themes of both the great and little traditions.

- Hirschkind, C. (2006). 'The Ethics of Listening: Cassette Sermons and Islamic Counterpublics'. *American Ethnologist*, 33(4), 623-635. Hirschkind's work focuses on the religious significance of music in Islamic cultures, particularly in relation to qawwali, and touches on how modern performances (the Great Tradition) resonate with traditional practices.

- Khan, R. (1996). *The Voice of Nusrat Fateh Ali Khan: A Musical and Cultural Analysis.* Oxford University Press. This work focuses on the life and influence of Nusrat Fateh Ali Khan, one of the leading figures in the global recognition of qawwali, providing insights into the Great Tradition of qawwali as a form of performance.

- Hussain, A. (2007). *Qawwali: The Devotional Music of the Sufis.* Zed Books. Hussain's work provides a thorough overview of the role of qawwali in Sufi religious practices, highlighting both local (Little Tradition) and global (Great Tradition) influences on the art form.

- Hood, M. (1985). 'The Ethnomusicology of the Sufi Mystical Music of South Asia'. *Asian Music*, 17(2), 3-30. This scholarly article explores the relationship between Sufism and music, providing important context for the practice of qawwali, and discusses how qawwali's performance context can shift from the local to the global.

- Nettl, B. (2005). *The Study of Ethnomusicology: Thirty-One Issues and Concepts.* University of Illinois Press. Nettl's work introduces key concepts in ethnomusicology that can be applied to the study of qawwali, including the distinction between Great and Little Traditions in performance and cultural contexts.

- Johnston, Sherilee. 'Poetics of Performance: Narratives, Faith and Disjuncture in Qawwali.' PhD thesis, University of Texas at Austin, 2000.

- Johnston, Sherilee. 'Performance as Discourse: '*Tamaashaa* in the Articulation of Ecstasy during 'Qawwali.' *Text, Practice, Performance.* 1 (1999): 23-34.

- Bhattacharjee, Anuradha and Shadab Alam. 2012. 'The Origin and Journey of Qawwali: From Sacred Ritual to Entertainment.' *Journal of Creative Communications,* 2012.

- Ghosh, S. 2012. 'The Role of Qawwali in Sufi Rituals'. *Journal of South Asian Studies,* 18(1), 71-90. This article discusses the deep religious and cultural significance of qawwali in Sufi rituals, particularly in the Little Tradition, and also touches on how these rituals intersect with public performances.

- Qureshi, R.B. 1986. *Sufi music of India and Pakistan: Sound, context and meaning in Qawwali.* London: Cambridge University Press.

- Newell, James. 'Experiencing Qawwali: Sound as Spiritual Power in Sufi India.' PhD diss., Vanderbilt University, 2007.

- Tiffany, J. 2019. 'Qawwali: The Art of Music and Mysticism'. *Journal of World Music,* 11(2), 255-273. Tiffany's paper looks into the cultural significance of qawwali as a form of musical mysticism and provides an analysis of its evolving role in both traditional and modern contexts.

- Baumann, G. 1999. 'The Complexity of Culture: The Role of Qawwali in the Sufi Tradition'. *Journal of Middle Eastern Music,* 13(1), 23-45. This journal article presents an ethnographic account of qawwali as it operates in both local and more globalised contexts, highlighting how qawwali retains both its religious and cultural relevance.

- Friedmann, A. (2018). 'The Globalization of Qawwali: From Local Shrines to World Music'. *Global Music and Media Studies.* This article provides insights into the globalisation of qawwali and its transition from local performances to international stages, offering a contemporary perspective on the relationship between the Great and Little Traditions.

- Adam Nayyar- 1998- Oriental Star Agencies, Ltd. Islamabad: Lok Virsa Research Center. http://www. osa. co. uk/qawwali_history. html (accessed 4/16/07)

- Atal, Y. (2001). Managing Multiplicity: The Insider-Outsider Duality. Economic and Political Weekly, 36(36), 3459–3466. http://www.jstor.org/stable/4411088

- 'Qawwali: The Mystical Musical Tradition of Sufism.' 2020. BBC Radio 3.

THE DECCAN STORY

Songs of the Heart, Songs of the Soul

Qawwals derive their significance from their personal connection to shrines and silsilas (spiritual orders), maintaining generational allegiance through the addition of the sacred name of the pir (master) like Warsi, Chishti, and Nizami to their own. Their life's journey unfolds through mehfils, singing in perpetual praise of the Almighty.

Qawwals Nazeer and Naseer Ahmad Khan Warsi, though based in Hyderabad, trace their personal connection to the shrine of Dewa Sharif, Barabanki, and its revered saint Waris Pak. Their ancestral journey from Awadh to Delhi to the Deccan, culminating in Hyderabad at the Nizam's invitation, has enriched their compositions with a seamless blend of regional dialects effortlessly woven into their music.

Songs of My Father, Songs for My Children

The brothers Nazeer and Naseer have established a unique legacy by founding a training centre in old Hyderabad, named after their grandfather. Here, they provide formal instruction in classical ragas and qawwali. Their training is meticulous and gives hope that future generations will follow the traditions of qawwali, even with the relentless onslaught of cinema music.

Qawwali, as a performance art, demands years of dedicated practice to be honed to perfection. The practitioner has to be versatile and understand the spiritual context of the words sung for the desired effect on the listener. Each qawwali is rooted in Hindustani classical music's raga system, requiring performers to captivate a randomly converged diverse audience through refined expertise.

A qawwali ensemble, known as a party, typically comprises eight or nine members: the lead singer after whom the party gets its name, one or two side singers, harmonium players, and percussionists playing the tabla and the dholak. The chorus of four or five men who repeat key verses follow the main qawwal who leads the verse, emotionally seeking the grace of the Almighty. They also follow his intense mood with their eyes on him following the emotional journey while maintaining rhythm through synchronised hand clapping, creating a transcendent musical experience. At the centre in old Hyderabad, they train students in all these aspects, some as the lead singers, others as chorus and many others as percussionists.

The oral tradition of qawwali passes from generation to generation, with young artists learning through immersion, observation and singing in mehfils alongside their elders.

Photographer: Dinesh Khanna
Qawwali Practitioners: Nazeer Ahmad Khan Warsi, Naseer Ahmad Khan Warsi
Text: Manjari Chaturvedi
Place: Dargah Hazrat Shah Khamosh, Nampally, Hyderabad, Telangana.
Project: The Qawwali Project

the deccan
story

QAWWALI AND URDU

An Entangled Relationship

Salil Misra

The leading nineteenth- and early twentieth-century Urdu poet Akbar Ilahabadi once wrote in a spirit of pun and taunt:

◆ ◆ ◆

Be hunar banke jo baitho, taana-e Hali suno
Ba hunar banke jo chamko, qaum se gaali suno.
Hamko to peer-e tareeqat ne yahi di hai salaah
Qissa-e Mansoor dekho, aur qawwali suno.

◆ ◆ ◆

(Loosely translated: If you are completely without any talent, you are likely to be ridiculed by Hali (the leading modernist poet of Urdu).
But if you excel and are talented, you would be ridiculed by the community. So, what to do! I have been advised by the wise old one to watch the story of Mansoor and listen to qawwali instead.)

Akbar was hinting in his own way at an Urdu-qawwali connectivity. In popular imagination, the two appear connected to each other through Islam. This affinity has acquired deep roots in popular mind, in spite of the fact that there is nothing distinctively Islamic about Urdu. Not only was no significant religious literature produced in mainstream Urdu, it actually developed a heretical attitude on religious matters, as will be argued later in this essay. The tradition of qawwali too posited itself in opposition to the tenets of high Islam. The mainstream qawwali represented an urge of a deeply spiritual journey towards

God. This access to God could be attained through personal explorations and was not to be mediated through any officially sanctioned doctrine. The major forms of expression that developed in qawwali were songs and dance. These militated against the tenets of high Islam. Sufism was the sacred vehicle qawwali attached itself to. Sufism developed two major forms of articulation—sober and ecstatic. The qawwali was a direct expression of the latter.

So, prima facie, the worlds of qawwali and Urdu do not appear to have any organic and structural link with high Islam. Given their orientation, the two could hardly be expected to find a place of pride within the sacred enclaves of high Islam. Interestingly, at a cursory level, Urdu and qawwali too do not appear to be connected to each other. Qawwali is ecstatic; Urdu, at least in its mainstream form, is abstract and sober. Qawwali is performative; Urdu contemplative. Qawwali is spiritual; Urdu is mainly heretical. Qawwali flourished in khanqahs (sites for the worship of Sufi saints); Urdu thrived on official patronage. Quite clearly, the trajectories of qawwali and Urdu flowed in very different directions.

However, in spite of differences, there are deep structural links between the two. This essay attempts to explore those linkages. This will be done by separately constructing the trajectories of qawwali and Urdu. The essay will then highlight the linkages between the two.

◆ I ◆

Qawwali as a distinct mode of literary, sacred and performative expression was rooted in the Sufi ethos. Sufism needs to be understood not as a single coherent movement but rather as a constellation of religious ideas, attitudes and activities that developed in response to high, doctrinal and scripturalist Islam. There was a great diversity to these attitudes. They took the form of reinforcement, modification, opposition and questioning. In some global studies of Islam, it has been argued that whereas in some cases Sufism posited itself as an alternative to high Islam, in some others, it became a substitute to it. In India, it often became a way (tariqa) of spreading Islam. Upon this view, Islam spread in India through the Turkana tariqa of coercion and conquest and the Sufiana tariqa of persuasion and dialogue. The Sufiana tariqa was more effective in spreading Islam in India than the Turkana tariqa.

As Sufism came to India, it developed three major strands—orthodox, syncretic and rebellious. Each developed its own style and mode of worship. The orthodox Sufism believed in all the tenets of high Islam, and the Quran to be the highest among the books of revelation. The syncretic Sufism tried to bring the tenets of high Islam closer to Vedantic and other Indic religious traditions. A heretical or rebellious Sufism developed towards the seventeenth century, partly as a reaction to Aurangzeb's policies of religious intolerance. They attacked the tenets of high Islam and treated the Quran and Prophet Muhammad (PBUH) at par with prophets of other religions. They celebrated idol worship and various other practices tabooed in high Islam, such as wine drinking.

However, one thing that was common to all these strands was a kind of local connectivity as against the insularity of high Islam. As high Islam sought to construct protective walls around it, Sufism of all brands reached out to other faith systems of the area. That helped to indigenise Islam. In north India, it developed connectivity with the Nath Panthis (a mystic sect withing Hinduism, prevalent in medieval India) and the bhakti tradition in general. This connectivity also led to mutual borrowing and sharing of styles. The bhajan-kirtan (singing of devotional songs) practice of Hinduism found its resonance in the qawwali. In a way, the qawwali was to Islam what bhajan-kirtan was to Hinduism.

Sufism accepted the basic tenets of high Islam, but did focus on alternative ways of establishing communion with God. One such was the way of singing and dancing to reach God. Qawwali became the accepted medium for this.

Qawwali proliferated in India during the Delhi Sultanate. With the establishment of the Sultanate, there was a great influx of scholars and poets from Persia, Arabia and Central Asia. They brought with them different religious styles and rituals. These different styles also played some role in giving qawwali its distinctive features.

Qawwali as a devotional form was fully established around the time of Amir Khusrau, the thirteenth-century poet of Persian and Hindavi, even though its roots go back to earlier times. Qawwali flourished in khanqahs and dargahs, shrines of Sufi saints. It popularised themes pertaining to Islamic cosmology, history and the life of Prophet Muhammad (PBUH). It upheld ideas of monism *(tawheed)*. The syncretic Sufism was also popularised by qawwali. Symbols of high Islam were indigenised and made compatible with local traditions.

The narratives of the birth of Prophet Muhammad (PBUH) were sung in regional languages also. One such narrative, popular in the region of Awadh went thus: *baaro ghee ke diye na/bhayile Amina ke lalana* (light the lamps of ghee/ Amina [Prophet's mother] has been blessed with a son). Likewise, a long qawwali by the Sabri brothers (Ghulam Farid Sabri and Maqbool Ahmed Sabri, leading qawwali singers from Pakistan, active during the 1950s to the 1990s) went into great lengths on the birth of Prophet Muhammad (PBUH): *Abdulla ke ghar se jahaan mein noor bikharne waala hai/Daai Haleema gode mein teri chaand utarne waala hai* (From Abdulla's house light is going to spread to the world/The moon is about to land in Halima's lap). Qawwali provided lyrical expression to all the major themes of orthodox Sufism.

Likewise, syncretic Sufism too received expression from qawwali. A major concern of the qawwali was also to explore devotional practices Islam shared with other faiths, particularly Hinduism. The life stories of Ram and Krishna were blended with Islamic mythology. Kashi and Mathura were sung about along with Mecca and Medina. Lives of Sufi saints were extolled along with those of Hindu poets such as Mirabai. Syncretic qawwalis became very popular and broke out of their sanctioned times and spaces. Qawwalis were originally sung and performed in dargahs and usually on Thursdays. In its syncretic form the qawwali broke out of this convention and reached out to general public platforms.

The third major thematic input was towards rebellious and heretical qawwali. In this form, heresy was celebrated and wine drinking was projected almost as a sacred act. The major tenets of high Islam were subjected to ridicule. One representative example of heretical qawwali is by Aziz Mian (1942-2000, leading qawwal from Pakistan): *Bakhsh deta to baat kuchh bhee na thee* ('Forgiveness should not have been difficult for you,' an appeal to God). The entire qawwali is addressed to God to consider granting mercy to the qawwal for all his sins and allow him a place in the heaven. Defiance, challenge and derision have all been employed in this appeal to God. All the institutions and authorial figures of Islam are ridiculed and subordinated to the qawwal himself who represents all humanity. The qawwal is the direct descendent of Adam and therefore the most rightful claimant of a place in heaven. It is part of his inheritance and cannot be taken away from him. The qawwal also questions the legitimacy of the angels who are going to pass the verdict on his conduct. The qawwal has sinned all his life. All the virtuous people should be grateful to sinners because it is only in relation to sins that virtues can be identified. Sins and virtues complement each other. If the sinners did not exist, who would ever praise the virtuous? The sinners also give God an opportunity to be merciful and thus do his duty. If the sinners did not sin, God would have nothing to do. If God did not forgive, he would fail in his duty. Therefore, there is a complementary relationship between sinners and God; sinners enable God to do his duty. The entire qawwali is sung in a blasphemous and defiant spirit.

In style it appears to be inspired by *Shikwa*, a long Urdu poem of complaint to God, written by Iqbal, the doyen of twentieth-century Urdu poetry.[1] *Shikwa* was written in 1909 and acquired a cult status in the pantheon of Urdu poetry almost immediately. Four years later, Iqbal wrote *Jawab-i Shikwa*, which was a reply from God to the complaints of Muslims. Iqbal's *Shikwa* elevated a mere act of complaint to the level of a literary genre. Aziz Mian's qawwali, *Bakhsh deta*... followed the same pattern of a complaining dialogue with God. But whereas in Iqbal's *Shikwa* the complainant is a faithful Muslim, unhappy with the plight of Muslims in modern world, the complainant in Aziz Mian's qawwali, is heretical and a sinner, very proud of his sins and yet a claimant to a place in heaven. Here are some chosen lines from the long qawwali:

◆

Hamne gunaah kiye to numaaya hua karam
Ham begunaah hote to kehta kareem kaun

◆

(It was only when I sinned, that the opposite of sin,
kindness appeared.
If I had remained sinless,
who would call you benevolent and merciful?)

◆

Tumko Kareem jaanke maine gunaah kiye

◆

(I sinned because I knew you were merciful, O God)

◆

Munkir-e Rahmat-e Khuda Rahna
Kufr hai itna paakza rahna

◆

(The real heresy is in being so pure and righteous.
It is a denial of the kindness of God.)

In its celebration of heresy, it really matches the mainstream Urdu poetry. The qawwali ends by denouncing the desire for heaven, by reciting the famous couplet of Zauq, the leading nineteenth-century Urdu poet:

◆

Aisi Jannat ko kya karoon lekar,
jisme laakhon baras ki hooren hon.

◆

(What use is heaven for me,
which has houries lakhs of years old?)

Qawwali became socially more popular when it broke free from Sufi shrines and entered the public sphere in general. It also entered Bombay cinema in the 1960s. Once in popular cinema, a whole range of themes—from romantic to patriotic—were added to it. From the 1980s, there has been a general decline of qawwali in Bombay cinema, even though as a popular medium it has continued to retain its charm and popularity.

◆ II ◆

The Urdu trajectory has been very similar to qawwali in many ways. Urdu may be considered a modern literary language with a very rich prehistory. Its prehistory connects with the history of qawwali. A proto-Urdu flourished in Delhi, Punjab, Gujarat and Dakan, through the medieval times, the same zones where qawwali also proliferated. It had a great Persian connectivity and borrowed many of its forms—ghazal, qasida (panegyric), marsia (elegy)—from it. However, even though Persian was a major influence, it was not the only one. Around the eighteenth century, Urdu carried within it multiple literary influences. It also took over many literary genres from Sanskrit, such as Barah Maasa (descriptions of the seasons) and Saraapa Nigaari (descriptions of physical beauty and body parts)—generally not found in Persian. These proliferated in Urdu in the eighteenth century. An Indic rootedness coexisted along with a Persian connectivity.

However, during the period after the eighteenth century, its Indic rootedness was considerably weakened and eroded, whereas the Persian connectivity got more entrenched. This happened at the level of architecture, form and content. Many terms of local Indic origin began to be discarded and replaced with their Persian and Arabic counterparts. This constituted a big break and the Urdu that developed from eighteenth century onwards was very different from its earlier literary expressions. It is however interesting that no such disjunction happened to the world of qawwali, in which all the older terms continued to be used with great gusto. This factor alone made Urdu and qawwali look different from each other. Words such as vastu, dehi, preetam, praan, pyaare, nain, mukh, sobha, hirday, ban, etc., (modified derivatives from Sanskrit and other regional languages) that were used abundantly in pre-Urdu, began to be discarded after the eighteenth century in preference to their Persian and Arabic counterparts. But they continued to be generously used in qawwali. There is another explanation why the languages employed by Urdu poetry and qawwali began to move apart from each other.

It has been argued by Amrit Rai in his book *A House Divided* that around eighteenth century there were three different Persian styles prevalent in poetry in India: Khorasani, Iraqi and Indian.[2] Urdu modelled itself on the Indian style that was ornate, 'florid turgid, full of exaggeration, with an abundant use of literary ornamentation', to convey complex and abstract philosophical ideas. Qawwali, on the other hand continued to use the old style that was simple, natural and musical.

However, at a deeper, more substantive level, Urdu and qawwali retained their thematic connectivity. Particularly two of qawwali's main concerns—heresy and syncretism—found full expression in Urdu also. The expressions of heresy, syncretism and rebellion against doctrinal Islam entered Urdu poetry through the eighteenth-century poet Mir Taqi Mir, arguably the greatest Urdu poet of all times. Since then, these traits became the dominant template of Urdu. Much of what Mir wrote was suffused with these traits. Some examples can be mentioned here:

• ◆ •

Mir ke deen-o mazhab ko ab poochhte kya ho unne to
Qashqa khaincha dair mein baitha kab ka tark Islam kiya[3]

• ◆ •

(Why do you ask about Mir's religion and faith?
He has drawn a sacred mark on his forehead,
sat in a temple and given up Islam a long time ago.)

• ◆ •

Kufr kuchh chaahiye Islam ki raunak ke liye
Husn zunnaar hai tasbeeh-e Sulemaani ka[4]

• ◆ •

(Islam needs to be decorated with some heresy.
Soloman's beads are beautified by the sacred thread
of Hinduism.)

• ◆ •

But parasti ko to Islam naheen kehte hain
Motaqid kaun ho Mir aisi musalmaani ka[5]

• ◆ •

(Something nice as idol worship does not exist in Islam.
Who is going to have faith in such Islam?)

• ◆ •

Ham na kahte the ki mat dair-o haram ki chaal chal
Ab ye daawa hashr tak Shaikh-o Barahman mein raha[6]

• ◆ •

(I warned you against following the ways of temple
and mosque. Let these battles be sorted out between
the Shaikh and the Brahman.)

⬩ ◆ ⬩

Yaaraan-e dair-o Kaaba donon bula rahe hain
Ab dekhen Mir apna jaana kidhar bane hai[7]

⬩ ◆ ⬩

(The stakeholders from both Kaaba and the temple
are calling out to me.
Now it is for Mir to decide where to go.)

All these ideas containing both syncretism and heresy were expressed in a lyrical form in qawwali also. They have brought Urdu very close to the basic orientation of qawwali. However, quite apart from being rooted in the same matrix of a thematic orientation, many other similarities of style and expression can also be discerned.

One of the earliest commentaries on qawwali highlighted the difference between the form and the content of qawwali. Whereas the form was singing and dancing, the content was the dissolution of the self in God. The commentary said: 'You must know that dancing *(raqs)* has no foundation either in the religious law (of Islam) or in the path (of Sufism), ... but when the head throbs with exhilaration and rapture becomes intense and the agitation of ecstasy is manifested ... that agitation is neither dancing nor foot play nor bodily indulgence, but a dissolution. Those who call it "dancing" are utterly wrong. It is a state that cannot be explained in words: "without experience, no knowledge."'[8] In this passage, the commentator tried to provide justification for the un-Islamic *forms* of qawwali by focusing on its essentially Islamic *content*. This distinction between form and content was highlighted centuries later by Ghalib who tried to provide a similar justification for the un-Islamic imageries employed in his poetry:

⬩ ◆ ⬩

Maqsad hai naaz-o gamza wale guftagoo mein kaam,
Chalta naheen hai dashna-o khanjar kahe baghair.
Harchand ho mushaahdah-e haq ki guftagoo,
Banti naheen hai baada-o saaghar kahe baghair.[9]

⬩ ◆ ⬩

(Loosely translated: Even when the purpose is to describe the beauty and manners of the lover, it cannot be done without referring to knife and dagger. Even when the discourse is about the eternal truth of God, it cannot be done without referring to the wine and the goblet.)

Most significantly, love (Ishq) was easily the most significant arena for the thematic affinity between Urdu and qawwali. As mainstream Urdu developed since the eighteenth century, it offered a range of perspectives on the theme of love and enlarged its dimensions. Vali Dakkani (late seventeenth-early eighteenth century, also known as Vali Aurangabadi), generally considered as the grand old man of Urdu poetry (Baba-e Rekhta), created a taxonomy of love—abstract and concrete, this worldly and otherworldly, of God and of fellow humans—and celebrated them all. One typical couplet of this flavour goes as follows:

• ◆ •

Shaghal behtar hai ishq baazi ka
Kya haqeeqi o kya majaazi ka

• ◆ •

(Indulgence with Love is a good idea. How does it matter whether it is other worldly or this worldly?)

With Mir, this simple celebration of love entered into a nuanced terrain. Mir's poetry was steeped in love, but the expression of love took multiple forms—lament, separation, cruelty, treachery, pathos and destructiveness. Mir has generally been considered a poet of 'wailing, moan and sigh', a poet of 'aah' as against 'waah'. Following are some examples of this melancholy:

• ◆ •

Shaam se kuchh bujha sa rahta hai
Dil hua hai chiraagh muflis ka

• ◆ •

(It feels cheerless and depressed with the coming
of the evening.
My heart is like a pauper's dimly-burning lamp.)

⬩ ◆ ⬩

Daaghe-e firaaq o hasrat-e vasl aarzu-e shauq
Main saath zere khaak bhee hangama le gaya

⬩ ◆ ⬩

(Pangs of separation, yearnings for union,
intense passion behold.
What a tumult I took with me into the grave!)

⬩ ◆ ⬩

Dil mujhe is gali mein le jaakar
Aur bhee khaak mein mila laaya

⬩ ◆ ⬩

(By luring me into the street of the beloved,
My heart has made me even more miserable
than before)[10]

However, in spite of these nuances, the older approach of fusing ishq-e haqeeqi and ishq-e majazi (otherworldly and this worldly love) and treating them as part of a single whole, continued with Mir also. In sharp contrast with the approach reflected in the couplets mentioned above, Mir also elevated love from its narrow, romantic confines and treated it as a universal, all-encompassing, omnipresent emotion:

⬩ ◆ ⬩

Ishq hi ishq hai jahaan dekho,
saare aalam mein bhar raha hai ishq
Ishq maashuq ishq aashiq hai,
yaani apna hi mubtala hai ishq.
Kaun maqsad ko ishq bin pahuncha,
aarzu ishq mudda' hai ishq.

⬩ ◆ ⬩

(Love is all over.
The whole world has been filled by it.
Love is the lover, and also the beloved.

In other words, love is its own entanglement.
Who was able to fulfil his/her objectives sans love?
Love is the desire, and also the purpose.)

And again,

⬩ ◆ ⬩

Dard hi khud hai, khud dawa hai ishq,
Shaikh kya jaane tu ki kya hai ishq
Ye na hove to nazm kul uth jaaye,
Sachche hain shaayraan khuda hai ishq.

⬩ ◆ ⬩

(Love is the agony and also the cure for agony.
O Shaikh [the righteous one],
what do you know what love is?
But for love, the whole system will collapse.
The poets are right in saying that love is God indeed!)[11]

It was this particular perspective on love which had a great appeal for qawwali and which was popularised in a big way by qawwali. The different forms of love fused in such a way that it was difficult to separate them. Also, love became a metaphor for unions of various kind. In qawwali, love became a template for a whole range of emotions and situations—romance, devotion, immersion, sublimation, interfaith harmony, and the ultimate union with God. Love was sacralised and transcendentalised. One qawwali from the film Barsat ki Raat (1960) written by Sahir Ludhianvi, captures this range in all its glory and splendour:

⬩ ◆ ⬩

Ishq azaad hai, Hindu na Musalmaan hai ishq,
Aap hi dharm hai aur aap hi imaan hai ishq.
Jisse agaah nahin Shaikh o Barahman donon,
Us haqeeqat ka garajta hua ailaan hai ishq.
Allah aur Rasool ka farmaan ishq hai,
Yaani Hadees ishq hai Quran ishq hai.
Gautam aur Maseeh ka armaan ishq hai,
Ye kaaynaat jism hai aur jaan ishq hai.

Khaak ko but aur but ko devta karta hai ishq,
Intiha ye hai ki bande ko Khuda karta hai ishq.

⬩ ◆ ⬩

(Love is freedom. It is neither Hindu nor Muslim.
It is its own faith and its own morality.
Love is the resounding declaration of reality,
which neither the Shaikh nor the Brahman is aware of.
Love is the mandate from God and the Prophet.
In other words, love is both Hadees and the Quran.
Love is the desire of both Gautam and Christ.
If the cosmos is the body, love is life in it.
Love turns dust into idol and idol into the deity.
Ultimately love transforms mortals into God.)

Urdu poetry and qawwali followed very different styles. But they were joined with each other through their great fascination and preoccupation with love, mysticism, heresy and syncretism. These themes brought both Urdu and qawwali together.

⬩ III ⬩

The exact relationship between qawwali and Urdu was quite complex and cannot be understood through simple categories of being similar or dissimilar. It would be more accurate to say that the relationship between the two was more like interpenetrating circles, in which some space was mutually shared and some space was exclusively occupied by each circle. In spite of being related to each other through concern and orientation, and also being distantly related to Islam, both qawwali and Urdu maintained their autonomous zones.

Qawwali developed in India through the Sufi route and played an important role in disseminating Sufi Islam through music and dance. These were considered the appropriate medium for a communion with God. Qawwalis were sung at Chishti dargahs and at urs (fairs in celebration of the death anniversary of Sufi saints). The initial themes were mystical love, praise for God and for Prophet Muhammad (PBUH), and a longing for the divine. In time to come qawwali developed a syncretic and a heretical dimension. The syncretic qawwali developed connectivities with the bhakti traditions and with other forms of popular Hinduism. The heretical qawwali acquired a blasphemous tone and subjected scripturalist Islam to ridicule. It celebrated idolatry and wine drinking. Qawwali employed a language that was Indic and borrowed heavily from many regional languages such as Awadhi, Sindhi, Punjabi and Dakni. In modern times it delinked itself from earlier support systems such as the Sufi centres and entered the public spheres. At all times, the qawwali was much less inspired by the elite and doctrinal traditions and much more by folk ones.

Urdu, by contrast, developed very differently. It acquired its distinctive features through an excessive Persianisation of a popular composite language tradition called Hindavi. Since the eighteenth century, mainstream Urdu moved away from the Indic literary traditions, of which it had been a part, and acquired an architecture that was heavily Persianised. In its Persianised incarnation, it appeared very different from qawwali, which had retained its Indic rootedness. However, even when their texture was very different, they remained deeply connected to each other, through their thematic orientation. Themes of love, syncretism and heresy remained very central to both Urdu poetry and qawwali. They both provided a wholesome expression to these themes, though in their own ways.

Given these common concerns, it is not surprising that both Urdu poetry and qawwali entered Bombay cinema in a big way, Urdu since the 1950s and qawwali since the 1960s. It may not be a coincidence that both have experienced a decline in the popular Hindi cinema since the 1990s. However, they have retained their charm and popularity and still continue to enthrall their lovers and followers.

Endnotes

1. Muhammad Iqbal, *Shikwa and Jawab-i Shikwa* (Complaint and Answer), Iqbal's Dialogue with Allah (SWT), translated into English by Khushwant Singh, Oxford University Press, New Delhi, 1981.

2. Amrit Rai, *A House Divided: The Origin and Development of Hindi-Urdu,* Oxford University Press, Delhi, 1991, p. 232.

3. Ali Sardar Jafri, *Deewan-e Mir*, 8.12

4. Ibid.

5. Ibid., 5.7

6. Ibid. 56.2

7. Ibid., 501.4

8. This essence of qawwali was explained in an eleventh-century passage by a patron saint of Lahore. Quote in Edward O Henry, 'The Rationalization of Intensity in Indian Music', *Ethnomusicology*, Vol. 46, No. 1, 2002, University of Illinois, Illinois, p, 39.

9. *Deewan-e Ghalib*, 60.6-7

10. All these selections and their English translations are from Muhammad Sadiq, *A History of Urdu Literature*, Oxford University Press, Delhi, 1984, pp. 132-33.

11. From Sri Ramnath Suman, *Mir* (in Hindi), Bhartiya Gyanpeeth, New Delhi, 1999, pp. 130-31.

Bibliography

- Bhattacharya, Haridas (ed.), *The Cultural Heritage of India,* Vol. IV, The Religions, The Ramakrishna Mission Institute of Culture, Calcutta, 1956.

- Chatterji, Suniti Kumar, 'Islamic Mysticism, Iran and India', in Chatterji, Suniti Kumar, *Select Papers,* Vol.1, People's Publishing House, New Delhi, 1972.

- Gellner, Ernest, *Muslim Society,* Cambridge University Press, Cambridge, 1981.

- Henry, Edward O, 'The Rationalization of Intensity in Indian Music', in *Ethnomusicology,* Vol. 46, No. 1, University of Illinois, Illinois, 2002.

- Iqbal, Muhammad, *Shikwa and Jawab-i Shikwa,* (translated from Urdu to English by Khushwant Singh), Oxford University Press, New Delhi, 1981.

- Jafri, Ali Sardar (ed.), *Deewan-e Gahlib,* Hindustani Book Trust, Bombay, 1958.

- Jafri, Ali Sardar (ed.), *Deewan-e Mir,* Hindustani Book Trust, Bombay, 1960.

- Rai, Amrit, *A House Divided: The Origin and Development of Hindi-Urdu,* Oxford University Press, Delhi, 1991.

- Robinson, Francis (ed.), *The Cambridge Illustrated History of the Islamic World,* Cambridge University Press, Cambridge, 1996.

- Sadiq, Muhamad, *A History of Urdu Literature,* Oxford University Press, Delhi, 1984.

- Safvi, Rana, *In Search of the Divine: Living Histories of Sufism in India,* Hachette India, Gurugram, 2022.

- Suman, Sri Ramnath, *Mir* (in Hindi), Bhartiya Gyanpeeth, New Delhi, 1999

FATEHPUR SIKRI

The Saint and His Magnificence

Shaikh Salim Chishti, a greatly revered Sufi mystic of the Chishti order in India, was known for his miraculous powers. Devotees believe that prayers offered at his mazar (shrine) fulfil wishes, leading to the tradition of tying threads at the marble windows of the dargah. These threads become symbols of aspirations, finally untied in gratitude when wishes are granted. The saint's legacy lives in this constant rhythm of hope and gratitude, marked by countless threads tied and untied at the pir's shrine.

Tell Me a Story, of Yesterday, of Today

The qawwals preserve and share stories of pilgrims seeking the saint's blessings. Among the most celebrated is that of Emperor Akbar, who walked barefoot through the desert to this sacred place, seeking an heir to his throne. After receiving Shaikh Salim Chishti's blessings, Akbar was blessed with three sons—the first named Salim in the saint's honour, later known to the world as Emperor Jahangir. Such was Akbar's devotion that he built the magnificent city of Fatehpur Sikri around the Saint's humble dwelling, creating the awe-inspiring tomb that stands today as testament to this spiritual legacy. The entrance to the shrine is through the majestic Buland Darwaza, that seems to reach to the sky. It leads people to the vast expanse of space that seems endless as the eyes try and grasp the vision of the serene white shrine set against the red sandstone fort. An architectural marvel.

This narrative of Akbar walking barefoot, seeking an heir to his throne, continues to draw people to the shrine daily, many seeking the miracle of parenthood. While the number of fulfilled wishes remains unknown, the legend of the saint's benevolence endures, woven into the fabric of the shrine's living history.

Of Faith, of Hope. All in a Song

Poet: Kaifi Azmi

Sookhi rut mein chhaayi badariya, chamki bijuriya saath
Doobo tum bhi sang mere, ya thaamo mera haath

Maula Salim Chishti, Aaqa Salim Chishti
Aabaad kar do dil ki duniya Salim Chishti

Jitni balaayein aayi, sab ko gale lagaaya
Khoon ho gaya kaleja, shiqwa na lab pe aaya
Har dard ham ne apna, apne se bhi chhupaaya
Tum se nahin hai koi parda Salim Chishti

Jayega kaun aake pyaasa tumhare dar se
Kuch jam se peeyengey, kuch meherban nazar se
Yeh sang e dar tumhara todeygey apne sar se
Yeh dil agar dubara toota Salim Chishti

Maula Salim Chishti, Aaqa Salim Chishti

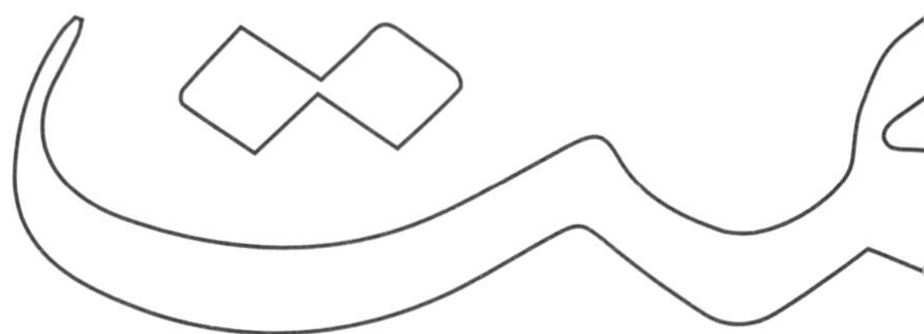

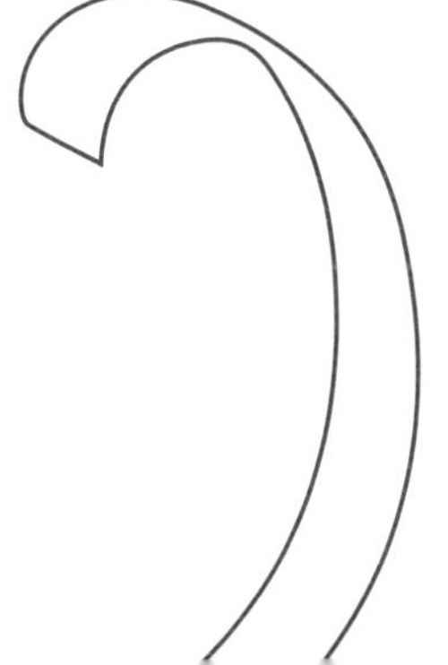

This is a favourite of the qawwals as they sit in the courtyard facing the entrance to the shrine and sing their hearts out for the benevolent sheikh. Their voices reach out to the skies. Nothing is hidden from the saint. He knows everything that is in the heart of the seeker, and he gives without any restraint. No one goes empty handed from the threshold of Sheikh Salim Chishti.

At the dargah, qawwali transcends mere performance to become a spiritual conduit between pilgrims and performers. Songs of varying length flow one into another as listeners sit in quiet contemplation, each finding their personal connection to the music, the saint, and the divine. The qawwals seek grace for everyone present, their voices becoming the collective prayer of the pilgrims.

Photographer: Mustafa Quraishi
Qawwali Practitioner: Qawwal Saleem Hasan Chishti
Text: Manjari Chaturvedi
Place: Dargah Shaikh Saleem Chishti, Fatehpur Sikri, Agra, Uttar Pradesh
Project: The Qawwali Project

fatehpur
sikri

Sanatani Qawwali

Manjari Chaturvedi

auwali Bahar*, a thirty-two page booklet, written by Pandit Mannilal Mishra and published in 1935 by Babu Baijnath Prasad Bookseller,[1] is an unusual document. It is written in Awadhi, a popular language spoken in a wide area in and around Uttar Pradesh. Notably, Awadhi is also the language of many literary works, including those by Goswami Tulsidas and a wide range of bhakti literature. This archival document is the main thrust of this essay—to assess the times and the cultural belief of society in which a writer, clearly a Brahmin pandit, uses qawwali, a music form associated with Sufi Islam, to write and compose devotional poetry for Hindu gods.

It would have been a regular Hindu religious document if it was simply a collection of poetry under the title of 'bhajans'. It is, however, titled 'Kauwali'. If viewed through the lens of our subcontinent's composite history and shared culture, there are numerous instances of Hindu poets writing marsiya (elegies) during Muharram (the sacred month of Muslims) and of Muslim poets writing on the Hindu gods Krishna and Rama. Here, in a unique manner the bhajan and the qawwali merge into one. Bhajans written as and called 'Kauwali'. The spelling of the word qawwali in the title of the booklet, derived from the way it is written in the Devanagari script, is unique too. The pronunciation, with a stress on 'au', the sound of the two vowels used together, is different from the way we pronounce qawwali today. Today, the word 'qawwali' lays more stress is on the phonetic sound of 'w' which is used twice in the spelling.

Historical Background

In 1935, when this was published, India was still undivided. This also brings forth the idea that qawwali was a popular music form and it was perhaps normal for qawwalis on Hindu Gods to be written and published without the fear of the book being banned.

The place where this is published is Benares (Varanasi). The city is well known as the city of Shiva since ancient times. It is closely associated with the Hindu religion and has great relevance for Hindus. Regarded as the spiritual capital of India, the city draws Hindu pilgrims who bathe in Ganga's sacred waters. It is also the chosen destination to perform funeral rites, and the river and the city are revered for this. Interestingly, along the city's winding streets are thousands of small and big temples which are at places interspersed with Muslim holy sites. The city of Benares is also of literary importance. It is largely a city of pandits, of Hindu scholars learned in Sanskrit and Hindu philosophy and religion, and of practising priests.

Scholar and academic Gopi Chand Narang opines, 'In its present form the qawwali is first and foremost an exquisite manifestation of the music and culture born from the interaction of Hinduism and Islam. As a music form it belongs exclusively to the Indian subcontinent and began to develop after the advent of Islam.'[2] He further states, 'It is also necessary to take into account aspects of the composite nature of Indo-Islamic society, of the shared culture and the obvious similarity between the qawwali and the Indian ritualistic temple singing known as bhajan-kirtan.'

This becomes clear and evident in *Kauwali Bahar*. The songs in the forty-odd bhajan-qawwali in this booklet span a wide range—from veneration of Indian Gods to the mythological stories that people are already well versed with. They are written in a lucid and understandable manner for the general public at large. Hence, instead of the formal Sanskrit language, it is written in Awadhi.

The famed *Ganga-Jamuni tehzeeb* emanates from the two major rivers that meander through most of north and central India, the Ganga and the Yamuna. It refers to the confluence of two different cultures, Hindu and Muslim. Most Hindu religious sites and important cities like Benares, Haridwar, Rishikesh are on the banks of the Ganga, while cities like Agra and Delhi, largely associated with Muslim rulers, are on the banks of the Yamuna. Vrindavan and Mathura, however, defy this stereotype. All of Lord Krishna's dalliance with the gopis and Radha Rani took place on the banks of the Yamuna and not the Ganga! Krishna, the Hindu god, even defies the Sufi Islam concept of the poetic content in qawwali, since we have a whole treatise written on Krishna which is sung by qawwals all over the subcontinent. Sufi saint Turab Ali Shah Qalandar and poets like Raskhan, Ibne Insha, Muztar Khairabadi have all written on Krishna, and their poetry is actively sung by qawwals. The qawwali *'Kanhaiya, yaad hai kuch bhi hamari'*, sung by Fareed Ayaz and Abu Mohammad, qawwals from Pakistan, is dedicated to Lord Krishna and has millions of views on YouTube. However, for argument's sake if we go along with the stereotype that the Ganga is sacred only for Hindus and that Varanasi is the holiest of Hindu cities, this particular document opens up layers of the city and its culture and cosmopolitan nature that we perhaps don't know.

Academics and historians are of the view that both Hazrat Moinuddin Chisti and Hazrat Nizamuddin Auliya, the two foremost Sufi saints of the Chishti silsila (Sufi order), credited with the creation of the qawwali as it exists today in the subcontinent, were said to be greatly influenced by the bhajan and rasgan traditions of Hindu temples. Scholar Jacob D. Fishel opines, 'If one were to witness people in India singing and dancing in glory of their God or praying and prostrating at the tombs of men they hold holy, one may think that these are Hindu devotees. And while Hindus do perform these activities, it is just as commonly performed by the Sufi orders that exist throughout the Muslim world and have had a home in India for centuries.'[3]

Poetic content of *Kauwali Bahar*

Pandit Mannilal Mishra's *Kauwali Bahar* has qawwalis for Lord Ram, on *Sita Haran* (the abduction of Sita), an invocation to Lord Ganesha, a qawwali on Lord Shiva (Kashi Vishwanath), on Hanuman, on Devi Durga and even a heretical qawwali for Lord Brahma. It tells us of a cosmopolitan and syncretic society that was completely at ease before the impending partition, a partition based on religion which happened only a decade later. There is no way of knowing the thoughts of Pandit Mannilal Mishra except by decoding the poetic content, where each composition is clearly titled as a 'Kauwali' and not a bhajan. The booklet begins with an invocation written for the Hindu god Ganesha.

॥ Prarthana Ganesh-ji Ki Kauwali ॥

dhyaun pratham tumhe Ganraj puran kaaj bananey wale
sohey lambodar ekdant, karivar aanan prabha anant,
bhraje char bhuja, chavivant, dushtan maan ghataney wale

'I take your name first, O Gajanan, the one who helps in completion of all works.' In Hinduism, Ganesha is primarily known as the 'remover of obstacles' and the 'lord of beginnings'. Ganesha, son of Lord Shiva, is always invoked at the start of rituals and ceremonies, as the one who can bring good fortune. Following this Hindu tradition, the first qawwali in this book is dedicated to Lord Ganesha. The various names of Ganesha used in this are typical of a bhajan: Lambodar, Ekdant, depicted with an elephant head. Then it goes on to describe the Lord with his four arms and modak (sweet) in one hand, trishul (trident) in the other.

Interestingly, there is a unique qawwali dedicated to Sanatan Dharma (the Hindu way of life) in the booklet.

॥ Kauwali Sanatan Dharm ॥

Arpan kari nij tan dhan dhaam mitron dharm sanatan paalo
Mano ved puran nigam ko, kije shradh pitr tarpan ko
Puja vipr sant gauwan ko, nish din hari pad preeti badhalo
Arpan kari nij tan dhan dhaam mitron dharm sanatan paalo

The poet describes the rituals of Sanatan Dharma and exhorts people to follow them and also at the same time rebukes Brahmins for not doing enough for the faith. 'O friends! Dedicate your body, mind, and wealth to preserving Sanatan Dharma; offer food to others in honour of your ancestors (shradh), perform the ancient rituals and be loving and compassionate to others. Establish sabhas (gatherings), educate and turn the fools into learned people, O Pandits! at least do some work and take some pains.'

॥ Kauwali Hanuman-ji Ki ॥

Dhan Dhan mahaveer Bajrang, Raavan Lank jaraney wale,
Aagya Raghunandan ki paaye, pahuche gadh Lanka mein jaaye

Krodhit ho di aag lagaye, Ram ke kaam banane wale
Dhan Dhan mahaveer Bajrang, Ravan lank jaraney wale

This is a qawwali dedicated to Lord Hanuman. It describes the antics of Lord Hanuman when he reaches Lanka and meets Sita to give her the message of Rama. Most of the popular stories from the Ramayana have been rendered as qawwalis in *Kauwali Bahar*. There is a qawwali, *'Kauwali Sita Haran Leela'*, that tells the story of how Ravana abducted Sita from the forest. There's also a qawwali on the separation of Lord Rama and Sita and the resultant emotional upheaval, *'Kauwali Ram Virah Leela'*. There's *'Kauwali Mandodari Vinay Raavan Se'*, where Mandodari pleads with Ravana to give Sita back to Rama, or else there would be only destruction and devastation.

॥ Kauwali Shriram Chandra Ki ॥

Dhan dhan Ram Chandra bhagwan lila lalit dikhane wale
Naumi chaitshukl guruvar, linho awadh nagar avtar,
Ghar ghar bhayo mangalachar, tribhuvan yash phailane wale
Dhan dhan Ram Chandra bhagwan lila lalit dikhane wale

This qawwali celebrates the birth of Lord Rama on the ninth day of Chaitra Shukl Paksh (the date according to the Hindu calendar). It goes on to describe the various deeds done by Rama, by saving Ahilya, the cursed wife of Rishi Gautama who had turned her into stone and who was finally released from the curse by Lord Rama. It also narrates the swayamvar of Rama and Sita, where Rama not only holds Shiva's bow, but also breaks it after which Sita garlands him. The poet's name 'Mannilal' finds a mention at the end of every qawwali.

Lord Krishna is the other popular Hindu god for whom many qawwalis have been written in this booklet on the various aspects of Krishna's life—his childhood *('Kauwali Baal Leela')*, stealing butter *('Kauwali Makhan Chori Leela')*, of him holding the mountain on his little finger to save the village from incessant rain *('Kauwali Govardhan Leela')*, of the raas (the mystical night of dance) with gopis *('Kauwali Raas Leela')*, of the gopis pining for Krishna when he moves to Mathura, of Radha Rani feigning anger and Krishna trying to placate her, of saving Draupadi (the wife of the Pandavas) from disgrace at the hands of the Kauravas *('Kauwali Cheerharan Leela')*.

॥ Kauwali Maniharin Leela ॥

Pahuche barsaney mein jaaye, ban maniharan shyam chabeeley
Nakh shikh saje shri yadurai, mohi murati lai banayi,
Radha ki dhyodi par aaye, thithhke sundar sajan sajilay
Pahuche barsaney mein jaaye, ban maniharan shyam chabeeley

This qawwali describes the joyful dalliance of Krishna with the gopis as he goes to Barsaney (the village of Radha Rani) playfully disguised as a maniharan (the bangle seller) and finds himself surrounded by gopis. Looking through the disguise, Priya-ji (Radha) asks the bangle seller, 'O deceitful one! Show me the bangles that would never break or open and will stay with me forever ... the eternal bangles.'

Gopi Chand Narang makes an interesting point which comes through in the booklet. 'The fusion of Muslim and Indian concepts, which could not be completely achieved at religious level, manifested itself fully in music and other fine arts. In Indian music the khayal is considered to be the invention of the Muslims. Not only did it become popular among the Hindus, but without its existence it is impossible to even conceive of Indian music. In the same way, the Muslims eagerly adopted the dhrupad, which is an ancient form of indigenous singing.'[4]

॥ Kauwali Kavi Chaturta ॥

Bhule Brahma-ji maharaj saari srishti banane wale
Kinhi kaarigari apaar, yukti se racha sakal sansar
Tis par bhi na kiya vichar, chuk gaye chatur kahane wale
Bhule Brahma-ji maharaj saari srishti banane wale

This qawwali is dedicated to Lord Brahma and is full of humour, exactly like what is witnessed in the heretical Urdu poetry in qawwalis. In Hinduism, Brahma is one of the three major gods (tridev). He is the creator of the universe, Vishnu is the preserver and Shiva the destroyer. It is believed that between these three gods they keep the balance of the universe intact. The poet mocks Brahma by addressing him thus: 'You created this world and yet you forgot to create discerning features in humans? For you should have given horns on the heads of the thieves and a clear long visible tail to liars, so that they were easily identified. You should have given small beady eyes to the lampat (lewd ones) so that they wouldn't see clearly and fall in every ditch on their own. These identifying features would have made it easy for decent and respectable people to stay away from unwanted ones.' Towards the end, the poet brazenly goes on to say that if someone with four heads ends up making such glaring mistakes, what can be said for simple one-headed people (like us). Brahma is traditionally depicted with four heads which symbolise his ability to perceive and oversee all aspects of creation and the universe.

॥ Kauwali Nasihat ॥

Hai yeh ishq bura janjaal pyarey ishq koi na karna
Aashiq shama pe ho parwana jalta hai, misle deewana,
Manni lal ishq manmaana, karna toh us rab ka karna.
Hai yeh ishq bura janjaal pyarey ishq koi na karna

॥ Kauwali Nasihat ॥

Bachna maashukon se yaar hain ye aafat ke parkale
Jisne kari buton ki chah, beshak ho hi gaya tabah,
Chhani khak darbadar, aah, aakhir hue jaan ke laaley
Bachna maashukon se yaar hain ye aafat ke parkale

The booklet even has a few qawwalis as above, those that counsel or preach (nasihat) and condemn (hikarat). Interestingly, these qawwalis use Urdu words like maashook (lover), ustad (master), kaafir (non-believers), aashiq (lover), zulf (hair), ishq (love). It is important to note that in 'Kauwalis' written for the Hindu gods, Urdu words are absent, while in the above ones Urdu words are freely used. This also suggests that the poet/author had equal knowledge of Urdu language to use that effectively as and when he desired.

Scholarly perspectives on the bhajan-qawwali bridge

Though the publication of the booklet demonstrates a bridge between the two musical forms of bhajan and qawwali, whether these were ever actually sung by qawwals cannot be said with any certainty. There is no record as yet. However, the bhajan–qawwali bridge exists even today and bhajan is an integral part of the popular poetic forms sung in qawwalis. We also see innumerable examples of bhajans being sung by regular qawwals who freely move from singing at the dargah to *mata ki chowki* (religious evenings for Hindu goddesses) and jagran (all-night religious soirees).

This again underlines the fact that the roots are the same, of bhakti and prembhav. As Donald Brenneis points out in his research paper of a time period before 1920 that 'in Bhatgaon, a rural Fiji Indian village, [the] Indian community who are the descendants of north Indians who moved to Fiji between 1879 and 1919 as indentured plantation workers, have weekly meetings of religious groups and linked through those events with such performance genres as parbacan (religious speeches) and bhajan kavvali (kavvali-style hymns)'.[5]

Gopi Chand Narang further states, 'From ancient times, India has been the cradle of ascetics, yogis and religious devotees. The Islamic concept of ishq (deep, frenzied love) fused with the similar bhakti concept of prem (divine love). In India devotional practice of bhajan kirtan had been customary since ancient times, and the use of musical instruments such as mridang, the jhanjh, the manjera, the iktara and the dholak was widespread in the temples and Shivalas. The Muslims thus began to acquire fondness for Indian music and this interest grew to such an extent that among them, many great masters and performers arose. This in spite of the fact that music was forbidden in Islamic worship in general, Muslim rulers granted it their patronage.'

Further, the chanting of Hindu Sanskrit mantras, which are repeated for a specific number of times (usually 108 times for the desired effect), popularly known as jaap, have been a popular religious or spiritual practice over the centuries. The emphasis here is on the repetition to create a meditative essence. Exactly the way it is done in most ancient pagan and spiritual traditions, including the zikr and dhikr in Sufi traditions.

Similar thoughts are echoed by Jacob D. Fishel. 'Like the veneration of saints mirroring Hindu puja, the themes and structure of qawwali shows influence from Indian classical music and Hindu mantras. A common theme in qawwali is the recitation of the names of God, like some of the most popular Hindu mantras. The two most prominent are the Shree Ram mantra which goes as follows: *"Shree Ram Jai Ram Jai Jai Ram"*; and the Hare Krishna mantra which is: *"Hare Krishna Hare Kirshna, Krishna Krishna Hare Hare / Hare Rama Hare Rama, Rama Rama Hare Hare"*.'

In qawwali, recitations of 'Allahu' and the titles attributed to Allah (SWT), such as 'the Compassionate, the Benevolent' are common and mirror the repetitive structure of the Hindu mantras listed above. Additionally, the melodic structures of qawwali have no distinctively Islamic origins, following instead Hindu musical patterns. This mixing of Indian structure with Islamic lyrics demonstrates the syncretism that is found in the religious cultures of India.[6]

This rare document gives us great insight into the musical heritage of qawwali as a shared culture between Hindus and Sufis. The journey from bhajan to qawwali and finally to qawwali as bhajan is a result of the flexible musical structure and versatile and fluid performance nature of qawwali. In a unique way, qawwali completes the circle and becomes a part of the religious practice amongst Hindus as this document demonstrates. The inherent cultural legacies of the land get influenced by outsiders, and as outsiders adapt themselves to the land and become natives themselves, these legacies in turn are also adapted. The divide blurs and traditions and legacies are taken forward by both, equally, with the same passion and fervour, because now it belongs to both and there is no 'other'. They are one. Fused.

The Kauwalis listed in Kauwali Bahar

1. Praarthana Ganesh-ji Ki Kauwali: Dhyaun pratham tumhe Ganraj puran kaaj bananey wale

2. Kauwali Shri Ram Chandra Ki: Dhan-dhan Ram Chandra bhagwan lila lalit dikhane wale

3. Kauwali Shri Kashi Vishwanath-ji Ki: Dhan-dhan Vishwanath Maharaj, Varanasi basaney wale

4. Kauwali Chetavani: Sukh chaho Ram naam ratt moodh, jhootey gaal bajaney wale

5. Kauwali Krishna Naam: Bhaj mann Murlidhar, Ghanshyam aawa gaman chudaney wale

6. Kauwali Shri Devi-ji Ki: Aayo sharan das kari aas ab toh Amb vilamb karo na

7. Kauwali Kavi Chaturta: Bhule Brahma-ji Maharaj saari srishti banane wale

8. Kauwali Shri Krishna Bal Leela: Kheley Nand aangan Gopal runjhun baajey pagan paijaniya

9. Kauwali Krishna Darshan Mahadev Leela: Thado yogi terey dwar Yashoda sut ke darash kara de

10. Kauwali Hanuman-ji Ki: Dhan-dhan Mahavir Bajrang, Raavan Lank jaraney wale

11. Kauwali Maniharin Leela: Pahuche Barsaney mein jaaye ban maniharan Shyam chabeeley

12. Kauwali Cheerharan Leela: Aisi chahiye tumhe na Shyam de do cheer adheer karo na

13. Kauwali Vanshichoran Leela: Lalita dijiye nek bataye meri vanshi kaun churayi

14. Kauwali Yog Leela: Aaye Udhouji Maharaj humko yog sikhane wale

15. Kauwali Makhan Chori Leela: Dhan-dhan Mohan Madan Gopal makhan chor kahane wale

16. Kauwali Govardhan Leela: Dhan-dhan Govardhan dhar Shyam Surpati maan ghataney wale

17. Kauwali Raas Leela: Dhan-dhan gopi sang Gopal, hil mil raas dikhane wale

18. Kauwali Gopi Vinay: Vanshi baja Dev Nandlal, sakhiyan man lalchane wale

19. Kauwali Khandit Maan Leela: Jaagey kaun bam dhig Shyam, jo mam dham prath uth dhaye

20. Kauwali Maan Leela: Kabse vinay karaun karjor, pyari itni maan karo na

21. Kauwali Radha Krishna Rahasya Leela: Kholo Radhey bhawan kivaad ko hai hamein jaganey wale

22. Kauwali Nagar Leela: Sunder shyamal gaur kishore nrap sut nagar dekhne aaye

23. Kauwali Sita Haran Leela: Ha chip rahi jaaye kehi auur hey Raghuveer pran ke pyaare

24. Kauwali Ram Birah Leela: Ha chip rahi aaj kehi auur hey Jaanki pran ki pyari

25. Kauwali Lakshman Shakti Leela: Vyakul bhaye Lakhan baldham shakti Meghnaad ne maari

26. Kauwali Mandodari Vinay Raavan se: Vinti karun dou kar jor de do piya Siya, Raghuvar ko

27. Kauwali Harishchandra Leela: Dhan-dhan Harishchandra Maharaj dharm maryada badhaney wale

28. Kauwali Paropkari Prashansa: Unko priya kab tak dhan dham, jo hain sajjan paropkari

29. Kauwali Prahlad Bhakt: Jab tak jiyun pita jag beech nis din Ram nam gun gaaun

30. Kauwali Bhagvadvinaya: Hey Prabhu doob rahi majhdhaar meri nayya paar laga do

31. Kauwali Shri Gangaji Ki: Mahima vidit sakal sansar dhan dhan taran tarani Gangay

32. Kauwali Sanatan Dharm: Arpan kari nij tan dhan dhaam mitron dharm Sanatan paalo

33. Kauwali Desh Uddharani: Soye behad aalas neend, jaago ab to Bharat wasi

34. Kauwali Holi Rangbhari: Aaye holi ki bahaar hardam hans hans rang dalaley

35. Kauwali Hikarat Jua: Khelo kabhi na koi jinhaar, yaaron jua bura hota hai

36. Kauwali Hikarat Sharaab: Hota jisse jigar kharab, chhodo sharab peena pyarey

37. Kauwali Nasihat: Bachna maashukon se yaar hain ye aafat ke parkale

38. Kauwali Nasihat: Hai yeh ishq bura janjaal pyarey ishq koi na karna

39. Kauwali Nasihat: Hogi muft zindagi khaar veshya se mat chashm lagana

40. Kauwali Buton Ki Buttebaazi Par: Sunta nahi koi fariyad in be-raham buton ne loota[7]

Endnotes

1. Pandit Mannilal Mishra, *Kauwali Bahar*, Babu Baijnath Prasad Bookseller, 1935

2. Muzaffar Ali (ed.), *A Leaf Turns Yellow: The Sufis of Awadh*, 2013, Bloomsbury

3. Jacob D. Fishel, Dr. Laura L. Cochrane, *Songs and Saints: An Exploration of Indian Sufism,* ANT 459WI, 2017

4. Muzaffar Ali (ed.), *A Leaf Turns Yellow: The Sufis of Awadh,* 2013, Bloomsbury

5. Donald Brenneis, 'Performing Passions: Aesthetics and Politics in an Occasionally Egalitarian Community,' *American Ethnologist* (1987), Wiley.

6. Jacob D. Fishel, Dr. Laura L. Cochrane, *Songs and Saints: An Exploration of Indian Sufism*, ANT 459WI, 2017

7. The booklet *Kauwali Bahar* has been obtained from the private archives & collection of Shri A.N. Sharma. There are ten pages missing in this booklet (pages 8,9,16,17,18,19,20,21,26,27)

॥ Kauwali Bahar ॥

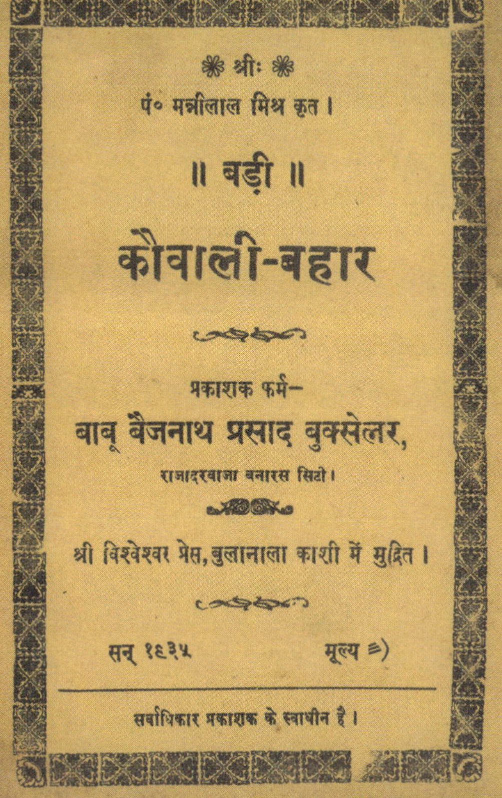

❋ श्रीः ❋

पं० मन्नीलाल मिश्र कृत।

॥ बड़ी ॥

कौवाली-बहार

प्रकाशक फर्म-

बाबू बैजनाथ प्रसाद बुक्सेलर,

राजादरवाजा बनारस सिटी।

श्री विश्वेश्वर प्रेस, बुलानाला काशी में मुद्रित।

सन् १९३५ मूल्य ≈)

सर्वाधिकार प्रकाशक के स्वाधीन है।

❋ श्रीगणेशाय नमः ❋

॥ कौवाली-बहार ॥

❋ प्रथम भाग ❋

॥ प्रार्थना गणेशजी की कौवाली ॥

ध्याऊँ प्रथम तुम्हें गणराज पूरण काज बनाने वाले। सोहे लम्बोदर एकदन्त, करिवर आनन प्रभा अनन्त, भ्राजै चार भुजा छबिवन्त, दुष्टन मान घटाने वाले॥ ध्याऊँ० ॥ १ ॥ ढरकै गंडन सो मदधार, तिनपै मँढ़े अलिन कतार, शोभित शीश छत्र छवि दार, कुण्डल श्रुति द्युति छानेवाले॥ ध्याऊँ० ॥२॥ दीपत रविसम चन्दन भाल, तापर साजि रह्यो बिधुबाल, धारे तनमें बसन बि-शाल, जनमन मुद उपजाने वाले ॥ ध्याऊँ० ॥३॥ मोदक एक हाथ सुखमूल दूजे हाथ लसे त्रिशूल, नाशै पलमें भव भय शूल, निगमागम गुणगाने वाले ॥ ध्याऊँ० ॥ ४ ॥ टारो सकल विघ्न भ्रम द्वंद, दीजै सब बिधिसे आनंद, वन्दत मन्निलाल ब्रजचन्द, संतन सब सुख पाने वाले ॥ ध्याऊँ प्रथम तुम्हें गणराज, पूरण काज बनाने वाले ॥ ५ ॥

❋ कौवाली श्रीरामचन्द्रजी की ❋

धन धन रामचन्द्र भगावन लीला ललित दिखाने वाले। नौमी चैतशुक्ल गुरुवार, लीन्हों अवध नगर अवतार घर घर भयो मंगलाचार, त्रिभुवन यश फैलाने वाले ॥ धन० ॥ १ ॥ कीन्हीं मुनि मखकी रखवारी, गौतम नारि अहिल्या तारी मोहे जनमपुरी नरनारी, कोटिन काम लजाने वाले ॥ धन० ॥ २ ॥ पहुँचे रंगभूमि दर्म्यान, तोड़ा सब राजन का कमान, जै जै पूरण

सुन चौरासी घण्टेवाली, काली भक्तन प्रन प्रतिपाली, कीजै पूरन इच्छा हाली, मन्नी अवसर अधिक रह्यो ना ॥ आयो शरण० ॥ ६ ॥

❋ कौवाली कवि चतुरता ❋

भूले ब्रह्माजी महराज सारी सृष्टि बनाने वाले । कीन्ही कारीगरी अपार, युक्ति से रचा सकल संसार, तिस्पर भी ना किया बिचार, चूक गये चतुर कहाने वाले । भूले ब्रह्माजी० ॥१॥ चोर और शाह रचे एकसार, सच्चे झूठे चतुर गँवार, कैसे पहिचाने नरनार बे चिन्हों के देखे भाले ॥ भूले ब्रह्माजी० ॥ २ ॥ अच्छे बुरे और बेइमान, कामी इन्द्रीजीत समान, इनकी करी न कुछ पहिचान, क्यों पी भंग भये मतवाले ॥ भूले ब्रह्माजी० ॥३॥ चोरों के सिर सींग जमाते, झूठों को दुमदार बनाते, लम्पट के लघु नैन लगाते फिरते गिरते ऊँचे खाले ॥ भूले ब्रह्माजी० ॥ ॥ ४ ॥ इस विधि रचते जो संसार, धोखा जरा न होता यार, करते खुशी से सब नरनार, अपना धर्मो कर्म सम्हाले ॥ भूले ब्रह्माजी० ॥ ५ ॥ एक मुख का है कौन हवाल, चारमुख वाले के ये हाल ज्यादा क्या कहै मन्नीलाल, चतुरानन के चरित निराले ॥ भूले ब्रह्माजी० ॥ ६ ॥ ७ ॥

❋ कौवाली श्रीकृष्ण बाललीला ❋

खेलैं नंद आंगन गोपाल रुन झुन बजैं पगन पैजनियां । शोभित सुंदर स्यामल अंग, दौरत इत उत सहित उमंग बिहँसत ग्वालन बालन संग, बोलत मृदुबचन सुखदनियां ॥ खेलैं नन्द आँगन० ॥ १ ॥ कबहू यसुदासो रिस ठान, मांगत माखन मिसरी कान्ह । कबहू हठ करि भृकुटी तान मटुकी फोरत गहत

मथनियां । खेलैं नंद आँगन० ॥ २ ॥ कबहू आँखमिचौनी इत उत छिपत परम छवि छावत, कबहुँ, चकई करन नचावत । उछलत गिरत मातु की कनियाँ ॥ खेलैं नन्द आंगन० ॥ ३ ॥ यहिविधि श्री बृन्दावनचन्द, मन्नी करत परमआनंद तरसत जोहिसुख हित सुरबृन्द, सो सुख लहत यशोमति रनियाँ । खेलत नंद आंगन० ॥ ४ ॥ ८ ॥

❋ कौवाली कृष्णदर्शन महादेव लीला ❋

ठाढ़ो योगी तेरे द्वार यशुदासुत के दरश करादे । चहिये और नाय कछु मोय, सांची बात बताऊँ तोय, पूरन सलक मनोरथ होय मोहिनी सूरत टुक दिखला दे । ठाढ़ो योगी तेरे द्वार० ॥ १ ॥ आया तजि अपनो अस्थान, कारण यही और नाजान, बीते छिन २ कल्प समान, करुणाकर तन तपन बुझा दे ॥ ठाढ़ो योगी तेरे द्वार० ॥ २ ॥ हैं ये त्रिभुवनपति करतार, भूमि भार उतारनहार, लीन्हों तेरे गृह अवतार, मन भ्रम अपनो सकल भुला दे ॥ ठाढ़ो योगी तेरे द्वार० ॥ ३ ॥ तूतो जाने मेरो लाल हैं ये सब दुष्टन को काल, बिनती सुनु मन मन्नीलाल बांकी झलक दिखा छबि छादे ॥ ठाढ़ो योगी तेरे द्वार० ॥ ४ ॥ ९ ॥

❋ कौवाली हनुमानजी की ❋

धन धन महाबीर बजरंग, रावण लंक जरानेवाले । आज्ञा रघुनन्दन की पाय, पहुँचे गढ़लंका में जाय, क्रोधित हो दी आग लगाय, राम के काम बनानेवाले ॥ धन धन महाबीर० ॥ १ ॥ रावन की वाटिका उजारी, मारा अक्षयकुमार सुरारी, फँस गये ब्रह्मफाँस एकबारी, लीला ललित दिखानेवाले ॥ धन धन० ॥२॥ चढ़ गये द्रुम असोक पर जाय, दीन्हों झट मुद्रिका गिराय,

॥ कौवाली नगर लीला ॥

सुन्दर श्यामल गौर किशोर नृप सुत नगर देखने आये ॥ मणिमय मुकुट शीश में धारे, कानन कुण्डल कलित सँवारे, जगवश करन हेत छबिवारे निरखत कोटिन काम लजाये ॥ सुन्दर श्यामल० ॥ १ ॥ मोहत मंद २ मुसक्यान, मारत चपल दृगनसों बान, कोमलकर धनुशर छबिवान शाभित तरकश कटि लटकाये ॥ सुन्दर श्यामल० ॥ २ ॥ ये ई मुनिमख रक्षा कारन ये ई गौतम नारि उधारन, ये ई असुरनवृन्द सँहारन आये इत अनुपम छबि छाये ॥ सुन्दर श्यामल० ॥ ३ ॥ सजनी ये बर श्याम सलोना. है सिय योग संयेाग बुगे ना, भरि दृग शोभा क्यों निरखो ना, बरबस लेते चित्त चुराये ॥ सुन्दर श्यामल० ॥ ४ ॥ ये ई शिवधनु भंजन करि हैं, ये ई जनक सुता दुख हरि हैं, ये ई त्रिभुवन आनंद भरि हैं मन्नीलाल मनहिं ललचाये ॥ सुंदर श्यामल० ॥ ३३ ॥

॥ कौवाली सीताहरण लीला ॥

हा छिप रहे जाय केहि ओर हे रघुवीर प्रान के प्यारे ॥ निश्चर निपट निलज अभिमानी, मानी एक न मेरी बानी, छल कर लिये जाय हठ ठानी, कैसी करौं कौन दुख टारे ॥ हा छिप रहे० ॥१॥ हो प्रभु सूर्य्य वंश सरताज, करुणासिन्धु गरीबनिवाज, राखत शरणागतकी लाज, असुरनवृन्द संहारनहारे ॥ हा छिप रहे० ॥ २ ॥ मोसो कौन चूक्र परिस्वामी, जो तुम सुनत न अन्तर्यामी, कीजे करुणा त्रिभुवन नामी, दशमुख दुष्ट न नीति निहारे ॥ हा

छिप रहे० ॥ ३ ॥ हा पतिपशी बीच दुखजाल, ले चल्यो सिंह को भाग सृगाल, कीजे जो इच्छा मन्नीलाल, बेबश भई विपति के मारे ॥ हा छिप रहे० ॥ ४ ॥ ३४ ॥

॥ कौवाली राम बिरह लीला ॥

हा छिप रही आज केहि ओर हे जानकी प्रानकी प्यारी । हे बटपीपर ताल तमाल, कदली कुन्दकदम्ब रसाल, दाड़िम चंपक कंज बिशाल, देख्यो किंने गई सुकुमारी ॥ हा छिप रही० ॥१॥ खंजन कीरकपोत कुरंग, गूँजत कमलन दलके भृंग देखो तुम गयंदगति भंग, सुन्दर अंगरंग छबिवारी ॥ हा छिप रही० ॥२॥ हा मम दृग चकोर मुखचन्द, बिंबाधरी सकल सुखकन्द, तव बिन बिकल भयो द्युतिमन्द चहुँदिसि ढूँढ़त फिरत दुखारी ॥ हा छिप रही० ॥ ३ ॥ जो नहिं प्राणप्रिया तोहि पाऊँ छिनमें चौदह लोक नशाऊँ पण्डित मन्नीलाल समझाऊँ कैसे मनमोहिनी सिधारी ॥ हा छिप रही० ॥ ४ ॥ ३५ ॥

॥ कौवाली लक्ष्मणशक्ती लीला ॥

व्याकुल भये लषन बलधाम शक्ती मेघनाद ने मारी । मूर्च्छित हो रणभूमि में सोये देखत दलयुत रघुपति रोये बोले हनुमत का मुख जोये, हे बलधारी परउपकारी व्याकुल० ॥ १ ॥ दीजै बंधु प्रानको दान, जीवन मम बिन लषन न जान, कीजे पूरन काज सुजान, तुम बिन हरै को पीर हमारी ॥ व्याकुल० ॥ २ ॥ सुनतहिं हनुमत लंका जाय, झटपट लाय सुखेन लिवाय॥ रातहिं रात सजीवन लाय, लीन्हे लक्ष्मण प्राण उबारी ॥ व्याकुल० ॥ ३ ॥ उठ बैठे लक्ष्मण हर्षाय भेंटे कटक सहित रघुराय

मल के, माया में दे टेढ़े चलके टक्कर मारे उछल उछल के इन दुष्टों को दूर हटा दो ॥ हे प्रभु० ॥३॥ दौड़ो २ नन्ददुलारे, कर पर धर कर देव किनारे, पंडित मन्नीलाल हमारे प्राण प्यारे दरश दिखा दो ॥ हे प्रभु० ॥ ४१ ॥

कौवाली श्रीगंगाजी ।

महिमा विदित सकल संसार धन धन तरन तारनी गंगे । हो तुम दीनन की सुधि लेनी, पलमें चार पदारथ देनी, छेनी अघ बैकुण्ठ निशेनी, भक्तन काज सारनी गंगे ॥ महिमा० ॥१॥ भागीरथि यश धर्म्मध्वजा हो विष्णु चरणी जन्हुसुता हो धारण किये अनंद प्रभा हो जग कीरति पसारनी गंगे ॥ महिमा० ॥२॥ ऐसो जम्यो तेरो आतंक तारे अगणित पतित निशंक रोवत यम कहि बचन मयंकहो ममपुरि उजारनी गंगे ॥ महिमा० ॥३॥ तव तट प्रातकाल नर आय मज्जन करता हिय हर्षाय, बुधि बल विपुल तेज यश पाय, कहै जय जन उधारनी गंगे ॥ महिमा० ॥४॥ जननी काटि विषम भ्रमजाल, कीजै, सब भाँतिन प्रति पाल वरणत पंडित मन्नीलाल, भवभय भीर टारनी गंगे महिमा ॥ ५ ॥ ४६ ॥

कौवाली सनातनधर्म्म ।

अर्पन करि निज तन धन धाम मित्रो धर्म्म सनातन पालो । मानो वेदपुरान निगम को कीजै श्राद्ध पितृ तर्पन को पूजा विप्र संत गौवनको निशादिन हरिपद प्रीति बढ़ालो ॥ अर्पन० ॥ १ ॥ सर्वोपरि ये धर्म तुम्हारा, फैला रविसम

जग उजियारा, दाता मुक्ति स्वर्ग को द्वारा, चाहै जब जिस दम अजमालो ॥ अपने० ॥ २ ॥ नितनव विद्यालय खुलवाओ हिलामिल सब कोइ पढ़ो पढ़ाओ, आपस में मिल प्रेम बढ़ाओ, मूढ़ों को विद्वान बनालो ॥ अपने० ॥ ३ ॥ मजहब नये हुए बहुजारी, उनसे बचो यही हुशियारी, होगी हरदम विजय तुम्हारी सच्ची बाणी बोलो चालो ॥ अपने० ॥ ४ ॥ खण्डें धर्म्म सनातन को खल, प्रगटे बहुत आज कल चंचल, पलमें करो परास्त उनका दल वैदिक विद्या चक्र चलालो ॥ अपने० ॥ ५ ॥ बिनती इतना मम सुन लीजे, स्थापित सभा हर जगह कीजै, मन्नीलाल जगत यश लीजै, पंडित तो कुछ कष्ट उठालो ॥ अपने० ॥ ६ ॥ ४३ ॥

कौवाली देशोद्धारिणी ।

सोये बेहद आलस नींद जागो अबतो भारतबासी ॥ पलटा कुछ एक दम जमाना, चेतो, नहीं होगा पछताना, करदो जारी चलन पुराना, होवे सारी दूर उदासी ॥ सोये बेहद० ॥ १ ॥ आपुस में मिल प्रेम बढ़ाओ, फौरन फूट फर्क बिलगाओ, नित नव मनमाने फल पाओ, विद्या बृद्धी करके खासी ॥ सोये बेहद० ॥ २ ॥ क्या थे पहले अब तुम क्या हो, सोचो धीर बिज्ञ बल बाहो, उन्नति भारत की टुक चाहो, घर२बनो सिल्प अभ्यासी ॥ सोये बेहद० ॥ ३ ॥ जो है दुखिया बंधु तुम्हारा, उसको हरदम देहु सहारा, कारज बने आपका सारा, मानो मित्र सकल गुणराशी ॥

FROM THE ARCHIVAL COLLECTION OF A.N.SHARMA

Book: KAUWALI BAHAR
By: PANDIT MANNILAL MISHRA
Publisher: BABU BAIJNATH PRASAD IN 1935

Poetic Forms in Qawwali

Suman Mishra

he captivating aspect of qawwali is its deep-rooted connection with the cultural symbiosis that flourished during the emergence of India's Ganga-Jamuni tehzeeb—the unique confluence of Hindu and Muslim traditions. Qawwali did not merely witness the formation of this composite culture; it played an instrumental role in nurturing it with its timeless melodies and poetic eloquence. Like an artist embellishing a vibrant tapestry, qawwali wove delicate motifs into the fabric of this harmonious civilisation, thereby strengthening its very foundations. For qawwals, this cultural legacy is an inheritance passed down through generations, preserving and perpetuating the spirit of unity and coexistence.

Qawwali did not merely remain a form of music in India; it became a mystical pathway leading the listener from the realm of self to the divine. It carves a narrow spiritual passage wherein, by immersing oneself at one end, one encounters the divine at the other.

Various forms of qawwali have flourished in India, evolving organically over time and enriching the tradition with their diversity. These forms are not merely musical expressions but are reflective of India's Ganga-Jamuni tehzeeb and the country's syncretic cultural heritage. A striking example of this harmonious blend is the inclusion of bhajans in qawwali. Whether it is the Krishna bhakti verses by Shah Turab Ali Qalandar or the composition *'Kanhaiya Yaad Hai Kuchh Bhi Humaari'* by Nawab Hilm, qawwali, in all its manifestations, serves as a conduit connecting the human soul to the divine.

Despite their historical richness, the various forms of qawwali remain relatively unexplored. Yet, they continue to thrive in all their majestic grandeur, particularly within the sacred precincts of Sufi shrines, where thousands of mystical verses composed by Sufi saints are recited on special occasions. These saints not only embraced Indian cultural motifs but also adorned them with golden embellishments through qawwali, thus enriching the tradition manifold.

The diverse forms of qawwali are as follows:

1. **Hamd:** A form of qawwali dedicated to the praise of the Almighty. Every qawwali session traditionally begins with a Hamd. This practice establishes the spiritual ambience, preparing the listeners to embark on a mystical journey.

Kaun sā ghar hai ki ai jaañ nahīñ kāshāna tirā aur jalva-ḳhana tirā
Mai-kada terā hai ka.aba tirā but-ḳhāna tirā sab hai jānāna tirā

Tū kisī shakl meñ ho maiñ tirā shaidā.ī huuñ terā saudā.ī huuñ
Tū agar sham.a hai ai dost maiñ parvāna tirā ya.anī dīvāna tirā

Mujh ko bhī jaam koī pīr-e-ḳharābāt mile terī ḳhairāt mile
Tā-qayāmat yūñhī jaarī rahe paimāna tirā rahe mai-ḳhāna tirā

Tere darvāze pe hāzir hai tire dar kā faqīr ai amīroñ ke amiir
Mujh pe bhī ho kabhī altāf-e-karīmāna tirā lutf-e-shāhāna tirā

Sadqa mai-ḳhāne kā saaqī mujhe be-hoshī de ḳhud-farāmoshī de
Yuuñ to sab kahte haiñ 'bedam' tirā mastāna tirā ab huuñ dīvāna tirā[1]

This Hamd, a devotional qawwali in praise of the Almighty, is written by Hazrat Bedam Shah Warsi, a revered Sufi poet from Awadh. Rooted in deep spiritual devotion, the poem transcends the boundaries of religious spaces, portraying the omnipresence of the divine. The poet declares that every sacred place—whether the Kaaba, a temple, or a tavern—belongs to the Almighty, emphasising the universality of divine love. Through metaphors of unwavering devotion, this calls for complete surrender, like a moth drawn to the flame, symbolising self-annihilation in the love of the divine. The final verses reflect humility, a beggar at the threshold of the Almighty, yearning for divine grace.

This Hamd exemplifies the mystical tradition of Sufi poetry, where divine love dissolves worldly distinctions, guiding the seeker towards spiritual ecstasy and unity with the Beloved. It sets the tone for a qawwali gathering, invoking an atmosphere of deep reverence and longing for divine proximity.

2. Naat: Naat are verses written in praise of Prophet Muhammad (PBUH). It is recited after the Hamd, reflecting devotion and love for the Prophet (PBUH). Naats are often composed in Persian, Urdu, and Arabic, maintaining the lyrical beauty of classical poetry.

Payaam laa.ii hai baad-e-sabaa madiine se
Ki rahmato.n kii uthii hai ghataa madiine se

Ilaahii ko.ii to mil jaa.e chaaragar aisaa
Hamaare dard kii laa de davaa madiine se

Hisaab kyaa ki nakiirain ho ga.e be-khud
Jab aa.ii qabr me.n Thandii havaa madiine se

Yahii to Kkhaana-kharaabii kaa ik thikaana hai
Chale kahaa.n dil-e-dard-aashnaa madiine se

Janaab-e-khizr ko zulmaat ne diye dhoke
Milaa to saagar-e-aab-e-baqaa madiine se

Hamaare saamne ye naazish-e-bahaar fuzuul
Bahisht le ke ga.ii hai fazaa madiine se

Na aa.e.n jaa ke va.nh se yahii tamannaa hai
Madiine laa ke na laa.e khudaa madiine se

Farishte sai.nka.do.n aate hai.n aur jaate hai.n
Bahut qariib hai arsh-e-khudaa madiine se

Isii kaa faiz hai duniyaa me.n ye vo chaukhat hai
Jo kuchh kisii ko milaa vo milaa madiine se

Ham us ko marja.a-e-maqsuud-e-ishq kahte hai.n
Dil-e-hazii.n kahii.n khoyaa milaa madiine se[2]

This Naat by Seemab Akbarabadi is a deeply spiritual and lyrical tribute to Prophet Muhammad (PBUH), capturing the poet's immense love and devotion for the holy city of Madina. The verses reflect the belief that Madina is a source of divine mercy, healing, and solace. The city is a place where every longing heart finds peace and where even the trials of the grave are eased by its blessed atmosphere.

The vivid imagery talks about the breeze from Madina carrying messages of divine grace and the Prophet's (PBUH) destiny-transforming presence, through which spiritual seekers attain eternal wisdom and sustenance from its sacred soil. Those who visit Madina never return, emphasising the unparalleled spiritual fulfilment found in the Prophet's (PBUH) proximity. This Naat exemplifies the tradition of devotional poetry, where love for the Prophet is intertwined with the longing for his city.

3. QAUL: The word qawwali is derived from the Arabic word 'Qaul', meaning 'to speak' or 'to declare'. It involves the repetitive chanting of sayings attributed to the Prophet (PBUH) and is typically recited after Hamd, Naat, and Manqabat. This repetitive chanting is believed to invoke a state of spiritual ecstasy.

Man kunto Maulā fa-hāzā Alīyun Maulā
dā-rā-dil-dā-rā-dil dar-dānī
ham-tum ta-nā-nā-nā nā-nā-re
yalā lī yalā lī yalālī-yalālī yā lā lī
Man kunto Maulā fa-hāzā Alīyun Maulā

This particular Qaul centres around the well-known declaration: *Man kunto Maula, fa-haza Ali yun Maula.* (Whoever accepts me as their master, Ali is also their master.)

This phrase, attributed to the Prophet (PBUH), highlights the spiritual significance of Imam Ali (RA) and is deeply revered in Sufi and Islamic traditions. The repetition of these words, interwoven with syllabic vocalisations which were introduced by Hazrat Amir Khusrau, such as 'yalālī yalālī yā lā lī', enhance the meditative and transcendental nature of the performance.

By engaging in this rhythmic chanting, both performers and listeners are drawn into a heightened spiritual experience, transcending the material world. The Qaul serves as an invocation of divine presence, fostering devotion and mystical reflection within the qawwali tradition.

4. Manqabat: Poetic verses written in praise of Sufi saints. Manqabat is usually recited to honour the saint whose urs (death anniversary) is being commemorated. These compositions emphasise the saint's spiritual stature, wisdom, and divine connection.

Dil me.n bharaa hu.aa hai josh-e-valaa-e-vaaris
ko.ii makii.n nahii.n hai is kaa sivaa.e vaaris

kyaa jaane kyaa kahaa thaa kyaa jaane kyaa sunaa thaa
kaano.n me.n aa rahii hai ab tak sadaa-e-vaaris

dekhuu.n to kis ko dekhuu.n chaahuu.n to kis ko chaahuu.n
aa.nkhe.n hai.n mahv-e-vaaris dil mutalaa-e-vaaris

ye ra.ng zindagii kaa rakhe khudaa hamesha
dil me.n ho dard-e-vaaris sar me.n havaa.e vaaris

meraa nishaan-e-madfan barbaad ho rahaa hai
is kii bhii kuchh khabar le ai khaak-e-paa-e-vaaris

'Muztar' kaa ye ta.dapnaa ba.ad-e-fanaa to kam ho
turbat pe aa ke jam jaa ai naqsh-e-paa-e-vaaris[3]

This Manqabat written by Muztar Khairabadi, is a poetic tribute to Hazrat Waris Pak of Dewa Sharif, a revered Sufi saint known for his spiritual wisdom, compassion and divine connection. The verses reflect profound devotion, portraying the saint as a guiding light whose presence and teachings continue to influence the hearts of his followers.

The poetry expresses an all-encompassing love for Hazrat Waris Pak, with a heart imbued with the saint's devotion, leaving no space for anything else. The echoes of the saint's words still resonate in his soul, the enduring impact of his spiritual guidance. The longing is so intense that the eyes remain fixated on the saint and the heart beats in harmony with his divine presence.

The Manqabat highlights the saint's lasting influence, with the seeker asking for a life immersed in his love and a heart that carries his pain and blessings. To remain connected to Hazrat Waris Pak, seeking solace at his sacred resting place, even in death. This Manqabat encapsulates the Sufi tradition of venerating saints, emphasising their role as spiritual intercessors who continue to guide and inspire seekers even beyond their physical existence. The saint's legacy, as depicted in these verses, remains a source of spiritual enlightenment and divine love for countless devotees.

5. **Rang:** Amir Khusrau referred to Rang as the 'Maha Rang' (the Great Carnival—Maha Raas), symbolising the mystical union of the human consciousness with the divine, a state where the physical and metaphysical realms merge, leading the devotee into an ecstatic state of mystical intoxication (fana). Qawwali sessions traditionally conclude with Rang during urs celebrations, signifying the culmination of spiritual ecstasy. It serves as a powerful conclusion to the spiritual journey experienced during a qawwali session, leaving listeners absorbed in the colours of divine love and unity.

Sab mil mauj manāo rī piyā ke kāran
hai so hai nāhīñ so nāhīñ

apnī sudh bisrāo rī piyā ke kāran
Hazrat Alī kī raini chadhī hai

rañg meñ aaj nahāo rī piyā ke kāran
prem kī dhārā meñ phāñdo 'vaqārā'

paniyā ban bah jaao rī piyā ke kāran[4]

This Rang by Hazrat Waqaruddin Qadri represents the culmination of a qawwali session, marked by the ecstatic union of the human soul with the divine. The words urge all seekers to immerse themselves in joyous celebration for the sake of their Divine Beloved (piya), emphasising the mystical concept that what truly exists is eternal and all else is transient. He calls upon devotees to relinquish worldly awareness and surrender to divine love.

With a reference to Hazrat Ali (RA), whose presence is often invoked in Sufi traditions as a symbol of spiritual strength and guidance, this encourages seekers to bathe in the colours of divine ecstasy. The imagery of flowing waters and surrender to this flow of love (prem ki dhara) further reinforces the theme of dissolution of the self into the boundless ocean of divine grace.

6. Ghazal: An exquisite form of Urdu and Persian poetry that has been profoundly enriched by Sufi saints, many of whom were prolific poets. Ghazals are widely recited at Sufi shrines, exploring themes of love, separation, and the quest for the divine.

Ze-hāl-e-miskīñ makun taġhāful durā.e naināñ banā.e batiyāñ
ki tāb-e-hijrāñ na-dāram ai jaañ na lehū kaahe lagā.e chhatiyāñ

Shabān-e-hijrāñ darāz chuuñ zulf o roz-e-vaslat chuuñ umr-e-kotāh
sakhī piyā ko jo maiñ na dekhūñ to kaise kāTūñ añdherī ratiyāñ

Yakāyak az dil do chashm jaadū ba-sad-farebam ba-burd taskīñ
kise padī hai jo jā sunāve piyāre pī ko hamārī batiyāñ

Chuuñ sham-e-sozāñ chuuñ zarra hairāñ ze-mehr-e-āñ-mah ba-gashtam āḳhir
na niiñd naināñ na añg chaināñ na aap aave na bheje patiyāñ

Ba-haqq-e-āñ-mah ki roz-e-mahshar ba-dād mā rā fareb 'ḳhusrav'
sapīt man ke durā.e rākhūñ jo jaa.e pā.ūñ piyā kī khatiyāñ[5]

This ghazal, composed by Hazrat Amir Khusrau, is considered one of the earliest Urdu ghazals and stands as a masterpiece of Sufi poetry. Blending

Persian and early Urdu (Hindavi), it exemplifies the mystical and emotional depth characteristic of the ghazal. The poetry explores themes of love, longing, and spiritual separation, reflecting the deep yearning of a lover—or a seeker—for the Divine.

The Beloved's indifference to the suffering of the seeker when he can no longer endure the pain of separation is described using rich imagery comparing the endless dark nights of longing to the darkness of the Beloved's tresses, while moments of union seem as fleeting as a short-lived life. The despair intensifies with the lament of the absence of communication, with no words or messages bringing solace. In the final verses, Amir Khusrau invokes divine justice, expressing his helplessness in the face of deception and distance. His language is layered with both earthly love and Sufi symbolism, where the Beloved represents the divine, and separation signifies the trials of the spiritual journey.

This ghazal, recited widely at Sufi shrines, embodies the essence of mystical devotion, portraying love as an all-consuming force that transcends the material world. Through its evocative verses, it continues to resonate with seekers on both a worldly and spiritual level.

7. **Sehra:** Sehra (a traditional floral veil or adornment worn by the groom) is a celebratory wedding poem traditionally recited within Sufi communities, particularly when the groom is a descendant of a saint. This glorifies the sanctity of marriage, symbolising the divine blessing upon the union of two souls.

Taabish-e-ruu-e-munavvar se munavvar sehraa
nig.hat-e-zulf-e-mu.ambar se mu.ambar sehraa

Shaan tarjiih kii maaduum hai in jalvo.n me.n
sehre se rukh kii ziyaa rukh se munavvar sehraa

Ho gayaa paas-e-adab josh-e-masarrat me.n fanaa
varna kyuu.n hai tirii dastaar ke uupar sehraa

Allaah Allaah ajab shauq-e-qadam-bosii hai
paa.nv tak aayaa hai nausha ke latak kar sehraa

Baarvar shaakh-e-mohabbat rahe daa.em baaham
nek saa.at me.n ba.ndhaa ho tire sar par sehraa

Maujzan aaj hai dariyaa-e-masarrat 'maikash'
is liye laa.e hai.n kashtii me.n lagaa kar sehraa[6]

This Sehra written by Maikash Akbarabadi, describes the sehra (a traditional floral veil or adornment worn by the groom) as radiant, illuminated by the groom's luminous face and fragrant tresses, signifying divine grace. The poetic imagery highlights the spiritual and aesthetic beauty of the moment, emphasising how the sehra and the groom's presence complement each other in magnificence.

The poetry reflects on the deep sense of respect and devotion surrounding the ceremony. In an act of humility and reverence, the sehra itself bows down as if eager to touch the feet of the groom, portraying the mystical charm of the occasion. The final verses offer a heartfelt prayer, wishing that the tree of love remains fruitful and the couple's bond flourishes under divine fervour. Through its rich symbolism and celebratory tone, this Sehra captures both the joy of worldly love and the sanctity of spiritual connection, reinforcing the Sufi belief that marriage is not just a union of two individuals but a sacred covenant under divine guidance.

8. Gagar: The ritual of Gagar is believed to have originated from the khanqah of Hazrat Sheikh Husamuddin Manikpuri. It is said that on the occasion of his pir's urs, Sheikh Husamuddin once went to fill water in a Gagar (water pitcher). His disciples (mureeds) accompanied him, carrying Gagars on their heads. As they walked with the Gagars, the qawwals sang mystical poetry (kalaam). Sheikh Husamuddin found this tradition profoundly moving, and from that day onwards, the ritual of Gagar became a tradition in his khanqah. The dargah of Hazrat Sheikh Sa'aduddin Khairabadi in Khairabad also observes the Gagar ritual, where qawwals sing special Gagar poetry.

Saadhu saadhu gaagar sar bhaarii
chalat dagar lachke panihaarii

saadhu saadhu gaagar sar bhaarii
madh kii bharii gaagar na sambharii

saadhu saadhu mai.n to piyaa haarii
saadhu saadhu gaagar sar bhaarii

bin madh piye bauraay jaat huu.n
jo dekhe jaane matvaarii

saadhu saadhu gaagar sar bhaarii
tumhre saadhe sakhii ab gaagar

nahii.n to jaat hai laaj hamaarii
saadhu saadhu gaagar sar bhaarii

khvaajaa-vaaris chaahe.n to 'bedam'
sigre khvaajan kii nainan me.n dulaarii [7]

This Gagar, written by Hazrat Bedam Shah Warsi, is dedicated to Hazrat Waris Pak of Dewa Sharif, a revered Sufi saint. The Gagar tradition is observed at several Sufi shrines, including Dewa Sharif, where qawwals sing mystical poetry while carrying water pitchers as a symbol of spiritual devotion.

In this kalaam, the Gagar represents divine love, overflowing with the intoxicating nectar of spirituality. The imagery of a panihaari (water bearer) struggling to balance the heavy pitcher reflects the state of a seeker overwhelmed by the burden of Divine love. The poetry expresses surrender to the Beloved (the Divine), acknowledging the transformative power of spiritual devotion. Even without consuming any material intoxication, the seeker is rendered intoxicated by love and longing for the divine presence.

The final verses invoke Khwaja Waris Pak, emphasising that only through the grace of the saint can a seeker attain spiritual enlightenment. An essential part of the Sufi musical tradition at Dewa Sharif, it beautifully encapsulates themes of surrender, divine intoxication, and the mystical bond between the seeker and the saint. It continues to be recited at urs celebrations, preserving the spiritual legacy of Hazrat Waris Pak.

9. Sawan: Sawan poetry is an essential part of Sufi musical traditions, evoking love, devotion, and the soul's yearning for its spiritual master, ultimately leading to divine union. Symbolic of divine grace and spiritual longing, the verses sung during the monsoon season draw parallels with the mystical union between the soul and the divine. These songs largely evoke feelings of longing and separation.

Saavan kii rut aa.ii
chalo sakhii jhuulan chaliye

hamre saiyaa.n ghar pa.daa hai hi.ndolaa
hil-mil dhuum machaavan chaliye

solaho-si.ngaar karke morii sajnii
apne piyaa ko dikhaavan chaliye

sa.nvarii morii sa.ng kii sahelii
apne saiyaa.n sa.ng khelan chaliye

Nijaamuddiin Auliyaa hai laadlaa meraa
gaa.e-bajaa.e rijhaavan chaliye

kahat 'Khaadim' apne safii suu.n
rahi-rahi gale lagaavan chaliye[8]

This Sawan poetry written by Makhdoom Khadim Safi reflects the spiritual symbolism of the monsoon season in Sufi tradition. Sawan (the monsoon season) is often associated with divine mercy and the soul's longing for union with the divine, mirroring the way the parched earth longs for rain. The poetry creates an imagery of joy, of devotion, where companions prepare to swing (jhoole) in celebration of the monsoon, signifying the ecstatic state of the seekers. The imagery of a bride adorning herself to meet her Beloved (saiyaan) symbolises the seeker's spiritual preparation to unite with the divine.

A key reference here is to Hazrat Nizamuddin Auliya, depicted as the beloved spiritual guide, whose presence brings joy and fulfilment to his followers. In the final verse as a personal significance, Makhdoom Khadim Safi mentions his own murshid (spiritual guide), Hazrat Makhdoom Safi, expressing deep devotion and longing for his guidance.

10. Salaam: Salaam in Sufi tradition is a prayerful invocation of peace and blessings, often recited in honour of Prophet (PBUH) , saints, and spiritual guides. It serves as an act of humility, gratitude, and submission, seeking spiritual connection and divine favour. A prayerful invocation for peace and well-being, it symbolises humility and reverence.

Nasl-e-aadam ke iftikhaar salaam
ai madiina ke taajdaar salaam

naazish-e-husn-e-kirdgaar salaam
ai hasiino.n ke shahryaar salaam

baa'is-e-ziinat-e-bahaar salaam
ai gul-a.ndaam-o-gul-'izaar salaam

dii gulaamii se tuune sab ko najaat
hurriyat ke payaam-daar salaam

ai yatiimo.n kii be-kaso.n kii hayaat
ai gariibo.n ke Gam-gusaar salaam

vaj.h-e-irshaad-e-'aalii-e-laulaak
fakhr-e-takhliiq-e-kirdgaar salaam

saare 'aalam se behtar aap kaa khulq
aap yaktaa-e-rozgaar salaam

aap duniyaa ke har hasii.n se hasii.n
aap qudrat kaa shaah-kaar salaam

ai mere markaz-e-ummiid-e-najaat
mere aqaa-e-naam-daar salaam

aap kii zaat par hazaar duruud
aap kii zaat par hazaar salaam

kaash 'Kaavish' bhii pa.Dh sake kisii roz
khud pahu.nch kar sar-e-mazaar salaam[9]

This Salaam by Abdul Hadi Kavish is a poetic expression of deep reverence and devotion towards Prophet Muhammad (PBUH). The verses celebrate the Prophet's (PBUH) unparalleled beauty, moral excellence and mercy, addressing him as the pride of humanity, the crown of Madina, and the beacon of liberation for the oppressed. The poetry calls out to his role as a saviour for orphans, the destitute, and the helpless, highlighting his compassionate nature and divine mission. It emphasises the Prophet's (PBUH) supreme status in creation, describing him as the epitome of perfection and divine artistry. The concluding lines express the longing to personally visit the Prophet's (PBUH) resting place in Madina, a sentiment shared by countless devotees who wish to offer their Salaam in person.

11. Holi: The Hindu festival of Holi is often linked to the story of Bhakt Prahlad, Hiranyakashipu, and Holika, symbolising the triumph of truth over falsehood, much like other ancient tales in Hinduism. In Sufi traditions, Holi transcends its conventional interpretation as a festival of colours and becomes a symbol of spiritual annihilation (fana)—the dissolution of the self into divine love and unity. It is the celebration of merging into the essence of the spiritual guide or guru, thus erasing the duality between the seeker and the divine. The poetry and teachings of Sufis and saints are imbued with this spiritual hue. In Sufi philosophy, Holi stands for the transcendence of the self, leading to a mystical oneness with the Creator, the annihilation of the ego and a dance of union with the divine. A manifestation of India's pluralistic tradition, Holi is celebrated at some Sufi shrines like Hazrat Waris Pak's dargah, accompanied by qawwali compositions reflecting the spirit of the festival.

Horī hoy rahī Ahmad jiyo ke dvaar
Nabī Alī ko rañg bano hai Hasan Husain khilār

Aiso anokho chatur khilādī rañg diino sansār
'Niyāz' pyārā bhar bhar chhidke ek hī rañg pichkār[10]

This Holi by Hazrat Shah Niyaz Ahmad Barelvi, a renowned Sufi saint and poet himself, emphasises the idea of unity in diversity, reflecting the pluralistic traditions of India. He beautifully blends Sufi mysticism with the vibrant essence of the Holi festival. The kalaam envisions Holi being celebrated at the doorstep of Prophet Muhammad (PBUH), where Imam Hasan and Imam Husain playfully partake in the festival, illustrating the universality of joy, devotion and divine love. The poetry describes a mystical Holi, where the colour of divine grace washes over the world, erasing differences and merging all into a single hue of love. The poem's concluding lines portray the seeker (Niyaz) joyfully immersed in the divine colour of love, standing for Sufi surrender and ecstatic devotion.

Holi exemplifies how Sufis embraced cultural and spiritual symbols to express their mystical philosophy, turning festivals like Holi into metaphors for divine union and self-transcendence.

12. Chadar: A ceremonial practice involving the offering of a decorated sacred cloth (chadar) at Sufi shrines, symbolising deep reverence and devotion. Chadar qawwali is sung during this ritual of laying a chadar which symbolises spiritual humility, devotion, and an appeal for divine blessings. It as an expression of love, respect, and spiritual connection to the saint whose shrine it adorns.

Huzuur-e-'vaaris-e-aalii-maqaam kii chaadar
habiib-e-hazrat-e-KHair-ul-anaam kii chaadar

iram se rauza-e-'vaaris' pe huure.n laatii hai.n
banaa-banaa ke daruud-o-salaam kii chaadar

ridaa-e-faatima-zahraa ye tasht-e-nuur me.n hai
ki hai husain alaihis-salaam kii chaadar

mirii balaa ko ho khurshiid-e-hashr kaa khatkaa
ki mere sar pe hai mere imaam kii chaadar

dar-e-huzuur pe haazir hai aap kaa 'bedam'
qubuul kiijai maulaa ghulaam kii chaadar[11]

This Chadar by Hazrat Bedam Shah Warsi describes the celestial significance of the chadar offered at the shrine of Hazrat Waris Pak. It poetically illustrates how heavenly beings bring forth a chadar imbued with durood (salutations) and salaam (peaceful blessings), linking the act of offering the chadar to the sanctity of Prophet Muhammad (PBUH) and his noble family. The poetry further connects the chadar to Hazrat Fatima Zahra (RA) and Imam Husain (AS), emphasising its spiritual purity and divine grace.

Hazrat Bedam Shah Warsi expresses his own humble submission, presenting himself as a devotee offering a symbolic chadar of love and devotion at the shrine. The imagery of light (nur) and divine radiance in the poem signifies spiritual protection and intercession, reinforcing the belief that such offerings serve as a means of attaining nearness to the saints and, ultimately, to the Divine.

13. Mubarak: Mubarak is a celebratory expression, traditionally recited to mark spiritual milestones such as the appointment of a Sufi successor, the establishment of a khanqah, or other significant events within the spiritual lineage. Mubarak conveys blessings, joy, and reverence for the occasion being honoured.

Ye ḳhusravī-o-shaukat-e-shāhāna mubārak
ye qasr ye ḳhuddām ye kāshāna mubārak

mastoñ ko mubārak dar-e-mai-ḳhāna ke sajde
mai-ḳhāna tujhe murshd-e-mai-ḳhāna mubārak

ai chashm-e-tamannā tirī ummīd bar aa.e
uThtā hai naqāb-e-ruḳh-e-jānāna mubārak

bulbul ko mubārak ho havā-e-gul-o-gulshan

parvāne ko soz-e-dil-e-parvāna mubārak
lo uth ga.e sab jalva-gāh-e-nāz ke parde
nazzāra-e-husn-e-ruḳh-e-jānāna mubārak

'sarmad' ko mubārak hoñ mai-e-sāf ke sāġhar
'bedam' hameñ durd-e-tah-e-paimāna mubārak[12]

This Mubarak by Hazrat Bedam Shah Warsi depicts a regal and mystical imagery, referring to Sufi leadership as a divine kingship and comparing the khanqah to a majestic palace. The lines highlight the sanctity of the gathering, where devotees (mureeds) express gratitude and devotion at the feet of their spiritual guide. The reference to the wine house (maikhana) symbolises the Sufi tradition of divine intoxication (fana or annihilation of the self in love for the divine), reinforcing the idea that the spiritual path is one of deep surrender and mystical ecstasy.

The poetry celebrates the unveiling of divine beauty (ruḳh-e-jānāna), symbolising the revelation of spiritual truths to the seekers. The nightingale (bulbul) and the moth (parwana) are metaphors for the yearning soul and the devoted seeker—both drawn irresistibly towards divine beauty and love. The concluding lines indicate the contrast between different levels of spiritual attainment—some drink from the pure goblet of divine realisation, while others find their place in the humility of accepting the humble dregs of spiritual wisdom.

14. Ghusl: Ghusl is recited during the ritual washing of a saint's shrine with rose water, symbolising spiritual purification, reverence, and divine grace. This tradition is particularly significant at the dargah of Hazrat Nizamuddin Auliya, where the sacred act of cleansing the mazar with pure water represents both physical and spiritual sanctification.

However, this tradition is not limited to the Chishti order alone; it is also practised in other Sufi orders such as Firdousi and Abululayi khanqahs. In khanqahs, on this day (as mentioned in *Auraad-e-Sharifi* by Hazrat Makhdoom-e-Jahan, Sheikh Sharafuddin Ahmad Yahya Maneri, R.A.), after sunrise, the following Arabic inscription is written on a banana leaf:

عليقـــاً مليقاً طليقاً انت تعلم ما فى قلوبهم مليقا

This leaf is then immersed in water, and the water is used for bathing. After bathing, a prayer for good health is also made.

According to another tradition, a different Arabic verse is inscribed on a banana leaf, which is then placed in water, and the water is drunk:

سلام قولا من رب الرحيم، سلام علی
سلام علیکم طبتم فادخلو ها
سلام علی موسیٰ وھارون، سلام علی الیاسین،
،نوحٍ فی العلمین، سلام علی ابراہیم
خالدین، سلام ھی حتیٰ مطلع الفجر

On this day, Hazrat Nizamuddin Auliya's shrine is bathed with rose water, and qawwali is performed throughout the night. During this night, qawwals repeatedly sing the same couplet:

• ◆ •

Meri Maili Gudariya Dho De Nizam,
Auron Ke Dhove Shale-do-Shale

• ◆ •

(O Nizam, cleanse my soiled cloak,
You cleanse the elegant robes of others)

Ghusl-e-marqad ko malak laa.e musaffaa paanii
chaahiye chashma-e-jannat ko achhuutaa paanii

un kii taqdiir-e-rasaa par hai farishto.n ko bhii rashk
urs-e-makhduum me.n laayaa jinhe.n daana paanii

tuu gale mil ke bajaa mujra.ii bahr-e-karam
sar se ab chashm-e-nidaamat ko hai uu.nchaa paanii

qabr-e-makhduum ko chhuune se jo mahruum rahaa
usii hasrat se hai dariyaa me.n ta.daptaa paanii

taalib-e-faiz huu.n mai.n pesh-e-mazaar-e-anvar
jaise maa.nge ko.ii pyaasaa lab-e-dariyaa paanii

dho.e jurm ahl-e-ma.aasii ke dam-e-ghusl-e-mazaar
bahr-e-altaaf-e-ilaahii kaa ubaltaa paanii

sa.ad ke dar se milo diida-e-giryaa.n ko 'vasiim'
kuchh na vasvaas kaaro paak hai bahtaa paanii[13]

The poetry by Waseem Khairabadi illustrates how even the angels (malak) bring pure, untouched water (musaffaa paani) for the ritual, emphasising its sacred nature. Blessed are those who participate in this spiritual act. Their fate (taqdeer-e-rasa) is so exalted that even angels envy them. The lines also evoke deep longing and humility, depicting seekers (talib-e-faiz) yearning for the saint's blessings, much like a thirsty soul longing for water at the edge of a river (lab-e-dariya).

The poetry describes how the water used in the ritual washing (ghusl-e-mazaar) holds divine significance, symbolising forgiveness and the cleansing of sins (jurm dhona). The imagery of a restless river longing to touch the saint's tomb signifies the sacred power of divine presence—even the elements yearn for connection with the saint's sanctity.

In essence, this poetry captures the deep spiritual emotions associated with the ghusl ritual and also portrays the transformative power of divine mercy and purification, making it a profound expression of devotion and humility.

15. Kamli: Ghusl Kamli is a devotional tribute to Prophet Muhammad (PBUH), who was known for wearing a black cloak (Kali Kamli). In commemoration of this, the ritual of Kamli is observed in Sufi khanqahs. Before the sama, the disciples hold the Kamli above their heads, and the qawwals recite the Kamli verses. Gradually, while moving forward, the Kamli is respectfully draped over the spiritual guide.

Ik kamlii vaalaa aayaa
sar pe rahmat haq kaa saaya

daaman me.n iimaan kaa saaya
aa.nkho.n me.n 'irfaan-e-darakhshaa.n

siine me.n qur.aan
ik kamlii vaalaa aayaa

nuur-e-sadaaqat ruu-e-jabii.n par
naqsh-e-amaanat lauh-e-jabii.n par

dil me.n zauq-e-yaqii.n aur lab par
Allaah kaa farmaan

ik kamlii vaalaa aayaa
'ilm-o-hunar kii daulat vaale

'aql-o-daanish hikmat vaale
sun ke us kii saada baate.n

sakht hu.e hairaan
ik kamlii vaalaa aayaa[14]

This poetry by Sufi Tabassum exalts the Prophet as the 'Kamli Wala' (The One with the Cloak)—a figure of divine mercy and enlightenment. This describes how the Prophet's (PBUH) presence brings spiritual illumination, with his forehead shining with truth (Nur-e-Sadaqat), his chest carrying the Quran, and his words embodying Allah's (SWT) command. The verses emphasise that even those endowed with knowledge, intellect, and wisdom are left in awe of the Prophet's (PBUH) simple yet profound teachings, highlighting his unparalleled wisdom and divine connection. This poetry, deeply imbued with love and reverence, reflects the Sufi tradition of honouring the Prophet's (PBUH) spiritual legacy, highlighting faith, divine wisdom, and the transformative power of his presence.

16. Joda: Before the sama, the disciples bring the Joda (clothes) of their spiritual guide on a tray (tashtari). The tray also contains a handkerchief, perfume, soap, and other items. The disciples stand with the tray balanced on their heads. As the qawwals recite the Kamli, the mureeds sway rhythmically, occasionally raising their hands in devotion. They then present the Joda to the murshid with great reverence. The murshid glances at the Joda and then distributes it among the disciples. After this ritual, the qawwals stop reciting the Joda verses and continue with the rest of the kalaam.

Banaa hai faiz-e-jahaa.ngiirii valiiullaah kaa jo.daa
ra.ngaa hai qaadrii ra.ng me.n naqiibullaah kaa jo.daa

ye rutba aur ye 'azmat mubaarak ho mubaarak ho
tujhe rahmat ne pahnaayaa rasuulullaah kaa jo.daa

muriido chuum lo ba.dh kar niraalaa faiz paa.oge
naqiib-e-rahmat-e-haq hai habiibullaah kaa jo.daa

karam se bhar rahii hai aaj har mohtaaj kii jholii
kuchh aisii barkate.n laayaa naqiibullaah kaa jo.daa

lagaa.o us ko aa.nkho.n se dilo.n me.n raushnii hogii
niraalaa maa'rifat kaa hai naqiibullaah kaa jo.daa

'fanaa' sar par rakho ban jaa.egii big.dii hu.ii qismat
ke faiz-e-bul-'ulaa.ii hai naqiibullaah kaa jo.daa[15]

The Joda by Fana Bulandshahri reflects the deep spiritual reverence and devotion associated with the ritual in Sufi traditions. It exalts the Joda as a sacred symbol of divine favour, tracing its spiritual lineage from Prophet Muhammad (PBUH) to great Sufi saints like Hazrat Naqeebullah and others. The poet describes the Joda as infused with divine grace and the Qadiri spiritual colour, bringing blessings, enlightenment, and transformation to those who receive it. The verses encourage devotees to cherish the Joda, as it serves as a conduit of spiritual illumination and mercy.

The poetry captures the essence of Sufi devotion, where even a simple garment becomes a vessel of divine blessings, capable of healing, uplifting, and guiding seekers on the mystical path.

17. SANDAL: Sandal is a ritual involving the application of sandalwood paste on the shrine, symbolising veneration. This tradition encapsulates the reverence towards and spiritual significance of the shrine and is a sacred tradition performed at Sufi shrines in Awadh.

Mushk-e-'ambar ko milaa kar jo banaayaa sandal
sandalii.n jaam me.n phuule na samaayaa sandal

us kii tarkiib-e-bahishtii ko niraalaa paayaa
'itr-e-firdaus se huuro.n ne basaayaa sandal

jinn-o-insaa.n ke sivaa saath thii huuro.n sii
mere khvaaja kaa ba.dii dhuum se aayaa sandal

nahii.n miltaa hai jo kaafuur pas-e-marg to kyaa
ho muyassar mujhe khvaaja kaa khudaayaa sandal

Allaah re ye shaan-e-kamaal-e-khvaaja
sar pe rizvaa.n ne ba-sad fakhr uthaayaa sandal

us ke sadqe ho.n ki rahmat se basaa kar jis ne
dard-e-dil ke liye iksiir banaayaa sandal

vajd me.n aa ga.e sab zaa.er-e-khvaaja 'siimaab'
huur ne aa ke jo dargaah me.n gaayaa sandal[16]

This Sandal poetry by Seemab Akbarabadi describes how the preparation of sandalwood paste is infused with divine blessings, elevating it beyond a mere ritual to an act of profound spiritual significance. The verses depict the grandeur of the ceremony, emphasising how the arrival of the Sandal procession at the shrine of the revered Sufi saint is met with joy, devotion, and mystical ecstasy. This expresses a longing to be blessed with the sacred sandalwood paste, equating it with divine grace and healing.

Through vivid imagery and mystical symbolism, the poetry captures the transformative power of the Sandal ritual, illustrating how it serves as an elixir for the hearts of devotees, deepening their spiritual connection with the saint and the Divine. There is also the mention of heavenly beings joining in the ecstatic celebration where the earthly and celestial realms unite in praise of the saint's spiritual legacy.

18. Phool: The ritual of offering flowers at Sufi shrines during gulposhi (floral tributes) has spiritual significance and is accompanied by qawwali compositions. The ritual of floral offerings conveys the profound spiritual bond between the devotee and the saint, where flowers become a medium of expressing faith, surrender, and divine connection.

Tumhaare dar pe jo baabaa cha.dhaa.e jaate hai.n
vo phuul makke madiine se laa.e jaate hai.n

faqiir apnaa muqaddar banaa.e jaate hai.n
dar-e-fariid pe dhuunii ramaa.e jaate hai.n

nigaah-e-lutf jo baabaa uthaa.e jaate hai.n
har ek Gariib kii big.dii banaa.e jaate hai.n

ataa ho sadqa khvaaja-piyaa gariibo.n ko
sadaa.e.n maa.ngne vaale lagaa.e jaate hai.n

namaaz-e-ishq adaa kar rahe hai.n diivaane
dar-e-fariid pe sar ko jhukaa.e jaate hai.n

sivaa-e-baabaa kisii kii talab nahii.n hai 'fanaa'
ham un ke ishq me.n hastii mitaa.e jaate hai.n[17]

This Phool by Fana Bulandshahri captures the essence of devotion as flowers, symbolising love, humility, and reverence, which are presented at the shrine of Baba Farid. The act of offering flowers is portrayed as a gesture of deep veneration, with devotees bringing blossoms from the sacred lands of Mecca and Madina, further emphasising the spiritual purity of the ritual.

The poetry highlights the transformative power of devotion, illustrating how faqirs (spiritual seekers) consider this act as a means to reshape their destiny and draw divine blessings. It speaks of the mystical connection between the saint and his followers, portraying how a single glance of grace (nazar-e-karam) from the saint can alleviate the sufferings of the poor and troubled souls.

The verses resonate with the deep emotional longing and surrender of the devotees who bow their heads in humility, seeking spiritual fulfilment and the saint's intercession. The concluding lines reflect the ultimate expression of love and devotion, with a willingness to annihilate the self in the love of the saint, aligning with the Sufi concept of self-dissolution in divine love.

19. **Basant:** A unique tradition attributed to Hazrat Nizamuddin Auliya and popularised by Amir Khusrau, celebrating the arrival of spring. It reflects the joyous confluence of divine love and spiritual renewal. A well-known story about Basant is associated with Hazrat Nizamuddin Auliya. His beloved nephew, Khwaja Taqiuddin Nuh, passed away at a young age, leaving Hazrat deeply grieved. In his sorrow, he would often walk in contemplation near his khanqah at the Chabutra-e-Yaran (the Pavilion of Friends). When Amir Khusrau, his most devoted disciple, learned of this, he sought a way to bring some joy to his master. It was the day of Basant Panchami, and people in Delhi were carrying mustard blossoms to offer at the Kalkaji Temple, believing that it would please the goddess. Curious, Amir Khusrau asked them about this tradition, and they explained the reason behind the offering. Inspired by this, Amir Khusrau picked some mustard flowers himself and went to Chabutra-e-Yaran, where he placed them at Hazrat Nizamuddin Auliya's feet. Seeing the yellow flowers, Hazrat asked, '*Cheest?*' (What is this?). Amir Khusrau playfully replied, '*Arab Yaar Toree Basant Manai*' (Oh Arab beloved, I am celebrating your Basant). A smile spread across Hazrat's face. From that day onwards, the celebration of Basant became an annual tradition in the Chishti and other khanqahs, symbolising joy, renewal, and the spiritual bond between the master and disciple.

ab ke basa.nt mohe bahut suhaa.e
ruuthe balam more ghar phir aa.e

dhan joban mai.n apnaa vaaruu.n
jo piyaa ha.ns-ha.ns garvaa lagaa.e

'Khaliil' piyaa ke bal-bal jaa.uu.n
bichh.de more ka.nt milaa.e[18]

This Basant by Khaleel Safipuri embodies the spiritual and emotional significance of the Basant festival in Sufi traditions, particularly within the Chishti order. Rooted in the above-mentioned legend of Hazrat Nizamuddin Auliya and Amir Khusrau, Basant is celebrated as a symbol of renewal, joy, and the spiritual reunion between the seeker and the divine.

The verses reflect the essence of longing and the joy of reunion, a recurring theme in Sufi poetry, where the Beloved (balam) symbolises the Divine or the spiritual guide. The delight at the return of the Beloved draws parallels to the blossoming of mustard flowers in spring, which represents hope, love, and spiritual rejuvenation. The imagery of surrender and devotion is also prominent, even offering the youth and beauty in devotion, reinforcing the Sufi ideal of selflessness and submission.

Additionally, the final verse conveys the poet's deep gratitude and admiration for the beloved, emphasising how separation (firaq) is transformed into union (visal) through love and devotion.

20. Bhajan: Sufi saints composed devotional songs in a language and style deeply rooted in bhakti traditions, fostering an enduring spiritual unity between different faiths. Reflecting the syncretic spirit of Indian Sufi tradition, bhajans are still sung at Sufi shrines, exemplifying cultural harmony. Notably, Qazi Ashraf Mahmood's bhajan 'Darshanollas' was melodiously rendered by Pandit Bhimsen Joshi and gained immense popularity.

Jag meñ aayā hai to pyāre jap le hari kā naam
jag-dātā-hari

apne man meñ ko.ū bichāre jap le hari kā naam
jag-dātā-hari

hridai meñ harī samā.e jo dhūñde so vā ko paa.e
hare hari haiñ jag ujiyāre jap le hari kā naam
jag-dātā-hari

paap kī gañgā meñ nahānā paapī bhañvar meñ duub na jaanā
nayyā lagā le pan ke kināre jap le hari kā naam
jag-dātā-hari

'sanjar' koī kaam na aave dhan-daulat sab yahīñ rah jaaye
jā.egā tu haath pasāre jap le hari kā naam
jag-dātā-hari[19]

This Bhajan by Sanjar Ghazipuri reflects the syncretic spirit of Indian Sufi tradition, emphasising the remembrance of the Divine (Hari) as the ultimate truth and source of salvation. In line with the Sufi philosophy of divine devotion transcending religious boundaries, this composition resonates with both Hindu and Sufi thought, advocating for constant remembrance (zikr) and surrender to the Divine.

The verses emphasise the impermanence of worldly possessions, urging the listener to chant the name of the Divine (Hari) before it is too late. The poet metaphorically compares sins to the Ganga's waters, warning against being engulfed in the whirlpool of worldly attachments. The imagery of a boat and reaching the shore symbolises the journey of the soul navigating the turbulent waters of life, reinforcing the need for divine guidance to attain liberation.

The closing lines serve as a powerful reminder of mortality, stating that wealth and material achievements will ultimately be left behind, and only faith and devotion will hold value in the hereafter. This aligns with the Sufi concept of detachment (zuhd) and reliance on the Divine (tawakkul), encouraging spiritual seekers to prioritise inner enlightenment over material pursuits.

Through its diverse and profound expressions, qawwali continues to be a living embodiment of India's pluralistic heritage, a mystical tradition that transcends religious boundaries, connecting souls to the divine. It is not merely a musical form but a spiritual experience that resonates with the harmony of human existence and the universality of divine love.

A Sufi is fundamentally an aesthete who, through poetry and actions, envisions a world that embraces all of humanity. It is a vast, inclusive universe where all beings share the same essence. Love unites all, dissolving distinctions and nurturing unity in diversity. In this imagined world of the Sufis, multiplicity harmonises into oneness, and diversity manifests as beauty.

The journey of qawwali echoes this mystical voyage that transcends boundaries and celebrates the union of the lover with the Beloved.

Excerpted from.

* Guldasta-e-Qawwali, Volume-1&2, Suman Mishra, Rekhta Books, 2019

Endnotes

1. Bedam Shah Warsi, Nurul-Ain: *Mosahhaf-e-Bedam* (p. 115), Shaikh Ata Mohammad, Lahore (1935)
2. Seemab Akbarabadi, *Tazkira Sho.ara-e-Warsia* (p. 115), Fine Book Printers (1993)
3. Muztar Khairabadi, *Khirman,* Part-3 (p. 20), Jawed Akhtar (2015)
4. Hazrat Waqaruddin Qadri, *Rang* (p. 359), Surood-e-Ruhani
5. Hazrat Amir Khusrau
6. Maikash Akbarabadi, *Maikada* (p. 42), Agra Akhbar, Agra (1931)
7. Hazrat Bedam Warsi
8. Makhdoom Khadim Safi, *Asrar-e-Haqiqat* (p. 55)
9. Abdul Hadi Kavish, *Sahba-e-Ishq*
10. Hazrat Shah Niyaz Ahmad Barelvi, *Diwan-e-Niaz-e-Be-Niaz* (p. 164)
11. Hazrat Bedam Shah Warsi, *Diwan-e-Bedam Shah Warsi* (p. 63), Hindustani Book Depot (1935)
12. Hazrat Bedam Shah Warsi, *Nurul-Ain: Mosahhaf-e-Bedam* (p. 112), Shaikh Ata Mohammad, Lahore (1935)
13. Waseem Khairabadi
14. Sufi Tabassum, *Kulliyat-e-Sufi Tabassum*
15. Fana Bulandshahri, *Deewan-e-Fana*
16. Seemab Akbarabadi, *Gulshan-e-Qawwali*
17. Fana Bulandshari
18. Khaleel Safipuri, *Khayaban-e-khaleel*
19. Sanjar Ghazipuri, *Diwan-e-Sanjar Al-Maruf Guldasta-e-Kalaam-e-Sanjar* (p. 120), Shaikh Ghulam Hussain and Sons Tajiran-e-Kutub, Kashmiri Bazar, Lahore

خبر تحیر عشق سن نہ جنوں رہا نہ پری رہی

خبر تحیر عشق سن نہ جنوں رہا نہ پری رہی
نہ تو تو رہا نہ تو میں رہا جو رہی سو بے خبری رہی

شہ بے خودی نے عطا کیا مجھے اب لباس برہنگی
نہ خرد کی بخیہ گری رہی نہ جنوں کی پردہ دری رہی

چلی سمت غیب سیں کیا ہوا کہ چمن ظہور کا جل گیا
مگر ایک شاخ نہال غم جسے دل کہو سو ہری رہی

خبر تحیر عشق سن نہ جنوں رہا نہ پری رہی

Poet: Siraj Aurangabadi

The Feminine in Qawwali

Danish Iqbal

Spiritual Egalitarianism and Gender Paradoxes in Sufism

ufi philosophy, at least in its theoretical underpinnings, has historically emphasised spiritual egalitarianism. Renowned female mystics such as Hazrat Rabia Basri, Lal Ded, Mirabai, and Zebunnesa Makhfi exemplify the deeply entrenched belief in the equal spiritual capacity of men and women. However, while Sufi thought has championed metaphysical parity, the practical realisation of this ideal has been undermined by prevailing patriarchal structures.

Hazrat Rabia Basri, an eminent female Sufi mystic of the eighth century, is widely acknowledged as a seminal figure in the articulation of romantic mysticism within the Islamic tradition. Her conceptualisation of ishq—unencumbered by conventional eschatological considerations of paradise and perdition—foregrounded an absolute and selfless love for the divine. Despite the patriarchal constraints of her time, Rabia's theological and mystical expositions transcended these limitations, establishing divine love as a central tenet of Sufi praxis. Her influence extended beyond the Arabic and Persian literary traditions, profoundly shaping the evolution of Sufi poetry in the Indian subcontinent.

As Annemarie Schimmel has observed, Rabia's mystical philosophy exerted a profound impact on subsequent Sufi poets, inspiring the development of female archetypes in Indo-Persian and vernacular mystical poetry. Figures such as Heer, Sassi, Sohni, and Marvi—enshrined in the literary and oral traditions of South Asia—emerged as allegorical embodiments of love's transcendental longing for the divine. This feminine narrative, rooted in Rabia's mystical ethos, played a foundational role in the evolution of *Ishqiya dastans* (narratives of divine love) and the broader tradition of expressing spiritual devotion through the feminine voice.

Although Rabia Basri's legacy legitimised the feminine presence in Sufi literary traditions, women's direct participation in qawwali performance remained circumscribed for centuries. Nonetheless, women exerted a discernible influence on male Sufis and actively patronised male poets. While *zanana mehfils* (female musical gatherings) provided a limited sphere for women's participation, their contributions rarely received the same recognition as those of their male counterparts. The imposition of purdah (seclusion) and the conservatism of shrine culture further constrained their ability to engage in public performances of qawwali.

Feminine Reclamation of Sufi Music: From Marginalisation to Prominence

The twentieth century witnessed a gradual reclamation of space by women in qawwali, both in public and private mehfils. In regions such as Sindh and Punjab, women had historically participated in the ritual of dhamal (whirling), an ecstatic practice associated with Sufi devotion. At the shrines (dargahs) of Lal Shahbaz Qalandar in Sindh and Data Ganj Bakhsh in Lahore, both men and women engaged in a localised adaptation of the whirling dervish tradition, particularly during the recitation of popular Sufi compositions. This participation, though informal, afforded women a degree of spiritual and performative agency within a domain from which they were otherwise excluded.

The evolution of qawwali reflects a complex interplay between spiritual devotion and human emotion, tradition and modernity, and inclusion and exclusion. While its origins are deeply embedded in the sanctified traditions of Sufi mysticism, the genre has undergone significant transformations, often challenging the rigid dichotomies imposed upon it by religious orthodoxy and patriarchal structures. The feminine presence in qawwali, though historically marginalised, has been instrumental in shaping its thematic and symbolic dimensions. Despite systemic barriers, women have continued to exert an undeniable influence on the spiritual and aesthetic discourse of qawwali, signalling an ongoing negotiation between tradition and contemporary expressions of Sufi musicality.

Scholars such as Shamim Barney Abbas argue that, paradoxically, the female voice occupies a central position within Sufi music and poetry, serving as the primary conduit for expressing love, longing, and divine yearning. The recurrent motif of the soul's aspiration for divine union is frequently embodied in the feminine voice, underscoring the complex relationship between gender, spirituality, and musical expression. Yet, despite this symbolic prominence, women's direct participation in Sufi musical traditions has been consistently circumscribed.

In the Indian subcontinent, the historical marginalisation of women in qawwali can be attributed to the interplay of doctrinal interpretations and sociocultural attitudes. Even within the khanqah (Sufi lodge) tradition, where spiritual inclusivity was theoretically upheld, women were often excluded from central performance roles. This disparity underscores the contradiction between the Sufi emphasis on spiritual equality and the patriarchal norms that have shaped its lived practice. Obviously, it is a paradoxical dimension of qawwali that despite its engagement with the feminine and despite the pervasive use of feminine imagery in Sufi poetry and music—where it served as a metaphor for longing, devotion, and the soul's yearning for divine union—the participation of women in qawwali performance has been systematically curtailed by entrenched socio-religious and patriarchal norms.

The historical hegemony of patriarchy has imposed significant limitations on women's agency within various cultural spheres, including their involvement in Sufi musical traditions. Although the feminine voice remains integral to the thematic and symbolic fabric of qawwali, women's direct participation in its performance has historically been marginalised. This exclusion is reflective of a broader societal and religious framework wherein men have traditionally dictated the contours of artistic and spiritual expression, thereby relegating women to the periphery of performance spaces.

The Gendered Division of Space in Qawwali Performance Traditions

Historically, qawwali performance traditions were deeply entrenched in familial and gharana-based structures, which monopolised the dargah space and established hereditary learning as the primary mode of transmission. These traditions, governed by patriarchal norms, frequently excluded women from performing in sacred contexts, citing concerns about the 'male gaze' as a justification for their marginalisation. Despite these restrictions, alternative spaces such as zanana mehfils continued to provide a platform for female participation, allowing the feminine voice to persist within the tradition, albeit in a limited and less publicised form.

Despite its inherently inclusive nature, qawwali has historically remained a male-dominated androcentric performance tradition. This exclusion of women can be attributed to prevailing gender norms within Islamic theological and sociocultural frameworks, which have often marginalised female participation in public religious and musical spheres. Orthodox interpretations of Sharia have further restricted women's engagement in qawwali, reinforcing a patriarchal paradigm that has shaped its historical development. Obviously, the absence of women in qawwali performances is not merely a theological imposition but also a reflection of entrenched sociocultural dynamics of Indian subcontinent. While doctrinal interpretations may have discouraged female involvement in public sama, women have engaged with qawwali in alternative, albeit peripheral, capacities. The persistent gendered structuring of qawwali has thus been a product of intersecting religious, social, and historical forces.

Comparative analyses indicate that while Sufi music traditions in regions such as Turkey and Central Asia permitted greater female participation, the Indian subcontinent witnessed a gradual erosion of women's involvement in sama and qawwali rituals. This shift can be attributed to the increasing influence of orthodox Sharia interpretations, which imposed stringent restrictions on women's participation in public religious expressions, including musical performances. Moreover, the broader socio-political landscape of medieval India reinforced gendered hierarchies that further marginalised female agency within Sufi traditions.

Unlike the relatively inclusive Sufi musical spaces in Turkey and Central Asia, the Indian practice of mehfil became increasingly male-dominated. While mehfil gatherings were initially accessible to both men and women, rigid orthodoxies gradually curtailed female participation, relegating women's spiritual engagement to private or domestic spheres. This evolution of exclusion was not merely a consequence of religious edicts but was also shaped by broader societal transformations that intensified patriarchal norms.

As noted by Manoj Kumar in his sociological study *Ritual and Music: A Sociological Analysis of the Dimensions of Qawwali*, the marginalisation of women in Indian qawwali traditions must be understood within a broader historical and cultural framework, rather than being solely attributed to theological injunctions. The interplay between religious doctrine, societal patriarchy, and shifting cultural perceptions contributed to the systematic exclusion of women from public qawwali performances.

The Dual Nature of Qawwali Lyrics and the Feminine Voice

Prominent scholars such as Annemarie Schimmel, in her seminal work *As Through the Veil*, have explored the intricate interplay between sensual and spiritual longing in qawwali lyrics. Schimmel highlights that the poetic metaphor of yearning for the beloved serves not only as a spiritual motif but also as a means of interrogating and critiquing prevailing social constructs. Within this interpretative framework, the feminine voice emerges as a crucial medium for articulating both individual and collective expressions of love and devotion, positioning it as a central element in the mystical discourse of qawwali.

It would be interesting to analyse women's influence on qawwali which ranges from passive engagement to active participation in an intricate and layered way. Regula Qureshi, a leading scholar on qawwali, has examined the historical role of women in this tradition, noting that their engagement was traditionally confined to the sphere of active listening rather than public performance. Women, although excluded from formal qawwali mehfils, played a pivotal role as cultural consumers who shaped musical tastes within the domestic sphere. This form of passive yet influential participation ultimately paved the way for the increased visibility of women in qawwali performances in later years.

Qureshi further argues that women's interaction with Qawwali through emerging media, particularly gramophone recordings, enabled them to exert cultural agency. This shift allowed them to influence the musical landscape and foster an evolving tradition in which both male and female listeners engaged more openly with qawwali. Such developments illustrate a broader process of reclaiming space for women within this historically male-dominated art form.

The evolution of feminine qawwali in India witnessed a transformative moment with the widespread popularisation of the song '*Lal Meri Pat Rakhiyo Bhala*' in the twentieth century. This traditional qawwali, reinterpreted through the incorporation of electric guitar and other modern musical instruments, transcended historical gender restrictions in Sufi musical traditions. Its immense popularity, particularly during the era of gramophone records, facilitated the emergence of the feminine voice in qawwali as a significant cultural force, breaking away from conventional constraints that had previously limited women's participation in this musical form.

The Influence of Bollywood on the Feminine Voice

The representation of qawwali in popular culture, particularly in Bollywood, has played a crucial role in reshaping perceptions of the feminine voice within this musical tradition. Artists like Shakeela Bano Bhopali reversed traditional gender norms in a domain historically dominated by men, and developed a performance style, blending emotive vocalisation, theatrical expressiveness, and a diverse repertoire that spanned Sufi, romantic, and socially reflective themes.

Benson Rajan's research, *Gendered Sufi Music: Mapping Female Voices in Qawwali Performance from Bollywood to YouTube Channels*, offers a comprehensive analysis of how qawwali attained a more heterodox expression through its cinematic adaptation. Bollywood's engagement with qawwali, particularly during the 1950s and 1960s, introduced a dramatic and visually spectacular reinterpretation of the genre, expanding its appeal to a wider audience.

A seminal example of this cinematic transformation is Guru Dutt's *Chaudhvin Ka Chand* (1960), which centred on themes of purdah and romantic longing. The film's narrative and visual composition encapsulate the romantic mysticism integral to Sufi thought, presenting a poetic meditation on the transitory nature of human love and divine yearning. The renowned couplet by Dagh Dehlavi, *Saaf chhupte bhi nahi, saamne aate bhi nahi* (They neither hide completely nor reveal themselves entirely) serves as a cinematic manifestation of this spiritual and romantic tension.

Guru Dutt's portrayal of qawwali in *Chaudhvin Ka Chand* also underscores the interplay between the male gaze and the elusive, veiled presence of the feminine. This thematic engagement not only critiques traditional gender norms but also reflects the broader cultural politics surrounding female visibility in public and sacred spaces. Through such cinematic interventions, Bollywood has contributed to the evolving discourse on gender, spirituality, and performance within the qawwali tradition, demonstrating the enduring relevance of the feminine voice in both historical and contemporary contexts.

The exclusion of women from formal qawwali spaces and their eventual return must be understood within the broader historical and societal structures that governed gender segregation and a delayed acceptance. Interestingly, male performers were also subject to exclusion unless they belonged to an inherited lineage or an accepted scholarly or musical tradition, but the restriction of female participation even within gharanas was particularly pronounced due to deeply ingrained notions of morality and decorum. The prevailing belief that a woman's voice could incite desire or emotional agitation among male listeners underscores the underlying patriarchal anxieties that shaped these practices. Ironically, this perspective implicitly positioned men as emotionally impressionable, reinforcing a gendered double standard that privileged male authority while limiting female agency.

Although such exclusionary practices may appear antiquated in contemporary discourse, it is imperative to situate them within their historical and cultural contexts, wherein gender segregation was widely accepted as a societal norm. The mid-twentieth century marked a gradual shift in these dynamics, with increased social interaction between genders facilitating a reconfiguration of qawwali performance traditions. The contemporary era has seen a significant departure from these rigid constraints, allowing for mixed-gender audiences and greater participation of women in qawwali, reflecting broader societal transformations in gender norms and cultural inclusivity.

Bibliography

- Qureshi, R.B. (1995). *Sufi Music of India and Pakistan: Sound, Context, and Meaning in Qawwali.* Chicago: University of Chicago Press. This is a seminal work on qawwali, exploring its historical, cultural, and spiritual dimensions. Qureshi provides an in-depth analysis of qawwali performances, their structure, and their role in Sufi rituals.

- Schimmel, A. (1975). *Mystical Dimensions of Islam*. Chapel Hill: University of North Carolina Press. This book offers a comprehensive overview of Sufism, including the role of music and poetry in Sufi practices. It provides context for understanding qawwali as a spiritual art form.

- Neubauer, E., and Doubleday, V. (Eds). (2006). *Ethnomusicology: A Contemporary* Reader. New York: Routledge. This collection includes essays on various musical traditions, including qawwali, and discusses its evolution and cultural significance.

- Manuel, P. (1993). *Cassette Culture: Popular Music and Technology in North India.* Chicago: University of Chicago Press. This book examines the impact of technology and commercialisation on traditional music forms, including qawwali, in South Asia.

Journal Articles

- Qureshi, R.B. (1986). 'Sufi Music and the Historicity of Oral Tradition.' *Ethnomusicology,* 30(3), 491–516. This article explores the oral traditions of Sufi music, including qawwali, and their historical development.

- Baily, J. (1988). 'Music of Afghanistan: Professional Musicians in the City of Herat.' Cambridge University Press, 12(1), 1–26. While focused on Afghan music, this article provides insights into the broader regional context of Sufi musical traditions, including qawwali.

- Katz, M. (2012). 'The Musical Journey of Qawwali: From Sufi Shrines to Global Stages'. Asian Music, 43(2), 1–25. This article traces the transformation of qawwali from a devotional practice to a globalised musical genre.

Chapters in Edited Volumes

- Qureshi, R. B. (2002). 'Islam and Music: The Case of Qawwali.' In *The Garland Encyclopedia of World Music: South Asia* (Vol. 5, pp. 185–197). New York: Routledge. This chapter provides an overview of Qawwali within the broader context of South Asian music and Islamic traditions.

- Ernst, C.W. (1997). 'The Spirit of Islamic Calligraphy: Qawwali and Sufi Poetry.' In *Sufism: An Essential Introduction* (pp. 89–112). Chapel Hill: University of North Carolina Press. This chapter explores the relationship between Sufi poetry and music, with a focus on Qawwali.

KAWALI

Its Earliest Gramophone Records in the Voice of Female Artists

Amar Nath Sharma

The conservation and reproduction of sound appears as a recurring motif across all traditions, both oral and written, grand and modest. The invention of sound recording and reproduction devices marks one of civilisation's greatest milestones. Until a century and a half ago, preserving a voice for posterity remained an elusive dream—what is now child's play was once the stuff of fantasy and fable.

The absence of sound-recording technology deprived humanity of countless historical voices that shaped our history and destiny. Imagine possessing audio records of Christ's Sermon on the Mount or Socrates's final words. In the Indian context, we might have preserved Lord Krishna's teaching of the Bhagavad Gita to Arjuna, the dialogues between Lord Rama and Lakshmana, or the discourses of Lord Buddha, Lord Mahavira, and Guru Nanak Dev-ji. Such recordings would have provided undisputed historical evidence of royal proclamations and significant events of their times. Recorded voices of kings and their era's pivotal events would have provided undisputed historical evidence for posterity.

In the realm of music, we might have treasured the legendary performances of Swami Haridas, the great Tansen, and Baiju Bawara. Yet all these voices remain lost to time, for before 1877, no recording or speaking devices existed.

Thomas Alva Edison invented and introduced the world's first sound-recording and reproducing device around 1877: the phonograph, which used 'Brown Wax Cylinders' (also called 'phonograms') as its recording medium. India quickly recognised the significance of this magical invention. The Bengali periodical *Sambad Prabhakar* published news of the first live phonograph demonstration in Calcutta (now Kolkata) on 21 December 1878:

> 'Messers Herbert Harraden (son of Mr. Samuel Harraden) has demonstrated in the Dalhousie institute a machine named the 'Phonograph', invented by [Thomas Alva] Edison. In this tiny machine, any kind of words and songs can be inserted and later the machine can reproduce the same without any alteration. A large crowd gathered during the exhibition. A Hindi song rendered by Mr. Dave Carson was clearly reproduced from this machine.'

The Bengali periodical *Samachar Chandrika* had first reported Edison's invention in its issue dated 9 January 1878. Later, an advertisement in *The Statesman* on 13 July 1885, featured E. Lafont's intriguing promise to demonstrate the phonograph – 'the wonderful talking machine' to speak, cough, laugh, and sing.

At this juncture, while the world remained spellbound by the phonograph, German scientist Emil Berliner introduced another marvel by the end of the nineteenth century—the gramophone, which used discs instead of cylinders for recording. This technology spread rapidly worldwide, and by 1902, India witnessed the arrival of its first commercial recording team in Calcutta, then the capital. The team, representing 'The Gramophone and Typewriter Ltd', was led by sound recordist William Fredrick Gaisberg with George Dillnut as his assistant.

Notably, Gaisberg had already recorded Indian performers in London in 1899. These early recordings included verses from Firdausi's satire on Sultan Mahmood, *Saki-Nama* by Hafiz Shirazi, and works by Ghalib and Zaheer Fariabi, in the voices of Mr Ahmed and Mr Hazrat. While these records bore 'E Berliner's Gramophone Record' as their trademark, none mentioned 'Kawali' against any released song.

Before commercial sound recordings began on Indian soil in 1902, a non-commercial era of recording had already emerged using Brown Wax Cylinders. Though cylindrography of complete recordings from this period are lost, my research documented in *The Wonder that was the Cylinder* indicates renderings and recordings of a few songs like *'Dil Se Jo Yaad-e-Khuda Karte Hain and Chehra Dikha Do Kamaliwale'* on cylinders, which appear akin to a Kawali song. But in want of their classification as 'Kawali' on these cylinders, we are unable to call them Kawalis.

As we move further, we note that in the first recording session in Calcutta of 1902, duly headed by W.F. Gaisberg, he did not cut any record of Kawalis. But in 1904-05, when sound recordists Willim Sinkler Derby and Max Hemp, representing the same company landed in India (Calcutta), to commence the second session of sound recordings on Indian soil, they recorded three Kawali recordings in the voice of Indians. The first one was in the voice of a male artist named Bijay Gopal Lahiry having the words *Dani-o-Dana* (Sindhu Kawali) [Bengali] and was released in the Indian market under a 7-inch dia gramophone record having the number G-2-12284. This was followed by another 7-inch dia gramophone record in the voice of a famous lady singer named Binodini Dassi of Calcutta. The record number was G-13625 with the words *Ki Aachhe Tomar Monay* (Hamir Kawali) [Bengali]. A third record was released in the voice of a female Bengali singer named Jadumani Dassi. This was also a 7-inch dia gramophone record and was represented by the record number G-2-12296, having the words *Dukhhara Tara Tomai* (Kawali Barwa) [Bengali]. Hereinafter it started recordings of many male and female Kawali singers in the days to follow.

As this chapter documents the earliest gramophone recordings of female artists of commercial sound recordings in India, for the convenience of our readers, I am providing a table that details fifty-one important Kawali recordings during this timeframe in the voice of female singers which have been specifically documented as Kawali.

Disclaimer: All records from the personal archival collection of A.N. Sharma. The representations of the record labels here have been used for illustrative purposes only and no claim is made in regard to exclusivity, and the 'trademarks' shown on these labels are the proprietary interest of the producing company only.

gramophone records
LIMITED EDITION
Broadcast

Gazal-Kawali
Sung by Sitangiri Dassi

Kawali
Sung by Sumati Bai

Ghazal-Kawali
Sung by Akhtari Bai

Ghazal-Kawali
Sung by Janki Bai

Kawali
Sung by Saraswati Bai Faterpekar

Gazal-Kawali
Sung by Akhtari Jan

Gazal-Kawali
Sung by Nawab Jan Aligarh

GAZAL-KAWALI
Sung by Miss Jawahir

GAZAL-KAWALI
Sung by Zaban

GAZAL-KAWALI
Sung by Azizan Jan

Kawali
Sung by Kali Jan

Gazal-Kawali
Sung by Benodini Dassi

Kawali
Sung by Keeti Jan

Kawali
Sung by Malka Jan

Miss Zohrabai Agrewali

Miss Amir Jan

Miss Nannhi Jan

Miss Manoda Sundari Dassi

Miss Janki Bai

Miss Gauhar Jan

Nawaban Tawaif

Miss Binodini Dassi

TABLE

Name of the Artist	Lyrics	Record No. and Make
1. Miss Binodini Dassi of Calcutta	'Ki Aachhe Tomar Monay' (Bengali- Hamir-Kawali)	Gramophone Record No. G7) 13625-" dia disc)
2. Miss Jadumani Dassi of Calcutta	'Dukhhara Tara Tomai' of (Bengali-Barwa-Kawali)	Gramophone Record No. G-(7) 12296-(2" dia disc)
3. Miss Banni Jan of Meerut	'Azi Haan Khwajaji Hamari Araj Sunio' (Kawali)	Gramophone Record No. G-(7) 12447-(2" dia disc)
4. Miss Asgari Jan of Agra	'Teri Yadein Rukh Mein Wah' (Ghazal Kawali)	Gramophone Record No. G-(7) 12468-(2" dia disc)
5. Miss Gauhar Jan of Calcutta	'Ke Tumi Nidiya' (Bengali-Desh-Kawali)	Gramophone Concert Record No. G.C. 10) 13864" dia disc)
6. Miss Bindubala Dassi of Agra	'Nipat Kapat Tuyo Shyam' (Bengali-Sindhu-Khamaj Kawali)	Gramophone Concert Record No. G.C. 13893
7. Miss Mumtaz Jan of Delhi	'Tumhi Sardar Aalim Ya Muhammad Mustafa' (Kawali)	Gramophone Record No. G. 7) 12436" dia disc)
8. Miss Shamim of Lucknow	'Ye Na Thi Hamari Kismet Ki Wisale Yaar Hota' (Kawali)	Gramophone Concert Record No. G.C. (10) 12221-(3" dia disc)
9. Miss Mehmuda Jan of Meerut	'Nikaalun Kis Tarah Tamanna, Sakhta Mushquil Hai' (Ghazal Kawali)	Gramophone Concert Record No. G.C. (13061-(3
10. Miss Nannhi Jan of Agra	'Mast Gashtam Az Do Chashme Sa' (Ghazal Kawali)	Gramophone Concert Record No. G.C. (10) 13117-(3" dia disc)
11. Miss Zeban Jan of Shaharanpur	'Tere Fayaz-e-Kadam ne Kar Diya Gulshan' (Ghazal Kawali)	Gramophone Concert Record No. G.C. (10) 13121-(3" dia disc)
12. Miss Mator Jan of Kasur	'Zara Washla Per Ho Ishara Tumhara' (Jangla-Kawali)	Gramophone Concert Record No. G.C. (10) 13152-(3" dia disc)
13. Miss Jhandi of Jhelum	'Chekunmaz Hairat Aaram Kezman' (Persian) (Ghazal-Zillo-Kawali)	Gramophone Concert Record No. G.C. (10) 13193-(3" dia disc)
14. Miss Keeti Jan of Meerut	'Aye Jaan Gam-e-dushman Mein' (Kawali)	Gramophone Concert Record No. G.C. (10) 12173-(3" dia disc)
15. Miss Nawab Jan of Aligarh	'Ya Rasool Allah' (Ghazal Kawali)	Gramophone Concert Record No. G.C. (10) 13293-(3" dia disc)
16. Miss Jankibai Chhappan-chhuri of Allahabad	'Ek Kafir Pe Tabiyat Aa Gayee' (Ghazal Kawali)	Gramophone Concert Record No. G.C. 10) 13642-3" dia disc)
17. Miss Malka Jan of Calcutta	'Humne Dekhi Na Sunee Aisee Dhumngar Aankhen' (Jhinjhoti-Kawali)	Gramophone Concert Record No. G-(10) 13529-(3" dia disc)

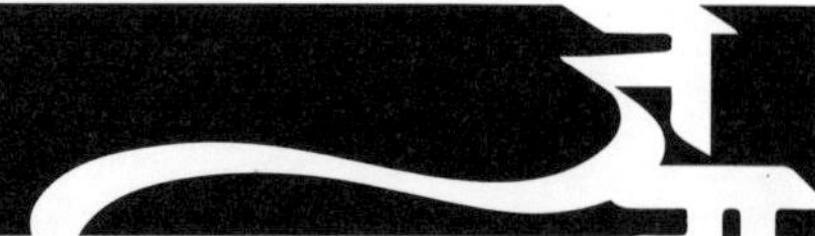

TABLE

Name of the Artist	Lyrics	Record No. and Make
18. Miss Manoda Sundari Dassi of Calcutta	'Bankima Thama' (Bengali-Bhairabi- Kawali)	Pathe Record No. 46878 (11" dia disc)
19. Miss Wazir Jan of Karnal	'Tu Mai Aur Aire Kamseen ke Liye' (Ghazal- Kawali)	Beka Grand Record No. D10) 659-" dia disc)
20. Miss Manik Baiji	'Paani Bhare Tu Kaun Albeli' (Kawali)	Beka Grand Record No. 21193 (10" dia disc)
21. Miss Wazir Jan of Benaras	'Fana Kaise Baka Kaise' (Ghazal Kawali)	Beka Grand Record No. 21613 (10" dia disc)
22. Miss Munnabaijee of Benaras	Hum Teri Raah Mein Mit Jayenge' (Ghazal Kawali)	Beka Grand Record No. 21258 (10" dia disc)
23. Miss Mungabai of Gwalior	'Fana Kaisi' (Ghazal Kawali)	Gramophone Concert Record No.G.C. (10) 13964-(3" dia disc)
24. Miss Achhanbai	Ishare-e-Nigah Ka Ruhe-e -Afhzah Ho Nahi Sakta' (Ghazal Kawali)	Gramophone Concert Record No.G.C. (10) 13975-(3" dia disc)
25. Miss Zohrabai of Agra	'Wo Mast Nazar Hashin Jalwa Dikha Raha Hai' (Ghazal Kawali)	Gramophone Concert Record No.G.C. (10) 13196-(4" dia disc)
26. Miss Amir Jan of Panipat	'Mere Dil Mein Aaja Har Dil Mein Aa Ne Wala' (Ghazal Kawali)	Gramophone Concert Record No.G.C. (10) 13128-(4" dia disc)
27. Miss Mohammad Bandi of Lucknow	'Hai Koi Aisa Jo Yaar Ko Jaana Chhod de' (Ghazal Kawali)	Gramophone Concert Record No.G.C. (10) 13205-(4" dia disc)
28. Miss Mubarak of Multan	'Karam Likhayo Soi Hona' (Multani) (Bhim Kawali)	Gramophone Concert Record No.G.C. (10) 13443-(4" dia disc)
29. Miss Nazir Jan of Bulandshahar	'Haseeno Ka Har Ek Aalam Main Shahara Ho Hi Jaata Hai' (Ghazal-Maand- Kawali)	Gramophone Concert Record No.G.C. (10) 13450-(4" dia disc)
30. Miss Zeban Jan of Jhajar	'Rang-e-Mehfil na Kaha, Isque Ka Saaman Na Raha' (Behag Kawali)	Gramophone Concert Record No.G.C. (10) 13091-(8" dia disc)
31. Miss Nawab Jan Tawaif of Meerut	'Aaz Sarsabj Gulistan-e-Sukhan Dekh Liya' (Kalingra Kawali)	Gramophone Concert Record No.G.C. (10) 13186-(8" dia disc)
32. Miss Hafizan Jan of Shaharanpur	'Kutchh Kar Laye Shringaar Chotur Sunder' (Bhairabi Kawali)	Gramophone Concert Record No.G.C. (10) 13108-(8" dia disc)
33. Miss Kadraji of Peshawar	'Dilwar Pe Maaj Di Girke Sel' (Ghazal-Nauroj-Jhinjouti Kawali) (Pushto)	Gramophone Concert Record No. G.C. 10) 8-13108" dia disc)
34. Miss Sandhan Jan of Ferozepore	'Saanjh Kolen Punnudala' (Kehare Kawali) (Sindhi)	Gramophone Concert Record No. G.C. 10) 8-13115" dia disc)

TABLE

Name of the Artist	Lyrics	Record No. and Make
35. Miss Illahijan of Patiala	'Man Bairagi Mora' (Piloo- Kawali)	Gramophone Concert Record No. G.C. 10) 8-13220" dia disc)
36. Miss Kali Jan of Delhi	'Rukh-e-Anwari Se Jara Parda Utha De Khwaja' (Kawali)	Gramophone Concert Record No. G.C. 10) 8-13530" dia disc)
37. Sitangini Dassi	Ghazal-Kawali	Gramophone Concert Record No. G.C. 10) 4-13276" dia disc)
38. Sumati Bai	'Tauba Na Ghadi Hui Aalam' (Kawali)	Odeon Record No. A 245817b (10" dia disc)
39. Akhtari Jan	Ghazal-Kawali	His Master's Voice I 10) 2-13848" dia disc)
40. Janki Bai of Allahabad	'Ek Kafir Par Tabiyat Aa Gayi' Ghazal-Kawali	Gramophone Concert Record No. G.C. 10) 3-13642" dia disc)
41. Miss Nawab Jan of Aligarh	'Ya Rasool Allah, Zeb-e-Khalique Yakta'Ghazal-Kawali	Gramophone Concert Record No. G.C. 10) 3-13293" dia disc)
42. Saraswati Faterpekar	'Ishq Mein Hue Badnam' (Kawali)	Broadcast Record Number B -3051A (10" dia disc)
43. Miss Akhtari Bai of Fyzabad	'Hai Mohabbat Hai Jawani' (Ghazal Kawali)	Megaphone Record Number OMC 10) 13273-1" dia disc)
44. Azizan Jan of Delhi	'Yeh Na Thi Hamari Kismet, Jo Visal-e-Yaar Hota' (Ghazal Kawali)	Gramophone Concert Record No. G.C. 10) 3-12202" dia disc)
45. Zaban of Delhi	'Tumhe Dil Mein Na Kyun Rakhon' (Ghazal Kawali)	Gramophone Concert Record No. G.C. 10) 3-12154" dia disc)
46. Kali Jan of Delhi	'Raham Ho Kab Sifat Teri' (Kawali)	Gramophone Concert Record No. G.C. 10) 3-12140" dia disc)
47. Miss Binodini Dassi	(Eman-Bhopali-Kawali)	Gramophone Concert Record No. G.C. 10) 3-13885" dia disc)
48. Keeti Jan of Meerut	'Ayi Jaan Gham-e-Dushman Mein' (Kawali)	Gramophone Concert Record No. G.C. 10) 3-12173" dia disc)
49. Malka Jan of Agra	'Humne Dekhi Na Suni Aisi Phumgar Aankhein' (Jhinjoti-Kawali)	Gramophone Concert Record No. G.C. 10) 3-13529" dia disc)
50. Mumtaz Jan of Delhi	'Tumhi Sardar-e-Aalam Ya Muhammad Mustafa' (Ghazal Kawali)	Gramophone Record No. 2-12436
51. Miss Jawahir	(Ghazal Kawali)	Gramophone Record No. 21300

List of Photographs

1. Miss Zohrabai of Agra (Courtesy *Bajanaama* by Amarnath Sharma)

2. Miss Amir Jan of Panipat (Courtesy *Bajanaama* by Amarnath Sharma)

3. Miss Nannhi Jan (Courtesy *Bajanaama* by Amarnath Sharma)

4. Miss Manoda Sundari Dassi (Courtesy Amarnath Sharma)

5. Miss Jankibai Chhappanchhuri recording a song in gramophone studio along with accompanists (Courtesy *The Music Goes Round* by F.W. Gaisberg)

6. Miss Gauhar Jan in the recording studio along with accompanists (Courtesy *The Music Goes Round* by F.W. Gaisberg)

7. Nawaban Tawaif of Meerut (Courtesy *Bajanaama* by Amarnath Sharma)

8. Miss Binodini Dassi (Courtesy Amarnath Sharma)

Bibliography

- *The Wonder That Was the Cylinder: Early and Rare Indian Cylindrical Records* by A.N. Sharma and Anukriti A Sharma, published by Spenta Multimedia, Mumbai

- *The Gramophone Company's First Indian Recordings* (1899-1908) by Michael S. Kinnear, Popular Prakashan, Bombay

- *The Gramophone Company's Indian Recordings* (1899-1908) by Michael S. Kinnear, Bajakhana P.O. Box II, Heidelberg, Victoria, 3084, Australia

- *Bajanaama: A Study of Early Indian Gramophone Records* by A.N. Sharma, Kathachitra Prakashan, Lucknow and Mumbai (India)

- A catalogue of Early Indian Beka-Grand Records

- *The Music Goes Round* by F.W. Gaisberg, The Macmillan Company, New York (1942)

Women Qawwals in Early Bombay Cinema

Yousuf Saeed

f you see qawwali primarily as an Islamic, devotional or Sufi genre of singing, you are probably missing out on a large-scale popular culture in South Asia where qawwali thrived as a mode of secular entertainment, devoid of its sacrality, especially via the Bombay film industry throughout the twentieth century and more. Since popular Hindustani movies are seen by some with disdain as they are filled with melodrama, hardly anyone has studied these movies seriously as part of our cultural history. But it is mostly through this cinema that qawwali emerged as a medium of mass entertainment where any types of lyrics—secular, romantic, mystical, funny or serious—could be sung through them, and in any kind of space, not necessarily only a Sufi shrine. Also, unlike a mazaar (shrine) where women are mostly discouraged to perform, it was cinema which gave female qawwals a space to express themselves in the most boisterous manner.

Qawwalis in Indian movies are as old as the earliest talking films of 1931. India's first sound film, Ardeshir Irani's *Alam Ara* (1931), although based on a fairy-tale-style Parsi play, contained several ingredients that could be considered Muslim devotional, such as the song *'De de khuda ke naam pe'* sung by Wazir Mohammed Khan. According to the author Akmal Hyderabadi, *Alam Ara* had six qawwalis while the second talking film *Shirin Farhad* (1931) had eight qawwalis,[1] although these claims are unconfirmed since the soundtracks of these movies are lost. In 1935, singer Jaddan Bai (mother of actress Nargis) emerged as the first woman music director in Indian cinema by composing for the film *Talash-e Haq*,[2] in which she apparently sang a qawwali *'Rasool-e Khuda O Kamli wale'* among other songs whose recordings are not available.

When sound came to Indian cinema, the very first female artists, whether for acting or singing, were mostly from the tawaif or courtesan background, many coming from Awadh or Lucknow since they were trained in Urdu poetry, Hindustani music as well as dance.[3] In fact, 'high society' women were initially discouraged from acting in the movies as the cinema itself was viewed in the same manner as the song and dance at the kothas (courtesan's quarters).[4] The courtesans were proficient in singing all sorts of songs including thumri, dadra, ghazal, qawwali, folk, as well as Islamic devotional ones, thus fulfilling the demands of the industry. Interestingly, some of the earliest gramophone records as well as radio broadcasts (between 1900 and the 1930s) have listed many well-known courtesans such as Gauhar Jan, Munni Bai, Miss Nawab Jan, and Miss Kali Jan as having sung qawwalis, without a chorus or clapping, their lyrics being devotional as well as romantic.

While examples of qawwalis in the movies sung by males can be found from as early as 1936, possibly the first qawwali in cinema in female voice was *'Aahen na bhareen shikave na kiye'* sung by Noor Jahan with Amirbai Karnataki, Zohrabai Ambalewali, and Kalyani Mitra for the film *Zeenat* (1945). It is a delightful song not only for its music and singing part (music by Meer Sahab) but also in its dramatics, featuring typical hand and facial gestures or musical/vocal nuances such as *haan haan, aahe, aji haan haan,* etc., that are used in a qawwali performance as we know today. One can spot actresses like Shashikala, Rehana, Shyama, Zohrabai, Zebunnisa, Kalyani, and Cukoo in the group of performers who joyfully sing for a large women-only audience.

For Shyama, originally baby Khurshid Akthar, this song was her debut at the movies at the age of nine,[5] whereas she would later appear in more important roles as qawwal. According to some, *'Aahen na bhareen'* became an anthem for women's liberation,[6] although this is not the first time women sang a qawwali. Singers like Zohrabai of Ambala and Amirbai Karnataki had been singing qawwali-like songs for radio and gramophone records since the 1930s. The following lines by Nakhshab Jarchavi talk of the flow of emotions that could not be avoided from being noticed by the lover, despite all the restraint:

• ◆ •

Roke to bahot aansu lekin,
kuchh ruk bhi gaye kuchh beh bhi gaye
Afsana kaha aur lab na hile,
ashkon se zuban ka kaam liya.

◆ ◆ ◆

(Tried much to stop the tears;
some stopped, but some flowed too,
I told my story without moving the lips;
the tears became my tongue)

'*Aahen na bhareen*' became so popular that its tune was used later in many songs including qawwalis. One of its lines, '*Kuchh keh na sake kuchh keh bhi gaye*', was used as the leading sher for a song by lyricist Akhtar Pilibhiti in *Shahnaz* (1948). Also, the tune of the song '*Sharma ke yeh kyun sab parda nashin*' of *Chaudhvi ka Chand* (1960) is somewhat similar to '*Aahen na bhareen*'. Its meter and tune were then adopted by lyricist Saba Afghani in the all-women qawwali '*Ansu bhi piye taane bhi sahe*' for *Night Bird* (1961) sung by Mubarak Begum and Chandbala. Several keywords and concepts like shikwe, aahen, qayamat, daaman were copied into this song from the original.

Zeenat was among the early Muslim social movies dealing with melodrama in a typical north Indian Muslim family. Another of its qawwali-like songs '*Dulhan ban javo*' is sung by a group of women on a dholak while the actress Noor Jahan is being made up a bride in the midst of Muslim wedding rituals and celebration. Many directors in the 1940 and '50s seem to have been fascinated by the idea of a women-only singing party, usually with a qawwali or qawwali-like song. From *Shikayat* (1948), *Sunehre Din* (1949) and *Bazaar* (1949) to *Wafa* (1950) and *Rajput* (1951), many films included qawwalis sung by women only. It was also common for women to enjoy poetry and attend mushairas (poetry soirees), probably sitting in enclosures separate from men. *Shikayat*'s qawwali '*Wo jo hum mein tum mein qarar tha*' sung by Miss Kalyani and Manik Varma and composed by Rashid Atre (who shifted to Pakistan in 1947), is a famous ghazal by Delhi's nineteenth-century poet Momin Khan Momin, a contemporary of Ghalib and Zauq. But a women-only space does not suggest that all their songs or movies were devotional or moralistic. Many of the lyrics and situations were romantic and flirtatious such as in '*Nazar se loot liya muskurane wale ne*' in *Wafa* (1950). Often, the all-girl qawwalis are sung to tease a coy heroine who seems to have fallen in love, for instance, '*Har baat poochhiye*' in *Chandni Chowk* (1954) or '*Jab ishq kahin ho jata hai*' in *Arzoo* (1965), and several others.

Today we know cinema qawwali to be sung mostly at a mazaar since that is how it has been visualised in many films: a protagonist comes to a Sufi dargah with a problem or quest, makes her prayer in the backdrop of a qawwali, and miraculously meets or confronts another protagonist there, who either holds the key to resolve her problem or could become a catalyst in her catharsis. But in reality, this is not how most qawwalis have been treated in the movies. Until the late-1960s, very few cinema qawwalis used the trope of the mazaar space. For example, *Mehndi* (1958), a Muslim social based loosely on Mirza Hadi Ruswa's novel *Umrao Jaan Ada,* starts with the scene of a family's visit to a dargah with a brief qawwali *'Allah ki rahmat'* followed at home by a domestic song for a little Muslim girl's initiation ceremony. The year 1958 had another mazaar-based devotional song *'Milti hai bheek maula tere huzoor se'* in *Sohni Mahiwal,* composed by Naushad. It's not a typical qawwali, but sung by women visiting a mazaar, led by Nimmi, to make an offering at the grave.

Qawwali has always been a medium of dialogue—between two singers or protagonists, two opposite teams, or the singer and the audience. It is difficult to say when or by whom were the qawwali muqablas or competitions between two facing groups started. Such a tradition is unlikely to exist at the Sufi shrines. But competitions of poetry and music were common in the courts of kings and nawabs in India. Many Bombay films have also depicted such poetic competitions usually between the lead male and female protagonists who are at loggerheads. *Nakli Nawab* (1962), *Mere Mehboob* (1963), *Ghazal* (1964), and *Dayar-e Madina* (1975) are some of the films that feature poetic rivalries which often lead to romantic union of the two protagonists. But the naive mehfils of mushaira that were hallmarks of adab (literature) and aadab (etiquettes) got catapulted to a more complex level of musicality, emotions and flirtation via qawwali muqablas. Though pre-1940s cinema doesn't seem to have any example of men-women qawwali muqabla, *'Muhabbat karne wale'* in *Shahnaz* (1948) or *'Haye yeh bholi soorat wale'* in *Char Din* (1949) seem to be some of the earliest men-women qawwali competitions, although the regular men-women group songs existed in the movies even from the mid-1930s.

Male and female teams fought in playful qawwalis from *'Muhabbat wo kare unse ke jiski shaamat aayi hai'* in *Bare Bhaiyya* (1951) and *'Haseenon se muhabbat ka bura anjam hota hai' in Albela* (1951) to *'Kisi ke teere nazar dil pe khaye baithe hain'* in *Dak Babu* (1954) and *'Muhabbat ne mujhe maara meri tauba'* in *Pehli Jhalak* (1954), mostly bringing relief after a tense scene in the movie. While these qawwali competitions were used in much of Bombay cinema, the classic songs from *Barsaat ki Raat* (1960) would always be placed at the top for the quality of their poetry and renditions. This film, set in Lucknow and Hyderabad, begins by surprising the audience with the prospect of two upcoming qawwal sisters being trained in music by their own father! The idea sounds daring not only because they come from a Muslim family, but especially so as they are in a lineage that professes music hereditarily. In general, music gharana families among Muslims discourage their daughters from performing in public,[7] unless they are courtesans, which the girls in this film are not. One of the sisters, Shama (Shyama), is in love with the Urdu poet Amaan Hyderabadi (Bharat Bhushan), who later happens to fall for another woman, Shabnam (Madhubala), as they accidentally meet during a rainy night (thus, *Barsaat ki Raat*).

As the two sisters struggle to compete with male qawwals in a muqabla, their first song, *'Nigahe naaz ke maaron ka haal'*, does not let them win. However, they perform much better the next time, managing to defeat their male counterpart Ustad Iqbal, albeit with the help of impromptu poetry from Amaan. Shyama who plays the lead woman qawwal here had earlier appeared as the singer and dholak player in the women's qawwali in *Zeenat*. The story of *Barsaat ki Raat (BkR)* seems to suggest that qawwali muqablas were part of real culture in Lucknow with some money being put up by the businessmen on betting. They use the phrase *karkhane ki chabi* (key for a factory or a building) for the prize—probably a piece of property. But what is most striking is the support and encouragement given by senior men to the girls for performing more and better qawwali.

The ultimate muqabla of the two sisters takes place opposite a much senior qawwal (actor Baalam) through the song *'Na to karvan ki talaash hai'* (Manna Dey, Asha Bhosle, Mohd. Rafi, etc.) which became the most loved cinema qawwali of all times. Wearing several medals on his chest, Baalam as a qawwal reminds one of a photograph of Ustad Fayyaz Khan of Agra. The lyricist Sahir Ludhianvi used the choicest poetic ingredients for the concept of ishq (love), often from the traditional repertoire of Amir Khusrau, Mira Bai and other poets, including some verses in Punjabi. The strong lyrics often compliment the real-life dilemma that Shama has on discovering that the person she passionately loves is already loved by someone else:

• ◆ •

Mere naamurad junoon ka hai ilaj koi to maut hai
Jo dawa ke naam pe zehr de, usi chara gar ki talash hai

• ◆ •

(If there's a cure for my unsuccessful passion, it is death.
The one who provides poison as medicine,
is the healer I seek)

Probably inspired by the success of *Barsaat ki Raat* and its qawwalis that popularised it, director P.L. Santoshi decided to make yet another movie based on qawwali muqablas. He and co-director Durgesh Kumar came up with a comparatively low-budget *Qawwali ki Raat* (1964) featuring several qawwalis in the voices of Mohd. Rafi and Shamshad Begum, often copying components from the songs of *Barsaat ki Raat*. The very first song, 'Qawwali ki raat hai', features the same actor Baalam as the lead male singer who had participated in *'Na to karvan ki talash'*. Probably following the same inspiration, there arrived another movie, *Muqable ki Raat* (1978), with qawwalis sung by Mohd. Rafi.

The year 1960 was a special year for qawwalis, Urdu and Mughal themes since some of their most representative movies, from *Barsaat ki Raat, Mughal-e Azam* and *Chaudhvin ka Chand* to *Babar, Basant* and *Aalam Ara ki Beti* were released that year. The memorable songs of K. Asif's magnum opus *Mughal-e Azam,* written by Shakeel Badayuni and composed by Naushad, have been visualised lavishly to create a Mughal palatial fantasy like no other. And among them is the qawwali *'Teri mehfil mein qismat aazma kar'*, a competition between two women teams led by Anarkali (Madhubala) and her rival Bahaar (Nigar Sultana) both of whom try to woo the Mughal prince in attendance. Like the poetry competitions called bayt baazi, each qawwali team in *'Teri mehfil mein'* recites its couplet or quatrain and then gestures towards the other team, as if saying 'over to you' with a slightly aggressive ending of '*... ham bhi dekhenge*' (we too shall see).

Two other songs of *Mughal-e Azam, 'Pyar kiya to darna kya'* and *'Jab raat hai aisi matwali'*, too are qawwali-like although with dance and no clapping.

There is no qualitative or stylistic difference between the poetry and music of the two songs. The only difference is visual—*'Teri mehfil mein'* is performed by two sitting groups who clap, but do not dance, whereas *'Jab raat hai aisi matwali'* is performed by a sitting group which doesn't clap, but is accompanied by a dance of young women. Although the director has left no stone unturned in depicting the grandeur of the Mughal courts and its entertainers, these songs are obviously present-day cinematic fantasies about the past—not historically accurate.

The royal courts shown in the qawwalis of other historical or Mughal-themed movies of that era, such as *Nausherwan-e Adil* (1957), *Babar* (1960) or *Razia Sultana* (1961), are not as lavish as those from *Mughal-e Azam.* A little later, *Mere Mehboob* (1963) carried several female songs which oscillate between a qawwali and a song-for-dance. While *'Tere pyar mein dildar'* and *'Allah bachaye nau jawano se'* are happy song-dances by groups of girls with no clapping, *'Mere mehboob mein kya nahin'* and *'Jan-e man ek nazar dekhle'* are sung (and casually danced) by two women, using instruments and some qawwali-like clapping. These are supposed to be regular songs with added visual nuances of qawwali for the affect.

Among other women's qawwalis, the wedding song *'Mere banne ki baat na poochho'* from *Gharana* (1961) is a friendly song-fight between members from the families of the banna (groom) and the banni (bride), trying to prove who is superior. The playful qawwali, voiced by Asha Bhosle and Shamshad Begum, is being performed in a Hindu family wedding. While Shakeel Badayuni penned its parodical lyrics, *'Mere banne ki'* is originally a Sufi qawwali/wedding song, sung in the past by Pakistan's Manzoor Niazi,[8] Munshi Raziuddin and Farid Ayaz-Abu Mohammad as well as Delhi's Meraj Nizami qawwals. Sufis use the imagery of a wedding or bridegroom to represent their ultimate wedding or consummation with the divine, although with the qualities of the groom described herein, it could even be a song praising the Prophet (PBUH) as a bridegroom.

It would be safe to say that Bombay cinema evolved a new genre of dance or mujra qawwali where a sitting group of men or women sing while another group or a single woman dances, often to enhance a muqabla between men and women. For example, *'Unse nazrein mili aur hijab aagaya'* in *Ghazal* (1964) is basically a kathak dance number with Meena Kumari singing the ghazal with a chorus and other women clapping. Similarly, *'Jao ji jao badi shaan ke dikhane wale'* in *Razia Sultana* (1961) is a dance qawwali muqabla where the women sing and dance while the men only sing. Usually the qawwali teams facing each other are placed in front of a chief guest/patron, such as a nawab or a villain, and the dancer/dancers in between, besides other usual guests/audience doing wah wahs (wows). A typical example could be a funny qawwali muqabla *'Badi door se chal kar aaye hain'* from *Jay Vijay* (1973), where the two male qawwali teams seem to represent Hindu and Muslim identities, fiercely but funnily competing with each other to impress a clownish king (Paintal) in his royal court where the women's dance teams seem to be representing the two sides.

In terms of the voices used in the qawwalis, the largest number of these songs have undoubtedly been sung by Mohammad Rafi. Almost all other regular singers—male or female—have given their voice for qawwalis, including Asha Bhosle, Manna Dey, Shamshad Begum, Mahendra Kapoor, Lata Mangeshkar, Kishore Kumar and Suman Kalyanpur, among others. But many traditional qawwals such as Ismail Azad, Yusuf Azad, Jani Babu, and Aziz Nazan were involved in cinema qawwalis. The most sensational female name in the cine and popular concert qawwali to emerge since the late-1950s was that of Shakila Bano Bhopali, not only for her musical talent but also for her looks and the queen-like stormy entries she made onto concert stages.

When barely in her teens, her talent was apparently spotted by Dilip Kumar and B.R. Chopra in the 1950s in Bhopal when they were shooting for *Naya Daur*.[9] She came to Mumbai and thrilled the audience with her concerts as well as movie appearances. She would enter smilingly with her all-girls team wearing the most elaborate shararas (Indian skirt), dupatta (scarf) and glittering jewellery, and speak to the audience with a handful of Urdu couplets thrown in with each sentence. While performing on stage she would make stylish actions such as rolling her choti (braided hair) teasingly with her hands, or even kicking an empty wine glass to end a qawwali about wine. Her enticing actions and facial gestures can be seen in many qawwalis, such as *'Milte hi nazar tumse'* in *Ustadon ke Ustad* (1963) or *'Kehte hain jis ko ishq'* in *Aaj aur Kal* (1963).

It is even said that when a B-grade movie flopped, they would add a Shakila Bano song in it and re-release it to make it a hit. In her early career, Shakila also acted in films such as *Rustam-e Baghdad* (1963), *Samson* (1964), *Tarzan aur Jadooi Chiragh* (1966), and *Gunda* (1969) where her songs were used. Her name as a charming female qawwal became so legendary that several films incorporated her concerts of qawwali and announced her real name, probably as an attraction for the box-office. She even wrote the qawwali *'Muhabbat bhara koi paigham de'* for *Humrahi* (1974) besides appearing in it as a qawwal. But the strangest fact about Shakila's career in the industry is that the films in which she appeared used her presence and name but not her voice. A probable reason for this is that her voice was rather rustic and folkish and not as refined as that of seasoned playback singers. The industry loved her looks and the alluring gestures, but her voice didn't fit her beauty, at least cinematically.

Indian cinema also created a stereotyped image of Muslims through the costumes and body language given to the qawwals: a shiny achkan (robe) and tirchhi topi (crooked cap), lips red due to munching of paan (betel nut), a flowing handkerchief in a hand, and a wicked smile. This is exactly how actor Pran appears in a birthday party qawwali *'Jeena to hai usi ka'* in *Adhikar* (1971) where he begins by introducing himself as Banne Khan Bhopali. So where did the shiny crooked cap, the most prominent costume of the cinema qawwals, come from? These inverted-boat-shaped thin caps, pointed upwards at the two ends, are almost never worn by the traditional male qawwals on stage or in a Sufi shrine. Among the earliest movie songs where one notices a women's qawwali group donning the crooked cap is *'Zara sunlo hum apne pyar ka'* in *Bazaar* (1948) featuring Nigar Sultana, the actress who later married the director K. Asif and appeared in the qawwalis of his *Mughal-e Azam* (1960), wearing much more embellished caps crowned with a feather. A similar highly embellished cap with a feather was also worn by the two women singers of the qawwali *'Pehchanta hoon khub tumhari nazar ko'* in *Barsaat ki Raat* (1960) and a ghazal singer (Bina Roy) in the royal court of *Taj Mahal* (1963) for the beautiful song *'Jurm-e ulfat pe'*. Also called Anarkali caps, these may have existed earlier as costumes for kathak or mujra dancers, in or outside cinema. These are definitely worn by women dancers in filmy kathak performances, such as by Vyjayanthimala in *Zindagi* (1964), Hema Malini in *Sharafat* (1970), and Helen in *Bahu Begum* (1971), besides others. But in qawwali performances, the Anarkali caps are seen mostly in the Indo-Muslim themed movies. They are missing in the qawwalis of films with non-Indic fantasies and adventures such as *Rustom-e Rome, Samson* (both 1964), *Tarzan and King Kong,* and *Raaka* (both 1965).

Poetically, almost all men-women qawwali muqablas tend to express the classic and often clichéd argument between beauty and love. While the importance of husn and jalwa (beauty, opulence) is mostly defended by the women team, the men seem to support dil, ishq and jazba (heart, love, emotion). In many cases, the lyrics presented by men are highly prejudiced against women, showing them inferior to men. But when their turn comes, the women too try to taunt the men in the choicest of words. Such gender debates, often witty, stand out in the qawwalis by the duo Yusuf Azad and Rashida Khatoon. Their well-known song *'Aise besharm aashiq hain yeh aaj ke'* for *Putli Bai* (1972) is the fiercest poetic debate to prove the superiority of men and women over each other, which even talks of how God selected some of the best and the worst ingredients when he decided to create man and woman. Interestingly, this musical argument is performed as an evening entertainment for Putli Bai, a woman dacoit, at her den full of rough drunkard dacoits, singing tributes to her bravery.

⬩ ◆ ⬩

Pehen ke sar pe dileri ka taaj bethi hai,
Jo ghar mein thi wo singhasan pe aaj baithi hai,
Agar jhuke to yeh dil kya hai jaan bhi dede
Jo sar uthaye to mardon ki jaan bhi lele.

⬩ ◆ ⬩

(She sits donning the crown of bravery,
The one who was homebound is now on a throne.
If she bows, she can give her heart or even life,
But if she rises, she can take the life of men).

The 1950s and '60s were a golden period of Bombay cinema that set a strong idiom of qawwalis for the next few decades. Until the late-1960s qawwalis involving women used classical Urdu poetry and romantic lyrics alongside funny and entertaining themes. The volume of qawwalis increased in the movies of the 1970s, where we saw more and more devotional or mazaar-based songs on one hand and comical qawwalis on the other. The stereotype of the Muslim community continued getting more intense and negative, for instance, often interspersing mazaar qawwalis with chase sequences involving Mumbai's underworld dons in the movies of the 1990s and the new millennium. Women were used in qawwalis mostly for their sex appeal and not so much to compliment the deep meanings of the lyrics. The only women's qawwali of recent times worth mentioning here is *'Suna hai ke unko shikayat bahut hai'* from the movie *Gangubai Kathiawadi* (2022) which tried to recreate the old time's stage qawwali with Bombay cinema's new-age visual idioms.

Endnotes

1. Hyderabadi, Akmal, *Qawwali Amir Khusrau se Shakila Bano Tak* [Urdu], Delhi: Lahore Fine Arts Press, 1982, pp. 106-07

2. Saraswati Devi also composed for Bombay Talkies' *Achhut Kanya* the same year

3. Bhasin, Shivani, 'Tawaifs' of Awadh: The first women of Hindi cinema', *The Hindu*, 30 August 2019

4. Sinha, Priyam, "Cultured Women" do not act in films: Tracing Notions of Female Stardom in Bombay Cinema (1930s–1950s)', *The Journal of Indian and Asian Studies*, Vol. 1, No. 2 (July 2020)

5. 'From Side Actress to Leading Lady: Yesteryear's Actress Shyama's Unknown Success Story', *Lehren*, June 20204, https://lehren.com/retro/flashback/shyamas-rise-the-journey-from-second-lead-to-leading-lady/10897/

6. Aziz, Ashraf, *Light of the Universe: Essays on Hindustani Film Music,* New Delhi: Three Essays Collective, 2003

7. This has been the usual trend, although broken recently by artists such as Zila Khan (daughter of sitarist Ustad Vilayat Khan), Riffat Salamat (daughter of Pakistan's Ustad Salamat Ali Khan) or Vusat Iqbal Khan (daughter of Dilli gharana's ustad Iqbal Khan), all of them incidentally doing 'light' music rather than the regular classical music

8. Https://www.youtube.com/watch?v=fLFicPcdIbY

9. PTI, 'Shakila Bano's friends mourn qawwal's demise', Mumbai Newsline, *Indian Express,* Mumbai, 17 December, 2002

Image: A gramophone record cover of 'Quwwalis from Films'
Courtesy: Yousuf Saeed

*Excerpted from Yousuf Saeed's forthcoming monograph 'Qawwali in Bombay Cinema' besides the Cinema Qawwali Archive he curated on https://cineqawwali.in

QAWWALI AND RESISTANCE

Songs of Protest

awwali compositions traditionally lay great importance on the words. The poetry is often so powerful that for centuries the poetic content has been used for social messages and even for social revolution.

The social impact of qawwali as an art form for resistance was visible at a protest site where this robust form of music was passionately sung by Qawwal Sarvjeet Tamta. He is one of the few Hindu qawwals who sings at mehfils regularly. Here the crowds listen to the performance and participate with the passion and fervour of resistance. The venue of protest drew large crowds of all religions and all genders. Poetry and music became the voice of the people protesting at the venue. Qawwali, a highly adaptive form, became a means of making a social statement.

At such venues the term 'urban qawwali' is used, which is a completely new genre of music that fuses popular Sufi music with modern rhythmic beats that often initiate a dance. This is popular among the new generation drawing crowds of people who perhaps have never even visited a Sufi shrine.

Photographer: MUSTAFA QURAISHI
Qawwali Practitioners: QAWWAL SARVJEET TAMTA, QAWWAL JUNAID LONAWA
Text: MANJARI CHATURVEDI
Place: SHAHEEN BAGH, NEW DELHI. DARGAH HAJI WARIS ALI SHAH,
DEWA SHARIF, BARABANKI, UTTAR PRADESH, INDIA
Project: THE QAWWALI PROJECT

qawwali
resistance

Qawwali Today: New Spaces, New Conundrums

Pragya Tiwari

On a balmy evening in early April I make my way through the maze of a South Delhi mall—entries, exits, corridors and escalators—to get to a concept bar and restaurant that hosts live qawwalis. One of the city's best known qawwali troupes is setting up as I walk in and look for my table in the dimly lit room. The stage is well appointed, framed by a gigantic Persian rug as backdrop and crystal chandeliers above. This opulence is in stark contrast to my last memory of their performance.

I had first heard this troupe over two decades ago, shortly after I had moved to Delhi, at the mausoleum of Hazrat Nizamuddin Auliya, the patron saint of the city. That first encounter comes to me now as a magic realist's dream. A cool breeze in the serpentine lanes and alleyways that open into the main courtyard, detours speckled with red and yellow flowers, air thick with the smell and haze of incense, a pale, gentle moon rising behind the canopy of twinkling lights, and the music of the qawwals giving wings to hundreds of prayers silently rising in the dusk.

In a quiet corner in the precincts, I found the tomb of Hazrat Amir Khusrau. If Nizamuddin Auliya was the patron saint of Delhi, Amir Khusrau, his foremost disciple, is the patron saint of music and poetry of the subcontinent. He invented musical instruments, experimented with Persian, Urdu, Hindi, Sanskrit, and northern dialects to enrich the language of the people, wrote reams of prose, riddles, and poetry, and innovated musical styles such as tarana and qawwali. Popularly known as Tuti-e-Hind (voice of India), Khusrau's oeuvre formed the basis of Ishq-e-Haqeeqi, the spiritual practice of love. Of seeking union with the Almighty who is cast as the ultimate beloved. His verses sung in the format of qawwali are meant to alter the physical and mental state of the seeker, evoking a trance in which one loses all sense of self and is aware only of the divine. Such is the power of this form that the Sufi saint Hazrat Qutubuddin Bakhtiyar Kaki is said to have gone into a state of ecstasy after listening to a qawwali and died three days later without ever having recovered from it.

Qawwali when rendered in its traditional setting is not transactional. Qawwals do not perform for a fee and while listeners can offer tokens known as vel to the singers, they are not obliged to. The rendition takes place on the floor, at the foot of the shrine, in the midst of throngs of devotees—the poorest of the poor, the homeless, the ailing but also the high and the mighty. It is believed that the saint holds the keys to power in the capital city, attracting leaders and rulers. Indira Gandhi was a frequent visitor too, even though, like all women, she was kept out of the inner chamber of the shrine.

The idea of music which comes from hallowed grounds, fostering values of equity, being performed in a mall, in an exclusive setting, with a formidable cover charge, is not of itself surprising. Capital runs our world and nostalgia for another time has no place in it. With old structures of patronage gone and the state failing to fill in, expecting custodians of musical traditions to continue with their craft altruistically while shunning the greasy pole of material wealth that the rest of us are on is disingenuous. Besides, in India, borders between the sacred and the profane have always been porous. I am curious simply to see how this medieval art form rendered by the twenty-third iteration of qawwali performers belonging to a single lineage will interact with contemporary consumption culture.

The interaction, I find, is mediated by three cardinal pillars of popular culture in India— 'Bollywood', social media and money.

The decor of the space is a nod to Bollywood Muslim social dramas with a door inspired by *Heeramandi*, a popular Netflix series based on the life of courtesans. The songs too are earworms with simple rhymes featured in either Hindi cinema or popular music albums. Here it is perhaps essential to say that Hindi cinema's own engagement with qawwali is an uneven terrain offering both the high art of poet Sahir Ludhianvi's *'Na Toh Karwaan Ki Talaash Hai'* from *Barsaat Ki Raat* to lyricist Anand Bakshi's lighthearted flirtation in *'Parda Hai Parda'* from *Amar Akbar Anthony*. But the one thing in common is that for the most part these songs speak of Ishq-e-Majaazi (romantic love) rather than Ishq-e-Haqeeqi.

Tonight it is not the metaphors that matter as much as the tempo that the singers raise further by interspersing the songs with chants of 'hey hey hey' in periodic interludes. The acoustics are designed to prioritise base and amplify the music to a deafening pitch. The set starts well past 10 p.m. and the audience is up on their feet almost instantly. Crowding the stage, waving bank notes, downing shots, ordering more bottles of vodka and pumping their hookah-holding fists in the air. In the mix, qawwali is yet another party drug that makes one feel numb and unassailable. The audience is in a trance as the saints of yore often were except unlike the latter their sense of self is not lost but heightened in their half-conscious state.

There are hierarchies everywhere. The upper deck is reserved for private parties and they have first dibs over requests. I send in one request, then another until the waiter patiently explains to me that if I am not padding my requests with cash I do not stand a chance. He is slurring his words and has moments ago told me to eat the food he had just served because 'everything is good here', even though I had ordered something else. Other waiters are taking drags of hookahs in corners before serving them, entreating customers to give them tips over the applicable service charge by flashing QR codes to payment gateways—'for better service, ma'am'. A fight has broken out at the bar because the barman has allegedly served cheaper whiskey than the now enraged customer paid for. The couple in front of me are sharing kisses and a hookah pipe until a young woman teetering on her stilettos falls on their table while trying to make her way to the washroom (make a left from a life-size portrait of Nusrat Fateh Ali Khan). To the right of me two men are moving confusedly, unable to decide whether they should film the musicians or dance to the music. They are not the only ones.

The qawwals keep interrupting their performance to wish select patrons on their special day. Happy birthday Rakesh-ji and Kaushik-ji. Happy Anniversary to Dolly and Jagdish, followed by *'Dulhe Ka Sehra Suhana Lagta Hai'*. The greetings are met with loud cheers, phones pointed at Rakesh-ji and Kaushik-ji and Dolly and Jagdish. Fragments of the night are being streamed on Instagram from hundreds of phones. From my table at the end of the chamber, the qawwals are visible to me only through other screens. It is clear that customers are paying first and foremost for the opportunity to fashion their online selves. We are here, we are living the dream, we have made it. The world is their oyster and the oyster is a photo-op. They are not entirely present for the music but that is alright because the pleasure is in anticipating how this moment will show up on their feed.

The writers I admire most excel at taking their readers with them into scenarios and making them really see what they are looking at. They bear witness, and they reveal what is hidden in plain sight. They do this because the first rule of good writing is 'show, don't tell'. Perhaps, also, because it is harder to tell. I can show you what I saw but how do I know what it really means?

We live in a time when culture wars define our politics. Our histories are being litigated and erased. Against this backdrop it is heartening to find songs that survive in our collective consciousness across generations. They may be written by lesser poets but they bind us amidst the powerful currents that threaten to tear our fragile, elusive connection apart, dividing shared memory along the lines of religion and language. But is this consolation enough?

Global capitalist forces flatten culture. They impose a uniformity of cultural practices that serve market consumption and a reductive form of Western modernity. This comes at the expense of local traditions that cannot mould themselves to serve profit-maximising set-ups. As incentives to carry on serving oral traditions pale before the allure of choices offered by the market and aspirations moulded by social media algorithms, future generations become reluctant to take on the mantle. Perhaps venues such as this one will ensure that qawwali does not die out by offering more than mere survival for the artists. But the irony is inescapable—the very forces that threaten the survival of music and performance arts such as qawwali offer market-led solutions for their 'revival'. What is lost in the process? A straightforward answer is diversity.

What started out as Amir Khusrau's experimentation with blending cultures has accumulated layers of influences over time—bringing together poetry, music, philosophy, spirituality and dialects of many regions, growing in many directions from that common root planted in the heart of Delhi in the thirteenth century. Every gharana, khandaan, dargah and khanqah brought their own history and mysticism to it. Strands of bhakti poetry, bhajans, shabad were woven in to create unique patterns until qawwali was as rich as India itself. The representatives of this vast universe on the Noah's Ark of qawwali 'resto bars' are romantic numbers closer to ghazal in character popularised by Bollywood and pop albums and performed by artists who are established in the concert circuits. This leaves the fate of other expressions of qawwali, including the offerings in praise of the Almighty, the Prophet (PBUH) and iconic saints, uncertain.

There is also a less straightforward question to be considered when examining the role of high-end venues in supporting qawwals and qawwalis. Can a tradition exist outside its historical and cultural context? Unlike the qawwali I am listening to in the South Delhi mall, traditional qawwali is not time-bound. It is not a set composition but improvised in both length and form by the performer. The spoken word is paramount despite the robustness of the musical setting. But the more egregious departure from tradition is in what is known as the usul-al-sama or the code of conduct of qawwali.

Custom dictates that three conditions must be met before one presents a qawwali. The first is zamaan, under which an appropriate time must be chosen for the qawwali, and the qawwal must be aware of when to present which kalaam. The second is makaan—qawwali is to be performed in a clean space conducive to spiritual ascension. And third, ikhwaan that requires listeners to be in tune with one another and with the performers, open to setting aside one's ego to experience closeness with the divine.

It is this final condition that lays out the delicate equation between the singer and the listener—one of mutual respect. The listener surrenders to the performer as she would to a spiritual practitioner, allowing the qawwal to lead the way to a higher plane. In this setting the equation is reversed. The paying audience calls the shots and the singers perform at their pleasure. They decide the songs played, and the pace, and they reward the performers for keeping the party going. Does performing outside the code of conduct change the fundamental nature of qawwali?

Evolution and change are par for the course when it comes to art forms. The thirteenth-century qawwal, for instance, may scoff at the centrality of harmonium in today's qawwalis. But at what point is the essence of the form lost? Adaptation is key to survival and continuity but at what point does it tip into cultural appropriation?

All that the writer can show you is a moment in time. Is that moment a portent for the times to come? Or perhaps, as in the myth of the churning of the ocean, the poison precedes the elixir. Writers don't have answers to questions like these.

The following week I go back to the dargah of Hazrat Nizamuddin Auliya on a Friday evening. Summer has begun to set in and an early summer dust storm is in the offing. A mellow orange sky is rapidly turning dark around the edges and a few stray fat drops of rain fall on to the Yaarana Chabutra where qawwali was first composed by Amir Khusrau. Today, the dargah is lit up for the 721st urs of Khusrau. Urs, literally meaning marriage, marks the demise of a Sufi master but instead of mourning, Sufis observe it as a week-long celebration believing that death marks the union of the Sufi with the beloved Almighty. The evening prayers have just concluded and qawwals take their position facing the shrine. Large crowds are milling around and in that din they begin with a naat in praise of the Prophet (PBUH) and followed by qaul—words of the Prophet (PBUH). Listeners from many walks of life sit in circles around them, hands raised or folded in prayer. As I turn to leave, the qawwals begin singing Khusrau's words. *'Chhaap tilak sab cheen li/ Mose naina milaa ke'*. Words that speak of losing one's identity to one's beloved Almighty. Words I had requested in the restaurant. A request that is granted here without my having to ask. I leave thinking, may a thousand qawwalis bloom.

THE QAWWALI PROJECT

An initiative by Manjari Chaturvedi

Started in 2011, this initiative examines the impact of modernity on the preservation of qawwali, a critical endeavour since oral traditions are often the first casualties of technological advancement. The project has successfully connected with hundreds of practitioners, bringing qawwali singers from smaller towns to metropolitan cities in India and international festivals, thereby providing them with a broader platform and increased visibility. Several collective and individual issues are addressed through the various activities of this project.

The primary objective of the project is multifaceted, focusing first on creating the first-ever comprehensive documentation of qawwali, preserving its rich history, diverse traditions, and evolving practices for future generations. Additionally, the project serves as a platform to bring together various organisations, scholars, academics and artists, fostering partnerships and collaborations that help support the livelihoods of qawwali practitioners. By increasing visibility and connecting artists with new opportunities, the project ensures that qawwali remains a sustainable art form, providing practitioners with opportunities to showcase their talent and gain recognition.

The project also explores the preservation challenges faced by this kinship-driven tradition in modern times, the malleable nature of qawwali that allows it to incorporate diverse traditions and concepts, and its predominantly andro-centric history while considering the poetic and spiritual influence of the feminine in its tradition.

Furthermore, the project understands the importance of field studies with strong follow-up strategies to support the musicians, especially those with limited formal education. This includes developing approaches to create sustainable livelihood opportunities for these artists. Through these efforts, the project seeks to ensure that qawwali continues to thrive as a living tradition, adapting to modernity while retaining its spiritual and cultural essence.

Under the umbrella of The Qawwali Project are the following initiatives:

i. **Understanding Qawwali Series** is an intelligently curated set of seminars aimed at fostering academic discourse around the traditional art form of qawwali. These interactive seminars bring together a diverse array of participants, including artists, students, film-makers, and academicians, on a unified platform. Through a blend of film screenings, lectures, performances, and discussions, the series seeks to bridge the gap between traditional performing arts and serious academic inquiry. The seminars cater to scholarly purposes and also engage large audiences interested in exploring India's rich cultural heritage. By examining various dimensions of qawwali, these symposiums delve into its historical, social, and poetic significance, shedding light on its evolution and contemporary relevance. This serves as a valuable platform for knowledge exchange, raising awareness about this spiritually rich and culturally significant art form.

Editions of Understanding Qawwali Seminars:

i. Edition 1, 2013 – Understanding the Traditional Art Form of Qawwali. Venue: India International Centre, New Delhi. Focused on introducing the audience to the foundational aspects of qawwali.

ii. Edition 2, 2014 – Exploring the Plurality of the Unified Art Form. Venue: India International Centre, New Delhi. Examined the diverse influences that have shaped qawwali over centuries.

iii. Edition 3, 2015 – The Anthropology and Social Impact of Qawwali. Venue: India International Centre, New Delhi. Discussed the cultural and societal implications of qawwali as a musical tradition.

iv. Edition 4, 2017 – The Poetic Content and its Social Impact with Regional Sensibilities. Venue: India International Centre, New Delhi. Highlighted the regional nuances and the impact of qawwali's poetic compositions.

v. Edition 5, 2019 – Understanding and Exploring Qawwali. Venue: Royal Opera House, Mumbai. Expanded the discourse to include the artistic and performative dimensions of qawwali in a metropolitan setting.

vi. Edition 6, 2021 – The Qawwali Project. Venue: India International Centre, New Delhi. Explored innovative approaches to documenting, preserving, and promoting qawwali in contemporary times.

2. **I Am a Qawwal** is an innovative ground-breaking self-documentation initiative aimed at empowering qawwals across India to represent themselves through photography, leveraging the internet and social media to increase their visibility and create new livelihood opportunities. This project emerged as a response to the challenges posed during the pandemic and serves as a unique effort to preserve and celebrate the lives of qawwals, especially those in small towns, who often remain unrecognised despite their vital role in carrying forward India's rich cultural heritage.

3. **The Q Project**, is a novel initiative that brings together the rich traditions of qawwali and jazz through a unique fusion of sounds. The project aims to honour the past while creating a future that resonates with contemporary audiences. The idea behind the project is to explore the shared history of improvisation in both qawwali and jazz, two musical traditions that thrive on spontaneous creativity and the free-flowing expression of emotions.

4. **Qawwali Mehfils** are curated performances featuring traditional qawwals singing both rare and popular compositions. This initiative aims to revive nearly forgotten treasures of qawwali while providing livelihood opportunities to practitioners struggling to sustain themselves. These mehfils are thoughtfully crafted, offering audiences an immersive experience of the music's spiritual and cultural depth. A narrator accompanies the performances, guiding attendees through the historical significance, stories, and context of the qawwalis being sung. This blend of music and storytelling celebrates the qawwali tradition and also educates listeners about its rich legacy.

5. **Qawwali Poetry Interactive** is a significant component that provides a unique, immersive experience for attendees and listeners. This features an intimate performance by qawwali practitioners, allowing the audience to witness first-hand the richness of the art form. The performances without amplification of sound, showcase a blend of popular poetic compositions alongside rare ones that are almost forgotten in contemporary times. These rare pieces provide a deeper connection to the historical and spiritual roots of qawwali. This helps preserve their legacy for posterity and also instils a renewed sense of pride in their roles within the society and to exhibit their connection to the sacred shrines they represent.

6. **Qawwali Capsules** where the practitionors speak, is a seminal initiative comprising short films that highlight the lives, artistry, and spiritual connections of qawwali practitioners where they share their own experiences, insights, and stories about their performance art, their lives, and their deep spiritual connection with the art form. Focused on musicians from smaller towns, this project highlights their practice of qawwali in an organic, non-commercial setting, emphasizing the spiritual nature of the music.

7. **The Qawwali Photo Project** is a pioneering initiative that marks the first-ever photo documentation dedicated to qawwali aimed at showcasing and disseminating the rich cultural heritage of this art form. This initiative was meticulously conceptualised to unfold the untold story of qawwali through images. It captures the lives of qawwali practitioners, their performances, and their deep association with the Sufi shrines where they perform. By capturing these moments and narratives through the lens it transcends a mere documentation, and serves as a tribute to the qawwals. It highlights their invaluable contributions to the preservation of this art form, and sheds light on their enduring significance in maintaining the cultural and spiritual fabric of the communities they serve.

This project, created in collaboration with leading photographers, offers an intimate glimpse into the lives of qawwals, providing a perspective rarely seen before – the qawwals in their everyday lives, interacting with their families and audiences, and highlighting the powerful connection between the performers and the devotees who visit the shrines, seeking grace.

One of the most heart-warming aspects of the project has been the reaction of the qawwals and their families, especially their children, upon seeing their images on display. For many, it was an emotional moment of recognition and validation, as their contributions to this deeply spiritual and culturally significant tradition were finally documented and celebrated. The practitioners are photographed amidst the people, in an organic and non-commercial setup, offering a raw and authentic look at their lives. For too long, the faces behind the qawwali music have remained largely faceless. People associate the name and music with qawwali but seldom recognise the individuals who create it. This project aims to change that by giving a face to the sounds, offering a visual identity to the qawwals who have passed down their musical tradition for generations.

In an age where technology often strips away the humanity behind the music, this project restores that human connection, capturing the essence of the people who bring this incredible art form to life.

Practitioners associated with the initiatives of The Qawwali Project.

1. Qawwal Nurul Hasan from Bilhera
2. Qawwal Haider Baksh from Lucknow
3. Qawwal Arshad Hasan Chisti from Kakori
4. Qawwal Rizwan Muazzam Ali Khan from Pakistan
5. Qawwal Fared Ayaz and Abu Mohammad from Pakistan
6. Qawwal Sabri Brothers from Jaipur
7. Qawwal Nazeer Naseer Khan Warsi from Hyderabad
8. Qawwal Danish Hussain Badayuni from Badayun
9. Qawwal Abdullah from Mehrauli
10. Qawwal Adil Hussain from Hyderabad
11. Qawwal Ali Waris from Mumbai
12. Qawwal Akeel Warsi from Dewa
13. Qawwal Anwaar from Jaipur
14. Qawwal Chanchal Bharti from Delhi
15. Qawwal Ehsaan Hussain from Hyderabad
16. Qawwal Gufran Aslami Khairabadi from Khairabad
17. Qawwal Hameed Sabri from Jaipur
18. Qawwal Hamsar Hyat Nizami from Delhi
19. Qawwal Hasnain Nizami from Delhi
20. Qawwal Jilani from Lucknow
21. Qawwal Saqlain Nizami from Delhi
22. Qawwal Mubeen Warsi from Dewa
23. Qawwal Niazi Nizami brothers from Delhi
24. Qawwal Niyaz Warsi from Khairabad
25. Qawwal Meraj Nizami from Delhi
26. Qawwal Furqan Nizami from Delhi
27. Qawwal Kamil from Hyderabad
28. Qawwal Shabih from Kakori
29. Qawwal Annu from Lucknow
30. Qawwal Aziz Chisti from Agra
31. Qawwal Shakeel Warsi from Lucknow
32. Qawwal Sultan Nizami from Delhi
33. Qawwal Yousuf Nizami from Delhi
34. Qawwal Raja Sarfaraz Darbari from Rampur
35. Qawwal Salim Chisti from Agra
36. Qawwal Shahid Sami Niazi from Rampur
37. Qawwal Ranjhan Ali from Punjab
38. Qawwal Zaki & Zakir Ali from Ajmer
39. Qawwal Wajahat Hussain Badayuni from Badayun
40. Qawwal Md Ahmed Khan Warsi from Rampur

Contributors

• **Affan Yesvi** is a Sufi scholar, columnist, and entrepreneur. As a descendant of the eleventh-century Sufi saint Khwaja Ahmed Yasawi—a mystic, poet, and founder of the Yasaviyya Sufi order in Central Asia—Affan carries a rich spiritual legacy.

A multifaceted entrepreneur, columnist, editor, and poet, and the founder of Rhyvers Publishing Group, Yesvi is known for his insightful writings on social issues. He contributes to prominent platforms such as *The Times of India* and *Huffington Post*. His weekly column, 'Sufi Soliloquy', for *The Times of India*, has captivated readers with its reflections on spirituality and contemporary concerns. •

• **Amar Nath Sharma**, I.R.S., a distinguished former Principal Commissioner of Customs and G.S.T., is widely respected as a collector and archivist specialising in gramophone records and recorded history of the Indian subcontinent. Driven by a deep passion for preserving the region's aural heritage, Sharma has spent more than three decades uncovering lesser-known aspects of India's cultural and musical legacy. He is the author of the acclaimed book *Bajanaama*, which explores the history of the earliest gramophone records by Indian artists, providing deep insights into the evolution of recorded music in India. Another of his notable works, *The Wonder That Was the Cylinder*, delves into the era of sound recording before the gramophone, focusing on the ground-breaking wax cylinder recordings. These extensive projects showcase his dedication to documenting history and also cement his legacy as a preserver of India's rich musical traditions, earning him a prominent place in posterity. •

• **Dr Dhruv Sangari** (Bilal Chishty), is a vocalist, lyricist, composer and Sufi scholar, lead singer of the bands Rooh Sufi Ensemble, Humble Mystic and the Washington DC-based National Sufi Ensemble: Interfaith sounds of syncretic South Asia. Trained in Hindustani classical by Shahana Banerjee and Ustad Iqbal Ahmed Khan, he also trained in qawwali under Ustad Meraj Nizami and subsequently the legendary Ustad Nusrat Fateh Ali Khan. Trained in tabla by Pt. B.S. Ramanna, Dhruv also holds a master's in music from the University of Delhi. Popularly known as 'Prince of Qawwali', Dhruv has several Bollywood, Hollywood, Television and Coke Studio, MTV singles along with motion picture music soundtracks to his credit. Having performed in more than fifteen countries, he has also recorded successful album collaborations and hit singles with music producers like Amit Trivedi, Mannan Shah and Nitin Sawhney. Showcased at festivals such as Silkroad GMW-Boston, WOMEX-Brazil, SXSW-Austin, Bhakti Utsav-Delhi, Jashn e Rekhta and the Sufi Route headlined by A.R. Rahman, his work has been frequently covered by the media and press. Empanelled with the Festivals of India Abroad, and the ICCR, Dhruv is also founder of Ektara India, recognised by UNESCO for its contribution to scholarship on Sufi-Bhakti and syncretic themes. Over the last two decades he has taught courses and performed as Artist in Residence at institutions such as NYU, Princeton, Johns Hopkins-Maryland, New England Conservatory-Boston, Hofstra-NYC, Colby College-Maine, Smithsonian, Kennedy Center-DC, Qatar Institute-DC, House of World Cultures-Berlin, Serpentine Gallery-London, Nehru Centre-London, Reed Society for Sacred Arts-Bethesda, Nita Mukesh Ambani Culture Centre-Mumbai and University of Baroda-India.

Currently based in New Delhi he is serving as an Intangible Cultural Heritage (ICH) Expert/Consultant with UNESCO, Delhi and co-founder/executive director at the Naadvistaar Foundation for Music, Delhi, India. •

• **Professor Danish Iqbal** serves as a professor at Jamia Millia Islamia's AJK Mass Communication Research Centre. As an acclaimed playwright and media professional, and a multifaceted individual with impressive accomplishments in both academia and the arts, he has established himself across numerous fields including theatre, academia, writing, research, cultural organisations, arts administration, and mass media.

His artistic and scholarly development has been influenced by collaborations with renowned theatre figures such as M.S. Sathyu, Amir Raza Hussain, and Dr Sayeed Alam. The recognition through more than fifteen national awards, including the Ghalib Award, Lassa Kaul Award, and Mohan Rakesh Samman, speaks to the quality and impact of his work. Beyond his professional pursuits, he has personal interests in table tennis, chess, and a refined appreciation for gastronomy. •

• **Dinesh Khanna**, a professional photographer with over thirty-five years of experience, Dinesh Khanna works across commercial and personal projects. His commercial practice for advertising and corporate clients includes food, portrait, and interior photography and for NGO visual documentation. His acclaimed books include *Bazaar* and *Living Faith*, with recent works *Right of the Line – The President's Bodyguard* and *Life in Rashtrapati Bhawan* commissioned by Rashtrapati Bhawan and Sahapedia. His photography has been exhibited at galleries internationally from Delhi to New York and Varanasi to San Francisco. Notable assignments of Dinesh include the Incredible India campaign and the Taj Mahal's 350th anniversary commission. Dinesh Khanna serves as Managing Trustee of Nazar Foundation, co-founded the Delhi Photo Festival, and curated photography for Serendipity Arts Festival. He teaches at institutions including Ashoka University, Jamia Millia Islamia, and MICA, while directing the Dhrish Academy of Photography at Museo Camera and serving as Visual Consultant with Sahapedia. •

• **Dr Kumkum Srivastava,** Born and raised in Old Delhi's composite culture, Dr Kumkum Srivastava's early years were shaped by her schooling in Karachi, Pakistan, where she developed proficiency in Urdu and Persian while absorbing Islamic cultural traditions. After completing her education at Presentation Convent, Delhi, she pursued her passion for history at Indraprastha College for Women, University of Delhi, earning both her undergraduate and postgraduate degrees with a specialisation in medieval Indian history.

Her academic journey continued at the University of Delhi, where she completed her MPhil and PhD. She additionally read social anthropology, focusing on the Sufi Order of the Qalandars. This research culminated in her acclaimed book, *The Wandering Sufis*, published by Aryan International in collaboration with the Indira Gandhi Rashtriya Manav Sanghralaya, Bhopal. She has to her credit various articles in numerous journals on history, Sufism, Punjabi proverbs, Punjabi folk songs and Urdu poetry.

Dr Srivastava's research spans diverse areas including Islam and Sufism, Urdu language and poetry, medieval Delhi, Punjabi folk songs, Muslim women, and Mughal architecture. She has conducted numerous heritage walks throughout Delhi and established herself as a prominent voice through her extensive writings and lectures on these subjects. She retired as an associate professor at Janaki Devi Memorial College (University of Delhi). •

• **Manjari Chaturvedi,** a classical dancer with professional Kathak training from Kathak Kendra, Lucknow, and a scientist with a master's in Environmental Sciences, University of Lucknow, has taken her obsession with classical dance and turned it into more than a mere stage expression. In her hands, it becomes a means of cultural renaissance and syncretism, a narrative form and dialogue. Nothing is more evocative of this than her two flagship projects: The Qawwali Project and The Courtesan Project, both unique research and documentation exercises, in which the recording of their histories in various forms have shaped ever-expanding archives in these subjects. These have taken the form of books, films, lectures, demonstrations, interviews, seminars, and stage performances. Her other projects which are reinventing the classical dance form are The Jugni Project, The 22 Khwaja Project, The Vrindavan Project, The Rumi Project and The Royal Gharana Series. These extensively researched and intricately worked-on projects are reclaiming traditions for the audience at large and she merges the barriers between art and academia. She is the founder of Sufi Kathak Foundation and Ganga Jamuna Culture Foundation, organisations that work on preserving and documenting performance art traditions. •

• **Mustafa Quraishi** is a documentary photographer based in New Delhi, India. In the past, Mustafa has worked with The Associated Press (2004-2013) and *The Indian Express* (1999-2004) as a staff photographer. Mustafa photographed major news assignments from Afghanistan during its historical pre- and post-Osama days to its parliamentary elections, from Nepal's removal of the monarchy to the tsunami in Andhra Pradesh amongst others. His career has spanned from the fame of being a Page 3 paparazzi in Delhi to working in extremely high-intensity areas with Maoist rebels in central and south India.

In 2007 Mustafa received a fellowship from the National Foundation of India to document Maoist rebels which became his long-standing body of work. Mustafa has been published in *The Newsweek, Time Magazine, Der Spiegel, The New York Times, International Herald Tribune, Geo, The Guardian,* etc. He has also worked with several NGO's like UNAIDS, International Planned Parenthood Federation (IPPF), Bill and Melinda Gates Foundation, Greenpeace etc. Mustafa currently works as a freelancer with NGOs and aid organisations. •

• **Pragya Tiwari** is a writer and editor and has written on politics and culture across national and international publications for the last two decades. She works as a culture consultant and edits *The Indian History Collective*. •

• **Rachna Atri Saksena** is the founding trustee of the Institute for Social Action and Research in Delhi. Her research focuses on the anthropological understanding of community and cultural heritage management, as well as social equity issues in policy frameworks and institutional practices. She curates performances featuring Hindi humour and satire, and collaborates on creating written and artistic works. After briefly working at ICICI Bank in New Delhi, she conducted research with several organisations including the Centre for Advocacy and Research in Delhi, CSSS (JNU), and the Indian Social Institute in Delhi.

Her writing as an anthro-poet appears in the anthology *Disguised*. She maintains life memberships in both the Indian Sociological Society and Indian Anthropological Association. Her academic credentials include training in cultural informatics (IGNCA), Social Anthropology (MPhil from University of Delhi), Social Work (MA from Lucknow University), B.Ed. from the Central Institute of Education, and History (Honours from University of Delhi). •

• **Professor Raziuddin Aquil** is Professor of History at the University of Delhi. His research and teaching interests encompass religious traditions, literary practices, and political cultures in medieval and early modern India. His authored works include *Sufism, Culture, and Politics: Afghans and Islam in Medieval North India* (Oxford University Press) and *The Muslim Question: Understanding Islam and Indian History* (Penguin). He has co-edited *History in the Vernacular* (Permanent Black) with Partha Chatterjee and *Literary and Religious Practices in Medieval and Early Modern India* (Manohar and Routledge) with David L. Curley. •

• **Reema Abbasi** is a distinguished Pakistani journalist whose work on gender sensitivity earned her UNESCO's Gender in Journalism Award in 2003. Her career path includes cultural reporting at *The News International*, socio-political writing for *The Herald Magazine*, and editorial work at *Dawn* newspaper, where she is currently employed. In 2014, she received recognition as the literary personality of the year with the Rajiv Gandhi Award at the Fifth Rajiv Gandhi Excellence Awards.

Secularism has been a central theme throughout her career. Her literary contributions include three books: *Historic Temples in Pakistan: A Call to Conscience*, which aims to stir a discourse that dispels the concept of religious power, and *Ajmer Sharif: Awakening of Sufism in South Asia*, which highlights Muinuddin Chishti's importance and Sufism's role in promoting justice and unity in challenging times, and *Sin*, translations of Wajida Tabassum's ground-breaking and progressive Urdu short stories.

Abbasi was educated at Sherborne School for Girls in England and St. Joseph's College in Karachi. Beyond journalism and writing, she is passionate about travel and arts and culture. •

• **Professor Salil Misra** has had a distinguished academic career, teaching history at multiple prestigious institutions: Jamia Millia Islamia from 1984 to 1987, Indira Gandhi National Open University from 1988 to 2010, and Ambedkar University Delhi from 2010 to 2024.

His scholarly publications include a monograph titled *A Narrative of Communal Politics: Uttar Pradesh, 1937-39* and a concise booklet in Hindi about the Swaraj Party, published by the National Book Trust. Throughout his academic career, Misra has published numerous articles exploring themes such as communal politics, language issues, Hindi and Urdu linguistics, the partition of India, social science education, and identity politics. Misra has been widely recognised in academic circles, having been invited as a sectional president by several regional history congresses, including the UP History Congress, Punjab History Congress, and Andhra Pradesh History Congress. Notably, he served as the president of the modern India section at the 81st session of the Indian History Congress in 2022.

In addition to his teaching and writing, Misra contributed to significant research projects. He was a member of the editorial team for the '*Towards Freedom*' project for the year 1942, sponsored by the Indian Council of Historical Research (ICHR), working alongside renowned historians Prof. Bipan Chandra and Dr Visalakshi Menon. During April to July 2009, he was a visiting researcher at the Centre for History of Emotions at the Max-Planck Institute for Human Development in Berlin. Currently Salil Misra is a Visiting Faculty at the B.M. Munjal University, Manesar. •

• **Suman Mishra** has established himself as a devoted Sufi scholar and poet. His interdisciplinary approach, particularly his engagement with music, has infused his Sufi studies with distinctive originality. Despite the understated elegance of his work, it has garnered recognition in prestigious publications.

Currently serving as managing editor for the Rekhta Foundation's Sufinama initiative, Mishra is actively developing multiple books on Sufism, with several already underway. His notable published works include the two-volume *Guldasta-e-Qawwali*, *Gramophone Qawwali*, and ground-breaking Hindi translations of Sufi saints' biographies and poetry—making these texts accessible to Hindi readers for the first time. •

• **Syed Zia Alvi** is a distinguished Urdu poet, writer and Sufi scholar.He hails from one of Khairabad's most prestigious khanqahi families in the Chishti order. His lineage traces back to Hazrat Makhdoom Sheikh Sa'aduddin Khairabadi, a revered Sufi saint. For over three decades, Alvi has been a prominent voice in spiritual discourse, delivering talks at dargahs and conferences across India and internationally.

His poetic journey spans more than thirty years, resulting in notable publications including the poetry collections *Qaus-e-Quzah* and *Fawaid-e-Sadiya*. Alvi's poetry has found resonance beyond the written word, with prominent Sufi musicians like Abida Parveen, Kavita Seth, Anita Singhvi, Radhika Chopra and Ali Waris recording his work in music albums. •

• **Professor Tanvir Anjum**, born in 1973 in Lahore, completed her education at Kinnaird College for Women, Lahore, before pursuing advanced studies at Quaid-i-Azam University, Islamabad. There, she earned her master's (1996), MPhil (1998), and PhD (2006) degrees. She joined the Department of History at Quaid-i-Azam University in 1999, where she now serves as a tenured professor.

Her academic interests span historiography and intellectual history of Muslims in South Asia, with particular emphasis on medieval Sufism. Her research explores state–Sufi relations, sociocultural aspects of Sufism, and Sufi literature, poetry, and music. Her scholarship has been enriched by prestigious fellowships, including a postdoctoral fellowship (2007-2008) at University of Carolina (UNC) at Chapel Hill, USA, and the Charles Wallace Fellowship (2001) at the School of Oriental and African Studies (SOAS), University of London, UK.

Anjum's scholarly contributions include three books, multiple monographs, and more than thirty-seven research papers in leading international and national journals. Her most significant work, *Chishti Sufis in the Sultanate of Delhi (1190-1400): From Restrained Indifference to Calculate Defiance* (Oxford University Press, Karachi, 2011), has become a notable contribution to the field. She has also authored numerous articles for the third revised edition of the *Encyclopaedia of Islam* (Brill, Leiden).

Based in Islamabad, she balances her academic career with family life, sharing her home with her husband and teenage daughter. ◆

◆ **Professor Vinay Kumar Srivastava** is professor of anthropology, University of Delhi. A PhD from the University of Cambridge, United Kingdom, Prof Vinay Kumar Srivastava has been a prominent figure in the field of anthropology. He served as the principal in Hindu University and returned to the department of anthropology in Delhi University in 2011. Authoring innumerable academic and research works including books, monographs, papers and articles, his areas of specialisation over the years have been comparative religion, caste system, family dynamics, medical systems, and anthropological theory and methods. Prof Srivastava had also been on the boards and committees of various universities and societies on anthropology and sociology. ◆

◆ **Yousuf Saeed** is a Delhi-based film-maker and researcher, working on the themes of South Asia's syncretic cultural traditions through his documentary films, writings, and multimedia productions. His films *Basant*, *Jannat ki Rail*, *Khayal Darpan*, and *Khusrau Darya Prem Ka* have been shown at several national and international film festivals, besides TV channels. He is currently the director of Tasveer Ghar Collective, a digital archive of India's popular visual culture, and is also the author of the book *Muslim Devotional Art in India* (Routledge). Yousuf is also working on an online multimedia platform titled cineqawwali.in that documents the qawwali songs featured in Bombay cinema. ◆

Photo: Mustafa Quraishi

bas ek daagh-e-sajda meri qainaat,
jabeenein teri aastaaney terey.

The mark is my universe—stamped on my forehead,
as I kiss your sacred ground,
The foreheads are yours, The thresholds are yours,
for nothing is mine.

Excerpted from a Ghazal by Poet Abdul Hameed Adam

ACKNOWLEDGEMENT

Muzaffar Ali Sahab introduced me to qawwali in 1994. That memory of a night of qawwali at the Dewa Shrine – the tears that flowed with the music – remains etched in my memory. It was inevitable that I would do this book. Today he is graciously part of this book. In 1998, I created Sufi Kathak, which explored dance with qawwali and it was the beginning of my own personal journey with this music. Hundreds of concerts, six seminars, multiple talks and presentations and after twenty six long years, it has rightfully culminated into this book.

The Sufi saints and under their umbrella, the people of their path, Pir-e-Tariqat Late Khwaja Afzal Nizami Syed Bhukari who always welcomed me with a smile and blessings; Khadim Late Mazhar Nizami; the present Khadim Haider Nizami and Qawwal Ghulam Rasool Nizami at the Nizamuddin Dargah. Bhai Afzal Safipur from Safipur Dargah, Bhai Jawwad from Ajmer Dargah, Bhai Jawed Qutubi from Mehrauli Dargah – all of them were instrumental in imparting the details of the oral traditions and giving special access to the photographers for shooting at the shrine on various occasions. The qawwals from Delhi, Punjab, Fatehpur Sikri, Hyderabad, Dewa, Lucknow, Kakori, Khairabad, Badayun, Rampur, Ajmer and Jaipur have been sources of untold wisdom and warmth. They have shaped my thinking profoundly and I hope this book is worthy of their faith in me.

This book will not have been possible without the India International Centre, their steadfast collaboration for the five editions of 'Understanding Qawwali' seminars and 'The Qawwali Photo Project', which is integral to the compilation of this book. At IIC I have experienced that rare combination of camaraderie and intellectual generosity that has led me on more than one occasion to confuse it as home for the one year during the process of completing this book. I am indebted to each one at the library for all their assistance and every single one at the tea lounge for the endless smiles with tea and atta biscuits.

This book is a product of intellectual community, of thematic solidarity and enduring friendships between lovers of Sufism and qawwali. In the past fourteen years, since 2011, from the early days of starting The Qawwali Project, I have amassed innumerable debts with the invaluable support of many academics, scholars, musicians and photographers. I am lucky to be able to call all the contributors in this book my friends and their influence can be felt in it. Words will not do justice to how much I have learned from them over the years and how much I value their steadfast belief and friendship. Shri Tarun Tejpal and Shri Divyabhanusinh, who gave their invaluable suggestions during the compiling and making of the book, Shri. A.N. Sharma, who generously shared with me his personal archives and gramophone records; Shri Yousuf Saeed who read the draft; Syed Zia Alvi and Shri Suman Mishra, who were ready with poetic inputs and corrections where ever needed. Bhawana Pandey and Ratn Sanjay whose support made this book possible.

The many young people whose assistance has been indispensible at various points in this project to help with organizing seminars, recordings, transcriptions and writing, navigating archives and library collections, include senior research associates Punita Kapoor, Arshita Singh, Ipshita Roy, Sarita Sharma, Shreya Jain, Tulika Varma, Mukib Ahmad and college interns Jaisika Parcha, Vasudha Sawhney, Shuchi S, Medha Goel, Aditi Sharma, Karan Tekwani, Aradhana Bardhan, Vinay Rathi, Harleen Kaur.

My publisher Shri Ajay Mago at Om Books for his steadfast faith in this first-ever literary book on qawwali. I owe special thanks to the brilliant mind of Shantanu Ray Chaudhuri for the close reading of countless drafts, hours of conversation and his ability to discuss the minute details of this project.

Shri Ashok Vajpeyi for graciously lending his support to this exceptional book.

Designers Chetana Vij and Daljeet Singh from the design team who have worked the intricate layout of this book while disseminating this valuable content.

Lawyer Dahlia Sen Oberoi who helped me navigate copyrights and contracts at various stages.

My final thanks are reserved for my family, who have graciously endured all the erratic hours and my unavailability for last fourteen years, owing to working on this impossible dream of The Qawwali Project. My incredible father Prof. R S Chaturvedi, a scientist, an academic, a professor who instilled in me the need for immaculate scholarship in whatever I pursued. My mother Sudha Chaturvedi and my sister Pallavi Chaturvedi for believing in my dream and having my back, as I moved ahead with impractical & demanding working schedules.

For my friends, you know who you are, who stand silently and at times vociferously in my support for the unusual, out-of-the-box projects and the unimaginable work I take on and do. I derive my strength from your support.

To each one mentioned above, a heartfelt, thank you.

MANJARI CHATURVEDI

• ◆ •

The compilation of this book has been generously funded and supported by Raza Foundation.